tear here

Top Ten Survival Hints for College Freshmen

10. Know the rules. Get a catalog and follow it exactly. Freshmen can get themselves in a lot of trouble by not knowing rules, regulations, deadlines, and so on. Schools try to educate new students through various orientation programs, but will ultimately hold students responsible for information published in their catalog. Read up on information such as tuition due dates, class drop deadlines, and grade point average requirements and be ahead of the game.

9. Get an academic advisor. Work with your advisor to select classes, majors, minors, and schedules. Make sure you're taking the classes you need as well as the ones you want.

8. Know your resident advisor, the upper-class student who supervises the dorm. RAs are an invaluable source of advice and assistance.

7. Budget your money carefully. It's hard for students to know how much money they will need per month for expenses. Set a budget and follow it.

6. Get involved in campus life. Join clubs, sports, and, if you are so inclined, fraternities or sororities. The social skills you develop can be just as valuable as the academic training you receive.

5. Don't be surprised if your grades are lower than normal at first. Moving away to college brings many changes and adjustments, some of which are more manageable than others for many students. It usually takes a semester to sort things out and learn the ropes.

4. Know what services are available on campus, including health services, counseling centers, and tutoring centers. If you need these services, use them.

3. "If you think you might be drinking too much, you are. If friends mention that you're drinking too much, then you definitely are. If drinking for the purpose of getting drunk is a valuable recreational activity for you, then you still need to grow up." —Terrence McGlynn, the University of San Diego

2. "As for the schoolwork itself, use a calendar, either on the wall or the computer. Put in your class schedule, note midterms and finals, days off for holidays, etc. Then add in extracurricular commitments. Now you know how much time you have for your assignments, readings, etc. It's great to be on your own with that first taste of freedom, but if you squander your time, you'll find yourself pulling ill-timed all-nighters that will leave you at less than your best." —Bob Greenberger, the State University of New York at Binghamton

And the #1 hint:

1. "Make sure you are totally ready to experience college before you enroll. If you force yourself (or someone else forces you) to go to college before you're ready, it affects many aspects of your life. Your grades will suffer, your self-esteem will suffer, and your friendships and family life will suffer.

   "It's okay to take a year or two off before you go to school. Work or travel. Find yourself. Then you'll appreciate school more when you actually go." —Pamela Smith, the State University of New York College of Technology at Farmingdale

ALPHA

P9-CDJ-499

College Packing Checklist

Clothing

____ T-shirts
____ Underwear (tops and bottoms)
____ Socks, stockings
____ Shorts
____ Jeans
____ Sweatshirts
____ Sneakers
____ Hiking boots or rain boots

____ Dressy pants
____ Dress shirt
____ Belt, tie
____ Blazer
____ Dress or two
____ Dressy shoes
____ Sandals
____ Rain gear (including umbrella)

____ Light jacket
____ Winter coat (if necessary)
____ Gloves, mittens
____ Scarves, hats
____ Pajamas
____ Slippers
____ Robe
____ Shower shoes

Furnishings

____ Blanket or comforter
____ Pillows
____ Sheets
____ Computer, disks
____ Door mirror
____ Extension cords
____ Fan

____ Bookshelf
____ Boombox or stereo
____ CDs and holder
____ Hangers
____ Light bulbs
____ Mini-vacuum
____ Posters

____ Power bar
____ Desk lamp, pole lamp
____ Telephone (if not provided)
____ Family photos
____ Small memo board
____ (Optional: rug, TV/VCR, cassette player)

Personal Hygiene

____ Comb, brush
____ Deodorant
____ Razor
____ Shaving cream
____ Cosmetics
____ Soap

____ Shampoo, cream rinse, etc.
____ Nail clippers
____ Shower bucket
____ Toothbrush
____ Toothpaste
____ Hair dryer

____ Towels (all sizes)
____ Cotton swabs
____ Personal hygiene products
____ Spare eye glasses, contacts
____ Contact lens solutions

Office Supplies

____ Notebooks
____ Pens, pencils, sharpener
____ Printer paper
____ Calculator
____ Batteries
____ White-out

____ Post-it notes
____ Ruler
____ Paper clips
____ Scissors
____ Highlighters
____ Reference books

____ Stapler
____ Envelopes
____ Address book
____ Stamps
____ Clear tape, duct tape
____ Printer cartridges

Health

____ Aspirin, Tylenol, etc.
____ Bandages

____ Prescription medication
____ Antibiotic cream for cuts

____ Upset stomach medication
____ Antihistamines, decongestants

Miscellaneous

____ Backpack
____ Athletic equipment
____ Water bottle
____ Cups
____ Plastic containers
____ Ziploc bags

____ Stuffed animal
____ Favorite candy
____ Room fan
____ Tissues
____ Laundry basket/bag
____ Detergent

____ Camera, film
____ Small sewing kit
____ Yaffa blocks (use for shelving or storage)
____ (Optional: folding drying rack)

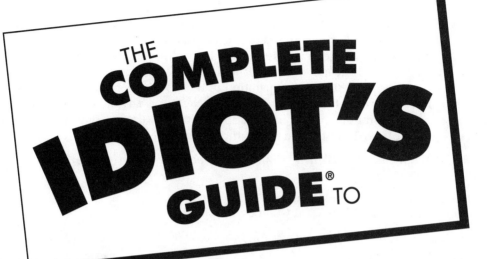

THE **COMPLETE IDIOT'S GUIDE**® TO

College Survival

by Laurie Rozakis, Ph.D.

ALPHA

A Pearson Education Company

Publisher
Marie Butler-Knight

Product Manager
Phil Kitchel

Managing Editor
Jennifer Chisholm

Senior Acquisitions Editor
Randy Ladenheim-Gil

Development Editor
Michael Thomas

Senior Production Editor
Christy Wagner

Copy Editor
Lisa M. Lord

Illustrator
Jody Schaeffer

Cover Designers
Mike Freeland
Kevin Spear

Book Designers
Scott Cook and Amy Adams of DesignLab

Indexer
Tonya Heard

Layout/Proofreading
Angela Calvert
John Etchison
Elizabeth Louden

Contents at a Glance

Contents

Foreword

For as long as I can remember, my mother has been giving me advice. When I was young, the advice was simple and succinct: "Eat your vegetables." "Pick up your toys." "Turn off your light and go to bed!" (I never really got the hang of that last bit—she still needs to remind me to sleep every now and again.) And from the very first time she told me not to touch the stove because it was hot, I figured out that she must know what she's talking about.

It sometimes gets to the point where I don't even realize how much my mother's advice helps me. But then someone will knock on my dorm room door at 3:00 A.M. searching for a can opener, a roll of duct tape, or a little mayo, and I'll be able to help them out because my mother insisted I always be well-stocked. Or I'll hear a story about one of my high school pals switching schools for the third time because they have no idea where they want to be or what they want to do, and I'll be thankful that my mother made me check out lots of schools and figure out which school was right for me.

Though I have no desire to upstage my mother, I would like to give a few tips from my experience as a college student. For the real deal, you'll need to read *The Complete Idiot's Guide to College Survival,* but here are a few starting points that I've always found helpful:

➤ **Don't get flustered.** College is chock-full of new experiences, and some of them will be a little overwhelming. Keep your cool—after all, you got in, so you *do* belong there! Remind yourself that you *can* handle college. Then read *The Complete Idiot's Guide to College Survival* to get the fine points. (It's like calling my mother, but much cheaper.)

➤ **Try everything.** If your school has an Activities Fair, sign up for anything that looks even vaguely interesting. You can always back out of something later that you're not enjoying, but give everything—especially things you've never done before—a chance.

➤ **Don't start a relationship during orientation week with someone you've just met.** If you can, avoid romantic entanglements for the first semester.

➤ **Don't be afraid to ask for help.** Professors, resident advisers, teaching assistants, counselors, and, of course, your parents are there to help you (even your fellow students, who may have can openers and duct tape). If there is something you're having trouble with on your own, it's okay to ask for help. Nobody is expected to do it all themselves.

➤ **Above all, remember that college is a whole new ballgame.** While you might have been a big fish in a small pond before, you're in the ocean now. Don't let being back at the bottom of the food chain get you down—you just have to work a little harder to get yourself back up there.

Occasionally, I'll get an e-mail from a high school senior who's looking to apply to my school, or who has gotten in and wants to know what to expect. Now, I don't have to spend hours drafting e-mails of my limited experiences—I can just refer them to this book!

In *The Complete Idiot's Guide to College Survival,* my mother answers every question you could have, drawing on both her experience as a professor and as the mother of a successful college student. You'll also find great advice from other students inside, because my mother interviewed every college student I've ever known. The treasure trove of knowledge in this book will be useful to every student out there.

Skim the book for the answers to your specific questions or read every word. Either way, any college student who follows the paths my mother sets out will not only survive college, but succeed in college and in life.

That said, start reading—but do remember to sleep at some point. I still forget that on occasion, and my dear mother's voice on the telephone reminds me, "Turn off your light and go to bed!"

Charles Rozakis

Charles Rozakis is a sophomore at Princeton University majoring in Economics. In addition to his course load, Charles is involved in many extracurricular activities. He even gets reasonable amounts of sleep. How does he do all this? He listens to his mother, of course!

Introduction

➤ What should I pack to bring to college?

➤ Help! I hate my roommate and don't know what to do!

➤ What classes do I need to take? When should I declare my major?

➤ Why am I having problems passing my classes? After all, I was an A student in high school.

➤ Should I pledge a Greek organization? If so, at what point in my college career?

➤ How do I write a term paper?

➤ I'm always broke. How can I keep track of my money and make it last?

➤ Should I get a job while I'm in college? If so, where? Doing what?

➤ What's all this I hear about alcohol abuse and date rape? How can I reduce the risks that I face?

➤ I think I want to get an off-campus apartment. How do I go about getting one?

➤ Should I study abroad?

As these questions suggest, going off to college is both exciting and terrifying. What to bring? What to expect? How to cope? It's a time of great change for students and parents alike as families make the big leap into the next stage of life.

In *The Complete Idiot's Guide to College Survival,* I'll help you cope with some of the most common—and upsetting—situations that arise when you go off to college. I wrote this book for the following people:

➤ High school students preparing for college

➤ College freshmen

➤ College sophomores, juniors, and seniors

➤ Newly minted college graduates

➤ Parents of college students

Today, having a college education is essential for keeping pace with the dizzying whirl of technological change. Whether you decide to pursue a two-year degree, a four-year degree, or graduate school, *The Complete Idiot's Guide to College Survival* will give you the tools you need to excel in college.

What You'll Learn in This Book

Far too many college students get derailed by the demands of dealing with sudden independence. Few students are prepared for the difficult classes, aloof professors, and peer pressure they encounter in college. Coping with roommates from different backgrounds, classmates from foreign cultures, and professors who refuse to coddle students increases the student's sense of disorientation.

The Complete Idiot's Guide to College Survival will give you the strategies you need to deal with the demanding college environment. I'll teach you effective study skills to help you do your best in class, including ways to deal with professors, teaching assistants, and the staggering workload. I'll help you learn powerful time-management techniques so you get all your work done—and have time to play.

Adjusting to college takes time and work, but the effort pays off. I can't promise you that going off to college will be a snap, but I *can* guarantee you that by the time you finish this book, you'll have the skills to succeed at college.

How This Book Is Organized

This book is divided into five sections that take you through the process of adjusting to college life. Here's what you'll find in each part of the book.

Part 1, "Campus Life," introduces you to choosing dorms and rooms and getting along with your roommate(s). You'll see how to pack what you need, too. Next comes the inside scoop on orientation, doing your laundry, coping with illness, and eating smart. I'll also show you how to get a handle on selecting classes, registering, and working with your advisor as you think about your major and minor course of study. In addition, you'll discover the importance of becoming involved in campus activities. This section concludes with effective strategies for coping with some of the bad stuff that can happen: homesickness, clinical depression, dissatisfaction with school, and academic failure.

Part 2, "A Class Act," shows you how to get a leg up on classroom success. You'll learn the importance of going to class, following the syllabus, attending office hours, and participating in class. Discover how to make the most of your study time by getting the right attitude, becoming a powerful reader, taking great notes, mastering memory tricks, and studying in groups, too. Then get the inside scoop on preparing for tests, taking tests, and learning from your test performance. Part 2 concludes with step-by-step instructions for writing great college term papers.

Part 3, "Money Matters," shows you how to budget your money, set up and balance a checking account, and use an ATM. I also teach you all about credit, focusing on how to make credit work for you during your college years—and after you graduate. Also find out how to finance your education through scholarships, grants, and loans and evaluate whether you should work while you attend college.

Part 4, "Reality Bites," educates you about sexually transmitted diseases, birth control, and rape prevention. You'll also learn to deal with intolerance on campus, including sexual harassment, racial and religious discrimination, and homophobia. Discover how to be a good roommate and what to do if you and your roommate just can't get along. This section concludes with frank advice about dealing with alcohol and drug use on campus.

Part 5, "Moving Up, Moving On," addresses issues you face as your college career progresses: moving off campus, studying abroad, taking time off, obtaining internships, and transferring colleges. I'll also help you identify your marketable skills, and prepare for being a college graduate. Then comes a chapter on commencement and taking your future into your own hands.

More for Your Money!

In addition to all the explanations and advice, this book gives you even more help when it comes to adjusting to college. Here's how you can recognize these features:

Below "C" Level

These warnings can help you stay on track. Each one makes it a little easier for you to avoid the problems that college students often encounter.

Extra Credit

These are interesting, useful bits of background information that give you the "inside edge" when dealing with the college culture.

Crib Notes

Go to the head of the class, thanks to the extra help these notes provide. These hints help you deal with many aspects of college life, including classes, classmates, and campus life.

Learn the Lingo

Here's where I explain the terms used by college officials, in college correspondence, and all around campus.

Dedication

My grateful appreciation, admiration, and deep respect for the gifted teachers in Farmingdale who have eased my own children's transition through school and into college:

Bob Andersen, math

Murray Cantor, assistant principal

Helen Citrano, physical education

Archie Defendini, math

Bradford DeMilo, music education

Joshua Golbert, music education

Flora Hartford, social studies/history

Barbara Lemming, guidance counselor

Michelle Lindsley, music education

Joanne Miltenberg, math

Jill Citrano Nimphius, foreign language

Ken Schwinn, English

Louise Skrzynecki, elementary school

Special Thanks to ...

This book would not have been possible without the generous help of many friends and friends of friends. My thanks to the following kind, intelligent, and gracious people:

Jimmy Anderson, the State University of New York College of Technology at Farmingdale

Drew Batchelder, Kenyon College

Barbara Bengels, Hofstra University

Kelly Betts, C.W. Post College (Greenvale, New York)

Emily Bloch, Queens College (New York)

Bonnie Bloom, University of North Carolina at Chapel Hill

Beth Bolger, the State University of New York at Cortland

Danielle Bobb, the State University of New York College of Technology at Farmingdale

John Buettner, Washington College, College Relations Staff (Maryland)

Nathan Buxhoeveden, Virginia Military Institute

Jennifer Ching, Seattle University

Maureen Colson, the State University of New York at Potsdam

Val Delaportes, the State University of New York at New Paltz

Deanna Deppen, Bryn Mawr College

Lynn Ekstrand, Quinnipiac University

Paul Faldetta, Nassau Community College (Uniondale, New York)

Melissa ("Issa") Ferrarese, Pennsylvania State University

Billy Fields, Indiana University

Mike Flynn, Georgetown University

Meish Goldish, Case Western Reserve (Cleveland, Ohio)

Bob Greenberger, the State University of New York at Binghamton

Danielle Guarracino, Cornell University

Doug Hamblin, University of Kentucky

John Hauff, the State University of New York College of Technology at Farmingdale

Patrick Holden, the State University of New York at Potsdam

Jonathan Hutzel, the State University of New York College of Technology at Farmingdale

Jonathan Kadishson, Lehigh University (Pennsylvania)

Kristel Kubart, Holy Cross College (Massachusetts)

Carol Lash, the State University of New York at Albany

Lason Leard, University of San Diego

Paul Lee, Princeton University

Gina Lewis, Boston University

Sharon Li, University of San Francisco

Marie Lilly, Clarion College (Pennsylvania)

xix

Kelly Madden, the State University of New York College of Technology at Farmingdale

Sapna Maloor, Fordham College (New York)

Lori Marlar, Murray State University (Murray, Kentucky)

Terrence McGlynn, Occidental College (undergraduate), the University of Colorado (graduate), the University of San Diego (professor)

Nneka McPherson, the State University of New York College of Technology at Farmingdale

Nick Monroy, Hofstra University (New York)

Stephanie Muntone, Oberlin College

Ellen Nelson

Mary Buell Nemerov, University of California at Berkeley

Syreeta Owens, the State University of New York College of Technology at Farmingdale

Scott Palma, Hofstra University (New York)

Jillian Palmieri, the State University of New York College of Technology at Farmingdale

Judith Pasko, California State Northridge

David Pucik, Columbia University (New York)

Danny Rivera, DeSales University (formerly Allentown College, Pennsylvania)

John Roach, the State University of New York College of Technology at Farmingdale

Jessica Roncker, The Evergreen State College (Washington)

Bob Rozakis, Hofstra University (New York)

Charles Rozakis, Princeton University

Chris Seifert, University of Illinois

Jill Semko, Indiana University

Lee Silverberg, Southwestern University

Pamela Smith, the State University of New York College of Technology at Farmingdale

Robyn Smith, Syracuse University

Mary Ellen Snodgrass, University of North Carolina at Greensboro

Lindsay Stern, the State University of New York at New Paltz

Michelle Stern, Mt. Holyoke College

Jessica Swantek, The College of William and Mary (Virginia)

Rob Swantek, Vanderbilt University (Tennessee)

Catherine Thomas, University of Maryland (College Park) and Pennsylvania State University

Michael Thomas, Eastern Kentucky University, University of Iowa

Erika Timar, University of California at Davis

Dan Vayda, Washington College (Chestertown, Maryland)

Christy Wagner, Ball State University (Muncie, Indiana)

Kathryn Werntz, Alfred University (New York)

Mark Wong, Academy of Art College, San Francisco

Susan Wright, New York University

Trademarks

All terms mentioned in this book that are known to be or are suspected of being trademarks or service marks have been appropriately capitalized. Alpha Books and Pearson Education cannot attest to the accuracy of this information. Use of a term in this book should not be regarded as affecting the validity of any trademark or service mark.

Part 1

Campus Life

"In my freshman year, I wasn't involved in anything except going to classes and working. However, because I smiled at my classmates and talked to them, I made a lot of friends. In the summer and fall of my sophomore year, I got more involved in my school's theater scene, and joined a student activist club, making even more friends and acquaintances. By keeping in contact with people you know, meeting new people, joining clubs, and just being friendly, you can make tons of friends."

—Emily Bloch, Queens College

Let's start by getting you settled into college life! In Part 1 you'll learn how to choose a dorm and get off on the right foot with your roommate(s). I'll show you what to bring and how to decide whether to take your car to campus. Next, you'll discover how to take charge on campus by participating in freshman orientation, doing your laundry, coping with illness, and selecting and registering for classes. You'll find detailed information on clubs, fraternities, and sororities. Part 1 concludes with a chapter on coping with some of the problems that can arise when you start college.

Movin' In

"When you're moving in, say 'Hi!' and meet new people. Some of the people I met the first day have turned out to be great friends."

—Patrick Holden, the State University of New York at Potsdam

No matter how anxious you are to begin your college career, it's scary moving out of your home and into a college dorm or apartment. Your world will suddenly be filled with new people, new places, new food. You're probably obsessing along these lines: "Will I like my roommate? Will he (or she) like *me?* Will I have the things I need? Will I be able to find my way around?" Relax. All freshmen and transfer students are thinking the same things.

Settling in isn't as difficult as you might think. There are likely to be a few stumbling blocks on the road to college adjustment, but most are easily avoided.

The Best Room in the House

Everyone has a horror story of the roommate from the Dark Side, but few people pay attention to the *dorm room,* which can be just as important as the *roommate.* Depending on your college's facilities, you might be able to choose the type of dorm you want. Here are some of the options:

Dorm Type	Description
Co-ed dorms	Male and females on the same floor or alternating floors
Single-sex dorms	All male or all female
Quiet dorms	Dorms with strict rules about noise
All freshmen	All newbies
Mixed classes	Freshmen, sophomores, juniors, seniors
Chemical-free dorms	No alcohol or drugs allowed
Off-campus housing	Apartments not on main campus

Crib Notes

In general, freshmen get the least desirable dorms; seniors, the best digs.

Some of these choices overlap. For example, you could have mixed-class off-campus housing or chemical-free, quiet, single-sex dorms.

Which one do you pick? If you're a party animal, do you really want to be in the quiet dorm? But maybe that's just the atmosphere you need to get your work done, at least at first. If you're Betty or Bobby Bookworm, it's tempting to seclude yourself in the nunnery or monastery (as the single-sex quiet dorms are often nicknamed). That might sound like an appealing choice, but shouldn't you use this opportunity to get out and meet people? I strongly advise freshmen or transfer students to avoid off-campus housing because it makes it more difficult to participate in campus life.

Bosom Buddies

It's not uncommon for friends to select the same college. You might even be attending the same college as your brother, sister, or cousin. Why not be roommates? After all, rooming with a friend or relative has to be easier than rooming with a stranger, right?

Yes and no. While it may seem like a great idea to be paired up with someone you've known for a long time, there are also disadvantages. The following chart summarizes the pros and cons. Study it to decide whether you really want to room with your high school friend or relative.

Rooming with a Friend or Relative

Advantages	Disadvantages
Built-in friend	Less likely to meet new people
May ease homesickness	Familiarity breeds contempt
Know each other's habits	May destroy the friendship

The Numbers Game

You might also have the option of choosing the *number* of roommates you have. Here are your choices:

Number of Students	Name of Room	Upside	Downside
one	single	privacy	loneliness
two	double	possible friend	possible murder rap
three	triple	possible friend	odd man out = bad feelings
four	quad	lots of friends	mass chaos

Only you can decide, but here's my recommendation: If you can get it, go for a quad. Odds are that the room will look like the Black Hole of Calcutta within a week, but a quad is the easiest way to make at least one close friend out of three. If you aren't getting along with one of your quad-mates, it's easy to misplace him or her in the mess.

The Odd Couple: My Roommate and I

Robyn Smith, a sophomore at Syracuse University, shared her first experience with a roommate:

> "I had a HORRIBLE roommate freshman year! We just didn't get along or respect each other. We sat down and talked about our issues calmly, and drew up a roommate agreement that we both abided by. We actually turned out to be pretty decent friends this year. We hang out a bit and have lunch together once a week. Your roommate isn't always going to be your best friend. If you

Grade: **D⁻** (!)

Below "C" Level

Not surprisingly, a person's sexual orientation is a key point of concern for many potential roommates. With few exceptions, roommate situations don't reach "red alert" on the basis of sexual orientation alone. More often, meltdown comes as a result of messiness, inconsiderate behavior, or immaturity.

expect that, and they aren't, it's going to be a big letdown. But if you both handle it maturely, it'll work out."

When you send in your acceptance letter and that big fat tuition check, you'll probably be asked to fill out a roommate questionnaire. Some colleges have a brief form; others send enough paper to cover a small continent.

Whether you have half a page or a book to fill out, take this questionnaire seriously. Paul Lee, a graduate of Princeton University, carries my advice one step further: "I encourage honesty on housing forms, but levity never hurts, and you might end up with someone with a sense of humor like yours, which could be a blessing."

University housing officials (along with everyone else on campus) really want you to be happy and to succeed at college. They recognize that matching you with a suitable roommate helps make the transition to college life easier. If you're lucky, your roommate(s) will become a friend(s). If not, you can coexist peacefully for a year.

Extra Credit

"In order to ensure I would not be paired with a roommate as a freshman at Princeton, I made sure to fill in my housing form with more detail than I think the housing people wanted. I discussed my being an only child and therefore being accustomed to getting my way in all matters, my rampant paranoia and xenophobia, and my need for personal space at odd hours of the day and evening. I concluded by saying that anyone compatible with my issues was more frightening than I was, and even I was not crazy enough to room with them. Whether or not I amused the housing folks, I did end up with a single room for my first two years. I needed that space to adjust to college life."

—Paul Lee, Princeton University

Truth or Consequences

"The only life lesson I learned in college was NEVER believe that people are what they appear to be—the showboats are as gauche and insecure as the rowboats. But they hide it better."

—Drew Batchelder, Kenyon College

If the questionnaire is brief, feel free to add information about personal habits that really matter to you. Remember, you and a total stranger are going to be confined in a room the size of a matchbox, so you're going to have to get along if you don't want to be tearing each other to bits.

Here are some issues to consider specifying:

➤ Drinking and drugging

➤ Lifestyle: clean or messy

➤ Respect for personal property

➤ Sleep habits: going to bed early or staying up late

➤ Smoking

➤ Taste in music

Below "C" Level

Don't wait for your roommate to make the first move! Call, write, or e-mail when you get your housing assignment packet.

First Contact

"I lucked out and got a really nice, considerate, easy-to-get-along-with roommate. Sometimes we don't agree, but it's important to not let those things bother me. I respect when she needs quiet time to study or sleep, but I don't always cater to her, either. I do what I want to do as long as it doesn't affect her negatively."

—Melissa Ferrarese, Penn State University

When you get your roommate assignment, the housing officials also include his or her address, telephone, and probably e-mail address. Make first contact as soon as possible to introduce yourself. My son lived in a quad his first year at college, so he had three roommates. One of his roommates, Nick, introduced himself by sending a letter scrawled in purple crayon. My son instantly knew that Nick had a great sense of humor and would be fun to live with. Time has proved him right.

In addition to establishing a common bond with your roommate(s), making contact ensures that you don't bring duplicate items—or forget something you really need. Since all dorm rooms are smaller than you'd like, who needs two sofas, two carpets, or two TVs? My son and his roommates contacted each other via e-mail to work out the crucial issue of their room's sound system. In the flurry of e-mails, the boys soon realized they had 12 speakers—but no stereo! My son nicknamed their system "Surround Silence" but arranged for one of the boys to bring the actual stereo.

Hints for Dealing with a Roommate

"I met Joan about the second week in my dorm. It turned out she had a TV and invited some of us down to her room one evening. She was a senior, living with another friend. We hit it off immediately, and that was it. There are only a few times in your life that you connect with someone in that way. We chose to room together the following year; she had one more semester to go."

—Carol Lash, the State University of New York at Albany

Nneka McPherson of the State University of New York College of Technology at Farmingdale suggests the following for getting along with roomates:

1. Be considerate. For example, don't claim a bedroom before other people have arrived. In fact, don't lay claim to any part of the room until everyone is present.

2. Be nice. Follow the Golden Rule: "Do unto others as you would like them to do unto you."

3. Don't buy large, hard-to-split items jointly. It's fine to share the jumbo-size laundry detergent, but dividing up a sofa at the end of the year can shatter even the closest friendships. I've heard roommates screaming: "Your friend broke the sofa's springs!" "No, your friend did it!"

4. Be careful about spreading tales. Loose lips sink ships and shatter budding friendships. Things said in confidence have a way of turning around and biting you in the butt.

5. Don't blow small issues out of proportion, but don't be afraid to communicate your concern about large issues.

6. When you discuss problems, offer constructive criticism. And take suggestions for improvement in the spirit in which they were offered.

7. Keep yourself clean. Take a shower every day. No one wants a smelly roommate.

8. Keep your half of the room clean. Pick up after yourself. Do your laundry so it doesn't smell up the room, take out your trash, and throw away any empty food containers.

9. Follow the dorm rules. Most dorms do not allow small electrical appliances such as crock pots, microwaves, and popcorn makers. Don't push the envelope and smuggle them in. You'll get yourself and your roommate in trouble.

10. Be considerate when it comes to dating. Never park your love interest in your roommate's bed!

Crib Notes

"Don't forget the stupid stuff—pillows and other small things you take for granted at home."

—Dan Vayda, Washington College (Chestertown, Maryland)

11. Stay out of your roommate's side of the room. Never touch your roommate's possessions without permission.

12. Always be yourself.

Packed to the Brim

> "If you can possibly arrange it, move in early. You're less likely to fight for elevators and stairway space. The less hassle you have moving in, the better you'll feel once you finish and the more you'll want to do something fun, like explore your new campus."
>
> —Dave Pucik, Columbia University

The experiences of countless college students prove that Einstein was correct: Two objects can't occupy the same space at the same time. Therefore, it's important to take what you need, and *only* what you need. (Of course, you've already spoken to your roommate[s] to make sure you're not bringing duplicate items.)

Remember, if you forget something or need something you don't have, it *will* be available. Many colleges allow vendors to set up tents during the first week of school to sell big items such as carpets and furniture, so you may not need to rent a van and lug these items from home. Upper-class students sell gently used refrigerators, carpets, sofas, computers, and futons at reasonable prices. Colleges often rent big items such as water coolers, refrigerators, and sofas, too.

Below "C" Level

"Avoid halogen lamps; they are a fire hazard because they get really hot really quickly."

—Jill Semko, Indiana University

Crib Notes

If you rely on prescription medication, *always* have a copy of your prescription with you as well as one on file in the Student Health Office. Further, if you have a serious medical condition, be sure to meet with health officials to discuss your medical history. You may want to share some of this information with your roommate and professors as well.

Everything but the Kitchen Sink

> "Moving into my room in college was extremely difficult. I packed for about a week before I left. It's hard to pack your whole life into just a few boxes in a short amount of time. It felt like I had so much stuff, but then when I thought about it, it was kind of sad that my whole life fit into our minivan."
>
> —Melissa Ferrarese, Penn State University

Melissa just told you what not to bring. I'll add something else—leave all your gold and diamonds at home. You're attending college, not a fashion show, and small valuables can disappear too easily.

Now, what *should* you bring? Consult the tear-out card in the front of this book for a checklist of items I recommend. Use it each semester you pack for school. As you pack, keep this thought firmly in mind: Some dorm rooms are even smaller than the law requires the minimum prison cell to be!

Crib Notes

"If you bring a computer/buy a computer/borrow Dad's computer/steal your sister's computer ... install current virus-checking software on it! I lost a disk of creative writing stories after printing an assignment in a computer cluster, and I have heard too many horror stories about papers/dissertations/everything they ever knew and loved being claimed by computer viruses to not spread this pearl around to anyone and everyone."

—Paul Lee, Princeton University

Here's some parting advice from Lason Leard, a senior at the University of San Diego: "Don't bring everything you own. You barely need anything. Each year I've cut back what I haul back and forth to campus in half, and now that I'm a senior, I still have too much. Only bring what you need, because not having a bunch of junk will make your life easier."

Below "C" Level

You can buy all your office supplies on campus, but you almost always pay less if you buy them at home when they are on sale.

Driving Ace

You can't live without your wheels—or can you? When you think about whether to bring your car to campus, consider these factors:

1. **The rules.** Many colleges do not allow freshmen to have cars.

2. **Public transportation.** Before you decide to bring your car, see what kind of public transportation is available in the city/town. Can

you get where you need to go on the bus, train, or trolley? If you're planning to tutor or work off campus, can you get there on public transportation?

3. **Parking.** The fees might be stiff. In addition, you might find yourself parking so far away from your dorm that you need a car to get to your car!

4. **Lend lease.** If you have a car on campus and your buddies don't, you're going to be driving a lot of people around, lending your car to your newfound friends, or feeling pangs of guilt that you're doing neither.

5. **Car care and cost.** Cars require a lot of care and expense to maintain. Who's going to pay for insurance? Repairs? In addition, if you have to park in a remote parking lot, your car is likely to be more vulnerable to break-ins and theft.

6. **Temptation to leave.** If you have a car, you're more likely to leave campus. You might frequent the bars in town, cruise the malls in the suburbs, or go home every weekend. Is this how you want to spend your college years?

Crib Notes

"Wear fuzzy slippers. Dorm floors can be miserably cold in winter."

—Mary Ellen Snodgrass, University of North Carolina at Greensboro

Money: Don't Leave Home Without It

"I still don't know how to handle money. I've never used an ATM machine and don't know where one is on campus. I deposited a check once and had to call home to ask how. I use cash mostly. The only thing I know how to do is write checks."

—Melissa Ferrarese, Penn State University

Now, Melissa is one of my favorite people, as bright as a new penny. She just never got around to learning how to handle money. That isn't going to happen to you, because I'm going to make sure you *are* financially savvy. (I'm also going to send Issa a copy of this book as soon as it's printed!)

Financial issues will be covered in detail in Part 3, "Money Matters," but having a handle on basic money issues before you move in is a must. Start here:

Learn the Lingo

Reconciling a checkbook is deducting any checks from your balance, adding any deposits, and making sure the bank has correctly computed your balance.

1. Learn how to handle your money *before* you go to college. Be sure you can make out a check, *reconcile* your checkbook, and use a credit card and a debit card.

2. Before the first day of classes, discuss with your parents how you will pay for your everyday expenses.

3. Check the ATM charges. Make sure you're not getting socked with stiff fees. If you are, change machines. If this isn't possible, take out larger amounts at a time to reduce the number of fees.

Below "C" Level

"Do not get a credit card if you don't have a job to pay the money back. Credit card companies prey on unsuspecting freshmen. Everywhere you turn there are credit card applications."

—Jill Semko, Indiana University

4. Set up a checking account in a local bank. Often, you can have the bank send you the papers you need to open an account. If not, open the account when you return for a school visit before the term starts. As a last resort, open the account when you move in (although the bank will be mobbed that day).

5. If at all possible, find a local bank that has a branch in your hometown. If Mom and Dad are forking over your spending money, a hometown branch makes it easier for them to make a deposit.

6. Most incoming students (and their parents) are unprepared for the costs of everyday living. As Rob Swantek from Vanderbilt University realized, "If you have a meal plan, try to eat on campus as much as possible. Eating off campus gets really expensive, really quick."

Let the Adventure Begin!

College is the beginning of a great adventure. You'll make new friends, explore new surroundings, acquire new skills, and embark on the road to adulthood. College can be the best experience of your life ... or one of the worst. In large part, it depends on how you approach it.

Now that you have the information you need to start off on the right foot, you can approach moving in, meeting your roommate, and beginning college life with a positive attitude and a smile!

The Least You Need to Know

➤ If you have a choice, select your dorm, room, and number of roommates carefully. Fill out roommate questionnaires thoughtfully and in detail.

➤ If a relative or friend is attending the same college, consider carefully whether you want to room with him or her.

➤ Contact your roommate(s) once you've been assigned and follow my suggestions for getting along peacefully.

➤ Pack judiciously. Room space is very tight.

➤ Under most circumstances, underclass students shouldn't bring their cars to school.

➤ Learn to handle your money *before* you go away to school. Talk about money with your parents, set up bank accounts, and budget carefully.

Chapter 2

Taking Charge on Campus

In This Chapter

➤ Attending orientation

➤ Getting around—without getting *too* lost

➤ Dealing with laundry

➤ Coping with illness

➤ Eating smart

"I can come and go, hang out with whoever I want, and do whatever I want to do, without explaining myself first. The lessons that you learn from these experiences are some of the most important lessons you can learn your whole college career. Taking control of your own life is a big responsibility. It's even harder when it all comes down to your own decision, 'cause Mommy isn't there making you do these things anymore."

—Maureen Colson, the State University of New York at Potsdam

So Mommy, Daddy, Biff, and Muffy wave good-bye. You choke back a few tears and sniffle a little, but you're secretly muttering, "Free at last! Free at last!" Then reality sets in like a smack in the face: You have to take charge of your own life. How do you begin? You begin by getting acclimated to your new environment.

Freshman Orientation

Some colleges go natural and offer incoming students three days in the woods to bond over marshmallows and mosquitoes. Others take the high road and invite you to renovate inner-city playgrounds or build Houses for Humanity. Still others hint at parties to come with weekends of water balloons, cotton candy, and three-legged races. Whatever form they take, all colleges run orientation programs the week before classes start to help you ease into campus life.

Like senior proms, homecoming bonfires, and Woodstock wanna-bes, college orientation programs are must-do events. These programs offer you a chance to meet a wide variety of students, from fellow freshmen to upper-class swells. (Juniors and seniors are eager to find new blood for their clubs, fraternities, sororities, and intramural teams, so they recruit at freshman orientation.)

Orientation programs offer another bonus: Professors, administrators, and support personnel such as administrative assistants also show up. The support staff are vital, because they're the people you'll need later to get replacement IDs, dorm keys, and other necessities of college life.

Crib Notes

Get your student ID as soon as possible. In most cases, it's your library card, meal pass, and security proof all in one. And keep it safe; replacement fees can be stiff.

The Golden Mean

Some students, like Jonathan Kadishson of Lehigh University, plunge in with gusto. Here's what Jonathan told me:

> "The college will probably sponsor a number of programs in the first few days to get you oriented, and for fun. Try to do as much as possible, just to get a feel for the college and the people around you."

Other students, however, find orientation programs too much of a good thing, like a weekend at an overpriced amusement park. These students suggest you do less at orientation. As Michelle Stern of Mt. Holyoke College advises:

> "Don't feel obligated to go to everything at orientation. The worst thing is not to be settled with personal stuff when classes start. You can still be decorating your dorm, but have your clothes and computer set up before classes begin. Not everything at orientation is mandatory, so pick and choose. Some things can be very helpful."

Learn the Lingo

Freshman orientation is the introduction program offered the week before classes begin. It often has a clever name, such as "Adventure Weekend." If in doubt, ask your RA (resident advisor) what the orientation program is called on your campus.

Walk This Way

Here's my advice:

➤ Take orientation seriously. Always get complete information on all activities offered.

➤ Read through all the materials and decide upon which activities to attend.

➤ Get some advice. As Dan Vayda of Washington College advises, "Talk to your RA and find out which programs to pay attention to."

➤ Know yourself. If you're already frazzled or tire easily, don't overdo it at orientation.

➤ While it's tempting to stay glued to your roommate's side, do this gig solo. You're at orientation to meet and greet, to make new friends, to get yourself used to college. If you're attached to someone else, you'll be far less likely to pay attention to your surroundings and form your own opinions about the college.

> **Crib Notes**
>
> "Seek out the important offices on campus and introduce yourself to the staff there, especially student affairs, financial aid, and the registrar's office. This may help in situations down the road. If possible, become known to the secretaries in these offices, for they are often running everything from behind the scenes and will help you out if you need it."
>
> —Dan Vayda, Washington College

Lost in Space

Most college campuses are astonishingly large—even a "small" campus can be spread over 350 acres! Fortunately, most of the buildings are usually clustered around a quad, but they all look staggeringly alike at first. Whether you're surrounded by hallowed halls of ivy-covered bricks or a postmodern masterpiece, it can seem impossible to figure out where you're going. Take a deep breath and do the following:

> **Below "C" Level**
>
> You often have to sign up for special orientation programs early on to ensure a space. Be sure to go through all the papers and send in any reservations and fees.

➤ **Get an individual map.** Easy as pie: It will be in your orientation packet. (Another reason to attend orientation and read all the handouts you get.) Mark the places you have to go to.

➤ **Use campus maps.** If by some chance you've forgotten your map, look for the campus map signs. They'll look like huge bulletin boards.

➤ **Find landmarks.** Yes, all the buildings look alike, so use trees, statues, gardens, sets of benches, fountains, and other landmarks to orient yourself.

➤ **Ask for directions.** You'll learn how to get to your destination and you'll meet some new people. You'll be pleased at how friendly people are, too; my fellow professors and I always walk lost students to their destinations on campus. We get to meet our freshmen and show off some of the most beautiful places on our campus.

A Clean Machine

"I never did laundry before college. I still mess up sometimes. I recently left one new navy blue sock in with my whites and now I have pale blue underwear and socks. Chalk it up to experience."

—Robyn Smith, Syracuse University

Now, some freshmen are not that eager to unlock the mysteries of laundry. What I like to call "Laundry Avoidance Syndrome" is more common than you might think. Jonathan Kadishson, a freshman at Lehigh University, advises: "Hold out as long as possible and take it home to your parents." (Little does he know that I have warned his mother, my dear friend Barbara Rogan, of his intentions.) Lee Silverberg, a graduate of Southwestern University, is more savvy since she has already completed her education. She suggests that you "bring lots of underwear to college." Despite the different approaches each student takes, you see the common thread: Laundry Avoidance Syndrome.

Extra Credit

A surprising number of colleges offer laundry service. You may also opt to take your laundry off campus to a Laundromat that will wash, dry, iron, and fold everything. Having someone else do your laundry has distinct advantages, but such service does not come cheap.

If you want people on campus to come within 10 feet of you, you're going to have to wash your clothes more than once a semester. Ditto on your sheets and towels. Your jeans need washing long before they can stand up by themselves. The "sniff" test isn't valid; maybe *you* can't smell them, but I bet my deodorant that someone else can. And they aren't fragrant.

Speed Read for Clean Clothes

Let's start with the most basic rule of clothing care: Some things can be machine-washed, and some things can't. You know that cats don't wash well; well, neither do garments labeled "Dry-clean only." *Always* read the garment label to see if your garment can be washed safely. Garment labels tell you the best way to wash, dry, and even iron clothing so it stays looking good and you stay looking even better.

Garment labels are either written in English or use symbols. Here's what you'll see on the label:

➤ **Wash.** The wash portion of the label tells you everything from which wash cycle to use to what type of detergent or bleach is recommended.

➤ **Dry cycle.** Garment labels specify which cycle—if any—to use to dry an item.

➤ **Ironing.** Some clothes need ironing, some don't—so check the label.

➤ **Dry-cleaning.** When a garment label indicates "Dry-clean only," remember that means do not put the item in the washer.

If you've cut off the label, the following chart shows general guidelines for fiber care. Use in case of an emergency.

Machine-Wash	Hand-Wash	Dry-Clean
cotton	most wool sweaters	wool garments
acrylic	some silk garments	some silk garments
nylon	rayon	
polyester	cashmere sweaters	

Using the Washing Machine

Using a washing machine is easy, once you learn a few simple steps. Work with me here because you'll get *far better* results by following these suggestions.

1. Sort items before laundering.

   ➤ Separate whites and colors.

   ➤ Separate sturdy cottons (such as jeans) from delicates (such as undies) and permanent press items (such as shirts).

   ➤ Wash lint-givers (towels) separate from lint-grabbers (permanent press items).

   ➤ Wash heavily and lightly soiled items separately.

2. Prepare the load.

   ➤ Empty pockets.

   ➤ Shake out cuffs.

   ➤ Close zippers and hooks.

   ➤ Repair any holes or tears—washing often makes them bigger!

Below "C" Level

When you're not sure whether to machine-wash or hand-wash a garment, have it dry-cleaned. Next semester, try not to bring any clothes that can't be tossed into the machine.

3. Pretreat any stains with a stain remover, sold in the same aisle as the detergents.

4. Make sure you know how to use the washing machine. When in doubt, read the instructions on the machine. They're most often printed on the inside of the lid.

Crib Notes

Try to remove stains as soon as possible. The longer they sit, the harder it can be to get them out. Use cold water for protein stains like blood or grass. Use warm water for oily stains, such as cosmetics or greasy foods.

Below "C" Level

Fabrics made from natural fibers such as cotton or linen wrinkle a lot. No matter how you wash them, they usually need to be ironed. Sorry!

5. Add water. Select the proper water temperature for best cleaning results.

   ➤ Use HOT water for whites and heavily soiled items.

   ➤ Use WARM water for most loads.

   ➤ Use COLD water for lightly soiled or brightly colored items.

6. When the machine is about half-filled with water, add detergent. Should you use powdered or liquid detergents? Powdered detergents work best on mud and clay stains; liquid detergents are good for cold water washing, pretreating stains, and removing greasy, oily stains. Be sure to use the recommended amount of detergent; when it comes to detergent, more is *not* better!

   You can also add bleach to remove stains, whiten fabrics, and improve cleaning. Chlorine bleach also disinfects and deodorizes. Check care labels and follow package instructions before use.

7. Add clothes. Yes, I know that you want to get all your clothes washed in one load, but be careful not to overfill the machine. The clothes won't wash well and you run the risk of cascading suds all over the floor. Very embarrassing.

8. Relax. This is a good time to study, meet the other students in the laundry room, or take a brief nap.

Using the Dryer

Dryers are wonderful inventions, as anyone who ever had a clothesline will tell you, but beware: Drying clothes on the high settings can turn your T-shirt into a doll shirt. In general, "warm" is usually the best setting. Don't overload the dryer, and keep a close eye on your clothing to make sure it's not crisping.

Some clothes (especially those made of 100 percent cotton) shrink even on the "cool" setting. You may want to invest in a drying rack for these items. These racks are inexpensive (usually $10 to $15) and fold up flat to store.

Other Tips

You can usually avoid ironing by doing your laundry correctly. For example, if you rinse permanent press fabrics in cold water, they'll wrinkle less. Here are some more easy hints:

➤ Use a permanent press cycle, especially if you're washing clothes in hot water.

➤ Don't pack the washing machine. This causes clothes to wrinkle more.

➤ Take clothes out of the dryer as soon as it stops running. The longer they sit, the more they'll wrinkle.

➤ Don't over- or underload the dryer.

➤ According to Lindsay Stern of Alfred University, "Girls: Don't put bras in the dryer! Hang them up!"

➤ According to Dawn Mandich of Alfred University, *always* check the lint trap in the dryer and empty it first. Built-up lint can destroy the dryer and even cause a fire.

Your clothes are expensive, so treat them right. In turn, they'll reward you with many years of loyal and attractive service.

Extra Credit

If your clothes come out of the washer tinted blue, green, purple, pink, red, or other colors, it usually means that dye from another garment washed in the same load wasn't colorfast. Since there's rarely any way to get color bleeds out, you're stuck with some strangely colored clothes until they're consigned to the rag bin.

Crib Notes

Some washers and dryers on campus take quarters; others take a special laundry card. You buy these cards at the bookstore or student center.

From Appendicitis to Upset Stomachs: Health Issues

Being sick is a drag under any circumstances, but it's especially upsetting to get sick when you're away from home and carrying a heavy load of responsibility.

College health infirmaries do their best, but they don't rank high among the students I interviewed for this book. For example, Lindsay Stern of Alfred University shared this terrifying story:

"In the beginning of October, I had flu-like symptoms, including an incredibly swollen throat. The health center gave me antibiotics and told me to wait it out. "In November, I started having a horrible earache on the left side, accompanied by what felt like a swollen gland on that side. I returned to the health center where a nurse practitioner gave me a decongestant. A few days later, the gland was more swollen and I decided go to a real clinic in the closest town. There I saw a different nurse practitioner who immediately gave me antibiotics for a HUGE tonsil and was concerned that it may be an abscess because it was only on one side and she told me to watch it closely. The next night, the mass in the back of my throat was so big I could hardly talk. Wednesday I went back to my school's health center where I FINALLY got to see a doctor who gave me a shot of antibiotics, finally realizing my problem.

"Thursday afternoon my roommate drove me to the hospital and the surgeon admitted me immediately. I was dehydrated from not being able to eat or drink. On Friday, I had surgery to drain the abscess and remove my tonsils and adenoids.

"What is the moral of this horrible story, you ask? Many health centers at schools are run by underpaid staff who see too many common colds and STDs to notice anything else. Learn about other options in your area and always know where the nearest hospital is."

Kathryn Werntz of Alfred University echoed Lindsay's experiences with this warning about the campus clinic:

"If you have ANY doubts about the health services provided on campus, GO ELSEWHERE. It may be worth a trip home to your personal doctor or to a knowledgeable nearby hospital. Personal and secondhand horror stories are atrocious ... I could go on and on about this one ..."

Unfortunately, I had no trouble gathering upsetting stories about campus clinic blunders. Try the following suggestions to make sure you don't end up a sad story in the next edition of this book!

1. Carry comprehensive health insurance. Try to stay on your parents' policy (if they have one) because it's usually far better than the college health policy. In most cases, if you choose the college's student health plan, you'll get treatment only in the campus infirmary. Pay the extra fee to get the option of treatment off campus.

2. Complete all health forms and make sure the campus infirmary has your medical history. Be especially careful to note any chronic conditions you have and medications you might be taking.

3. Always wear identification (not carry—*wear*) if you have a serious condition such as diabetes, epilepsy, or potentially fatal insect or food allergies. There are special medical alert bracelets designed for just this purpose. Don't make health officials guess what treatment you need if you're passed out on the lawn.

4. Be sure you have *all* your inoculations, even the extra ones. All colleges require you to have the basics, such as MMR (measles, mumps, rubella) and tuberculosis. Get the extra shots because contagious illnesses spread like wildfire in close quarters. I strongly recommend hepatitis and flu shots to start.

5. Use common sense. Never share razor blades, toothbrushes, or anything that can come in contact with blood products. (Yes, I know it's gross, but "sleepover guests" have been known to share grooming aids on groggy mornings.)

6. Know your own body and don't ignore the signs of sickness. If you feel sick, you probably are.

7. Take immediate steps to get well if you're sick. Get a fast diagnosis and start taking any medication you're prescribed. Don't say, "I'll wait this one out. I'll feel better soon." Walking around with pneumonia for a week is rarely conducive to quick recoveries.

8. Know what's "going around." If everyone on your floor has a stomach virus, this might not be the night to do the "All-you-can-eat taco bar" and tango the night away. It's probably the night to eat light and get to bed early.

9. Go home if you get seriously ill. Before you leave, speak to all your professors and make arrangements to keep up with the work. If you anticipate needing extensions on your work, have the dean of students intervene and send an official letter about your condition.

10. Give yourself the best chance at staying healthy. Get enough sleep. Eat a balanced diet with fruits, vegetables, and carbs. Exercise. Keep a positive attitude.

Food, Glorious Food

"Whether you eat in college dining facilities or eat off campus, at least a part of your life at college is about eating. What you choose to do really depends on the school itself. Despite popular contention, some campuses actually have very good food. Others, you may not want to touch any of the cafeteria food with a 20-foot pole. At least not without anti-radiation gear. Then there's also the cost. Why should you pay for an off-campus cheeseburger if your meals are included in your housing costs?"

—David Pucik, Columbia University

College food has been much maligned, and there's a good reason for it: Most food served in schools is loaded with fat, salt, and calories. And if that isn't bad enough, it doesn't even taste good. (How can anyone make fat and salt taste bad? I think it's the steam table effect.)

Humor aside, Dave is right: Some colleges really *do* have good food. This raises another problem: If the food at your college is yummy, you're apt to fall prey to the dreaded "Freshman 15," the tendency of freshman to overeat and pack on 15 pounds the first semester. Emily Bloch discovered this her first semester at Queens College:

> "I don't drink, but, boy, do I have a sweet tooth. If the parties don't get you, the desserts definitely do. That brownie with the 16 grams of fat doesn't look TOO harmful in the face of stress and fatigue—but it is!"

Emily offers this advice: "It's good to treat yourself, but try to buy your own snacks in the healthy section of the local supermarket to get you through the day."

Robyn Smith of Syracuse University made this suggestion:

> "Take advantage of the salad bars and vegetarian entrées. I'm not much of a vegetable eater, but a salad with a good fat-free or low-fat dressing really hits the spot now. And, if you eat a salad at the end of the meal instead of the beginning, it helps with the digestive process and soothes your stomach from the 'mystery meat.'"

Below "C" Level

Ask upperclassmen about the quality of food on campus and what they do when they've got those midnight cravings. If you can only eat kosher, make sure you can get kosher.

Sometime during the summer before college starts, you'll most likely be asked to select a meal plan. Most plans have two parts:

➤ The number of cafeteria meals you pay for

➤ The number of "flex points" you can use at various campus eateries, such as delis, coffee shops, and grills

I recommend that you sign up for a plan that guarantees you at least 14 dining hall meals a week. This gives you lunch and dinner every day. You can keep some cereal, milk, and fruit in your room for a healthy breakfast. Having your meals set gives you one less thing to worry about as you settle into college life. Further, the cafeteria is a great place to meet people, hang out, and relax. Jonathan Kadishson, a freshman at Lehigh University, agrees with my advice:

"I have a 14-meal plan, which I find is perfect. Some people have 19, and I don't know anyone that can eat more than 15 in a week. The food isn't great, but there are usually plenty of options. Have healthy food and drinks in your room. As for the Freshman 15, if you are the type that gains weight, you better run or hit the gym, because it's not a myth."

To make the most of whatever meal plan you select, visit different cafeterias around campus and get to know what's served where. Check special dining halls, too, such as the kosher kitchen (if your campus offers one). Not only will shopping around get you the best selection of eats, but you'll also meet a wide variety of people—teachers as well as students.

The Least You Need to Know

➤ Attend orientation activities.

➤ Immediately start finding your way around campus. Use a map and ask for directions, if you need them.

➤ Wash your clothes often and properly.

➤ Have health insurance, up-to-date health forms, and *all* your inoculations.

➤ Get enough sleep, at a balanced diet, exercise, and keep a positive attitude.

➤ If your college offers a meal plan, take it. You can eat well on campus if you select food carefully.

Chapter 3

The Class Experience

In This Chapter

➤ Understanding degree requirements

➤ Working with your advisor

➤ Registering for classes

➤ Buying and selling textbooks

➤ Selecting majors and minors

"If you are thinking about trying something, do it ... the worst thing that can happen is that you don't like it. This is much better than regretting the fact that you did not pursue a class, topic, sport, or club."

—Dan Vayda, Washington College (Chestertown, Maryland)

Dan's advice is solid gold—especially when it comes to planning your class schedule.

End Game

Let's focus here, freshmen: Despite the wonderful whirl of clubs, parties, and plays, you're in college to take classes, get an education, and earn your degree.

The following chart shows the most common undergraduate degrees you can earn. Your college will offer some or all of these degrees, depending on its size and mission:

Degree	Abbreviation	Duration
Associate of Arts	A.A.	2 years
Associate of Science	A.S.	2 years
Bachelor of Arts	B.A.	4 years
Bachelor of Engineering	B.E.S.	4 years
Bachelor of Fine Arts	B.F.A.	4 years
Bachelor of Science	B.S.	4 years
Bachelor of Business Administration	B.B.A	4 years

Learn the Lingo

Core requirements are classes that every student must take regardless of his or her major. **Electives** are free-choice classes.

Crib Notes

In addition to a set number of credits and classes, you may need a minimum cumulative grade point average (GPA) to graduate. At Indiana University's Kelly School of Business, for instance, the required GPA is 2.0 out of 4.0, a "C" average.

Credits and Classes

To earn your degree, you need a specific number of credit hours and a specific set of courses. All classes fall into one or more of the following three categories:

➤ **Core requirements.** Classes that every student must take to graduate.

➤ **Major requirements.** Classes you must take to earn your specialized degree.

➤ **Electives.** Classes you choose according to your preferences. Electives go with your core requirements and major requirements to complete the total number of credits you need to graduate.

According to Emily Block of Queens College: "Required core courses aren't always so bad. In my college, for example, you have to fulfill certain required subjects, like humanities and sciences, but you can choose which courses you want that fall under those subjects. I sometimes get stuck with a course I don't like, but I make the most of it, and try my best."

Most nonlaboratory classes carry three credit hours; most lab classes carry four credit hours. At Indiana University's Kelly School of Business, for example, a student needs a minimum of 124 credit hours to earn the Bachelor of Business Administration degree. Of this number, at least 48 credit hours must be in business and economics courses, and at least 50 credit hours must be in courses other than business and economics.

No Flex Here: Requirements

Not only do you need to amass a specific number of credits, you must also satisfy specific requirements. To earn a B.A. in English at Hofstra University, for example, students must complete 39 credits in literature and 3 credits in English or American history.

➤ 9 credits in foundation courses: ENGL 41 and 6 credits chosen from ENGL 40 or 43, 42, and 51 or 143.

➤ 3 credits in ENGL 100.

➤ 3 credits in major authors chosen from ENGL 107, 115, 116, or 119.

➤ 24 credits of electives chosen from any of the 100-level courses in the English department. At least 6 of these credits must come from courses dealing exclusively with literature written before 1800.

Every program has specific course requirements. Refer to the program of interest in your college class bulletin for specific information. Billy Fields, a graduate of Indiana University, gets right to the point:

"Make sure you know exactly what classes to take and have a plan for getting all the credits you need. I remember one of my good friends went through the graduation ceremony and found out a week later that he was missing two credits and had not, in fact, graduated. I hear this sort of thing happens often."

Below "C" Level

"Especially second semester, you want to talk to as many people as possible to figure out which electives are good, which are hard, interesting, etc. But don't listen to the smartest kid in your hall when he tells you Dynamics of Physics and Rotational Optics is easy, and don't drop out of Intro to Economics because some kid you met at a party said it's hard."

—Jonathan Kadishson, Lehigh University

Dazed and Confused

Selecting classes isn't that difficult if you know what you want. But what if you don't have a clue what you want to study? Try these suggestions:

➤ Sign up for core requirements so that you get them completed up front.

➤ Always include at least one interesting class in a subject you have never explored before, such as economics, geology, computer science, anthropology, or engineering. This helps you discover where your interests and abilities lie. As Patrick Holden of the State University of New York at Potsdam advises, "Whenever you have the chance to take something not pertaining to your major, do it. Not only is it cool to learn new things, but it helps you decide what you want to do with your life."

➤ Attend as many guest seminars and lectures as you can to broaden your horizons. Most colleges have guest programs open to the entire campus nearly every day.

➤ Speak to your advisor about different courses of study and careers.

➤ Ask other students what they are studying and why.

➤ Seek out brief internships in local businesses, companies, and firms to explore different careers firsthand. Internships are a great way to spend part of winter and summer vacations.

A Friend Indeed: Your Advisor

You will be assigned a faculty advisor whose job it is to help you decide which classes to take and to help guide you through the maze of the course catalog. Your advisor is just that—an *advisor,* not someone who calls the shots. The actual selection of classes is completely up to you. Since you're not obligated to follow your advisor's suggestions, it's tragically easy to slip through four years without taking what you need. You'll be the one left carrying the bag—not your advisor. In college, there's no one to blame for screw-ups but yourself.

For example, let's say that your college requires four years of physical education. Perhaps you really do mean to take volleyball, but somehow you never seem to get around to signing up. Or maybe gym isn't your thing, so you decide the rules somehow don't apply to you. Wake up and smell the coffee: They do. Even if you scream, "My advisor never told me!"—and you're right—it won't matter. If you don't complete your requirements, you won't graduate on time.

Here's what you should expect from your advisor:

➤ Reliable information about course contents

➤ Dependable information about university requirements

➤ Suggestions for majors and minors

Extra Credit

You don't have to be best friends with your advisor, but you *do* have to be paired with someone knowledgeable who will spend time helping you. I was blessed with a gracious, generous, and brilliant undergraduate mentor/advisor, Dr. Ruth Prigozy. Ruth, this acknowledgment doesn't begin to thank you for your gentle and consistent guidance.

However, most advisors also take a genuine interest in your academic career and try to help you settle in and prosper. The really top-notch advisors also act as advocates if you need some extra help along the way. And if you're really, really lucky, your advisor will become a mentor and even a friend. I was that lucky.

If you and your advisor don't click, you can usually request another advisor. But first, carefully assess the reason for the friction. It may just take a few weeks for the two of you to get along, so don't be too quick to bolt.

Mama Said There'd Be Days Like This: Class Registration

"First semester freshman year, I hated my classes. But I got through them and learned which classes to stay away from. Philosophy and sociology courses have a lot of reading, so stay away from taking too many heavy-reading courses in one semester."

—Robyn Smith, Syracuse University

Now that you know you have to take core classes, electives, and perhaps even classes in your major, it's time to register for them. Follow these steps to register:

1. **Choose your classes.** Study the class bulletin to see what you *need* to take. Then decide what you *want* to take. Add the two together to make your choices. Don't sign up for a class just because it sounds good. Be sure you understand what the title means and what the course requires you to do.

2. **Check requirements.** Most classes have requirements, called *prerequisites*. For example, you can't take English 2 until you take English 1. Furthermore, nearly all freshman are tested to make sure they have the skills they need to succeed. Melissa Ferrarese, a freshman at Pennsylvania State University, had the following experience: "To sign up for classes before my first semester, I had to go to Penn State in the summer to take placement tests and then schedule. Based on when you are scheduled to go do this, it is possible to get blocked out of many classes."

3. **Consider time.** As you pick your classes, keep meeting time in mind. Some classes meet Tuesday and Thursday only. Other classes are given on Monday, Wednesday, and Friday, or

Crib Notes

As you plan your schedule, leave yourself time to get from class to class, especially if you have to cross campus. Allow for a lunch break, too.

just Monday and Wednesday. You can even take classes that meet only once a week for three hours.

Be sure the class times don't overlap. For example, if a class meets Monday and Wednesday from 9:00 to 10:00, you can't also take a class that meets Monday and Wednesday from 9:30 to 10:30.

4. **Make several alternative schedules.** As a freshman, you're going to register last, so your odds of getting the exact schedule you want are about zero. Janice Race, a graduate of Queens College, described how she planned her schedule: "I would prepare three or four schedules and then decide which I liked best, next best, and so on. Since I am a prehistoric creature, the tool of choice was tracing paper. This way I could lay one sheet over another to see what I would end up if I made different combinations." This method also allows you fall-back plans if you don't get what you want.

5. **Be sensible.** If you have a hard time getting up in the morning, don't schedule an 8:00 or 9:00 A.M. class. "Don't delude yourself with the excuse 'It will make me get up earlier in the morning,'" says Jill Semko, a graduate of Indiana University. "It won't. You'll fail the course because you will never go," she adds.

6. **Know what you're getting into.** Introductory classes in large universities are often huge, containing hundreds of students. My first semester as an undergraduate, I was shocked to discover that Psychology 101 was held in the theater. The professors used microphones as they strode across the stage. As I poured out my dismay to a friend at Cornell, she shared her experience: The class was so large that the overflow watched the class on television! Keep this in mind when you sign up for intro classes.

Below "C" Level

"Another place where the time/credit ratio is very high is in costume shop for drama people and in studio for art people. PE classes probably have the best ratio of all. Not something to avoid, so much as be prepared and plan for going in."

—Bonnie Bloom of the University of North Carolina, Chapel Hill

7. **Balance your workload.** You've got enough to adjust to without overloading yourself with work. Bonnie Bloom of the University of North Carolina, Chapel Hill, put it this way: "I wish I had known that the actual credit hours you get for a class may not accurately reflect the amount of time you will put into it. I came to college thinking my labs would be fun. Then I realized how many hours of work, in and out of the lab, I was putting in. And all for one credit! Suddenly, I realized that not having any term papers in my classes didn't quite make up for having a lab report nearly every week due for my chem, physics, and bio labs. I was actually doing more work than my roommate, an English major!"

8. **Don't procrastinate.** Jonathan Kadishson, a freshman at Lehigh University, offers this excellent advice: "Registration differs at every college, but in general, get it done AS SOON AS POSSIBLE. I waited 5½ hours in line at the registrar's office the day before classes started, and it took exactly 20 seconds to fix my schedule."

9. **Don't give up if a class is closed.** Yes, as a freshman you are on the bottom of the barrel, but there are strategies for getting the class you really want. Start by putting your name on the waiting list. If that doesn't work, try Judith Pasko's great idea: "Put a letter in the teacher's mailbox explaining a very good reason why you should be first on the waiting list: required class, heard about the teacher's brilliance, a possible major, and so on. Double-check spelling and punctuation and border on the obsequious: 'If there's a desk and chair for just one more student, I guarantee that the work I put into your class will make your job no harder than it already is. Thank you so much for considering my request.'" Judith (of California State Northridge) reports that this approach worked with a known curmudgeon who never let anyone in!

10. **Deal with special needs.** If you have special needs, before you enroll in a college, contact Disability Services personnel so you can make sure campus facilities and services are adequate to meet your needs. If you haven't been able to make these arrangements earlier, better late than never. Contact Disability Services as soon as possible to get what you need: interpreters, wheelchair-accessible facilities, readers, van services, and so on. As you register for classes, make sure your needs are going to be met. If they aren't, you often have legal recourse under federal law.

Bonus step: If you really, really, really want a specific professor or a specific class and it's likely to be closed out, see if it's offered at an unpopular time, such as 8:00 A.M. or 8:00 P.M. Other students will often be unwilling to take the class at one of those times, so some seats will likely be open.

The Process

There are two typical methods by which colleges schedule their students: the sadistic method and the smarty-pants method. The sadists make you stand in line until your feet go numb; the smarty-pants allow you to register online, by phone, or through the mail.

While the smarty-pants method is clearly more humane, you have a better chance of getting the

Crib Notes

"Work for the registrar's office. Granted, things may be different in your college, but at mine [Georgetown] I got to register early and never got closed out of a class."

—Mike Flynn, Georgetown University

classes you want if you appear in person. That's because professors and department chairpeople often work registration. If the class is full, you can make an instant appeal to the person with power.

Book Smart

"Buy your textbooks used, with highlighter markings. Sell them at the end of the semester."

—Judith Pasko, California State Northridge

Be prepared for serious sticker shock: Textbooks are expensive. You may want to keep your textbooks or resell them at the end of the semester. If you think you'll be reselling them, be sure to cover your books and keep them as pristine as possible. This will get you more money at resale—but nowhere near what you're expecting or think you deserve. You might be able to save some money buying your books through online "bookstores," but you're still looking at a big pile of money for a small pile of books.

In the Major League

"As a freshman, don't worry about knowing what your major will be. Worry about it near the end of your sophomore year. (Though if you know you're into the sciences, do your prerequisites early.)"

—Terrence McGlynn, Occidental College (undergraduate), the University of Colorado (graduate), the University of San Diego (professor)

Your *major* is the subject you've decided to specialize in, such as English, computer science, pre-med, or physics. Usually, you must complete 36 to 45 credits in a major. A *minor* is a subspecialization, such as "American Literature" within the major "English." A minor is usually around 18 to 21 credits.

Learn the Lingo

A **major** is the subject you specialize in; a **minor** is a sub-specialty.

Your major and minor can be related, but they don't have to be. You could major in business and minor in theater, dance, or ecology. Obviously, you can't have the same major and minor. Some students earn a double major, which obviously requires a full credit load in both subjects. For example, I had a double major in English (36 credits) and education (36 credits).

At some point in your college career, you'll have to select a specific major. This is called *declaring* a major.

In most cases, you don't have to formally declare your major until junior year. Problems with declaring majors fall into two ends of the spectrum:

➤ **Declaring a major too soon.** Try not to declare your major in your freshman year, even if you've wanted to be a vampire slayer ever since you first saw *Buffy*. Give yourself time to decide if you'd really rather chase UFOs, for example.

➤ **Declaring a major too late.** No matter how you feel about waiting for inspiration to strike, you can't put off this decision forever. And you don't want to be a senior taking 21 credits a semester in a vain attempt to graduate on time.

Crib Notes

"After the first year or two, take a good look at who your friends are and think about why you enjoy them and what fields/majors they are involved in ... it may help you judge whether you're really in the right major. Do you hang out with your classmates and discuss topics in your major, or do you hang out with other friends and discuss completely different things? A friend said this to me. It really made me think and did actually help me. I was a psych major, but all my closest friends were music or art majors. I'm now in a completely different field."

—Kathryn Werntz, Alfred University (New York)

What major should you select? Here's some advice from Paul Lee, a graduate of Princeton University. Paul is currently in an M.D./Ph.D. program in neuroscience at the University of Maryland. At Princeton, Paul majored in neuroscience, but he now realizes that he should have majored in creative writing.

"If you have a choice, as I did, between majoring in what will lead to the medical school/law school/graduate school/Wall Street job, etc., of your choice, or in majoring in something that does not directly lead to those paths, choose the latter (which I did not). College is the last chance you have to immerse yourself in something without material gains being a major issue. Neuroscience would be a very noble major and Mom will be very proud, but that is what the Ph.D. work is for—don't miss a chance to stay up late writing what is probably not going to be the Great American Novel but will let you explore a facet of yourself that you may not have the chance to indulge later when the rent is due."

Emily Bloch, a freshman who has already declared her major at Queens College, offers this advice:

"In terms of a major, I would say think long and hard about what really interests you. I'm a theater major, because theater and acting are two things I truly love and can picture doing for the rest of my life. Check out academic advising on your campus, because they might have a book or program to help you figure out what you really want to do. Don't worry about impressing your friends and family too much. Think of backup plans, but do what you want to do."

The Least You Need to Know

➤ Take the right number of classes that satisfy major and core requirements so you can complete your degree in a reasonable length of time.

➤ Advisors can provide valuable help.

➤ When you register, check requirements, consider when the classes are offered, and have backup schedules. Balance your work load, register as soon as possible, and deal with any special needs you may have.

➤ Books cost a lot. Keep them in mint condition and you may be able to resell them and recoup some of your outlay.

➤ You must declare a major (the subject you specialize in) at some point in your college career.

Chapter 4

Making the Club Scene

In This Chapter

➤ The importance of extracurricular activities

➤ Which organizations to join

➤ How to make your choices

➤ A few points to keep in mind

How much of your time do you think you spend *outside* the classroom in college? Pick one:

(a) 25 percent

(b) 50 percent

(c) 75 percent

(d) 90 percent

The answer may shock you—it's (d)! You spend a full *90 percent* of your time in college *not* sitting in the classroom. That's because the average college student takes four to five classes per semester. Usually, each class meets for three hours per week. The math is simple:

3 (hours) × 5 (classes) = 15 (hours)

So, you've got 15 hours a week devoted to actual class time. Add a lab or two and you're still well under 20 hours. That's it.

There are 168 hours in a week. Subtracting time for studying, eating, and even sleeping still leaves a lot of time for social pursuits. Clubs are often the cornerstone of a super college social life.

Be There or Be Square

"How can you make the most of your college years? Get out and meet people! Join school clubs, sports, intramurals, the newspaper, the radio station, theater, debate club, or whatever. Many colleges now boast about their broad range of student activities in their ads. There's bound to be something there nearly every student can enjoy."

—Christy Wagner, Ball State University (Muncie, Indiana)

Christy's right: Colleges offer so many social activities that you're bound to find the one (or more!) that's perfect for you.

Why should *you* get involved in extracurricular activities? After all, you could use that extra time to sleep, watch television, get an off-campus job, or contemplate your navel. Besides, aren't you busy enough attending classes, keeping up with homework, and doing your laundry? Why take time away from studying?

There are many reasons you should plunge into the college social scene. Here are my 10 favorites:

Top Ten Reasons for Getting Involved in College Activities

10. **To improve your grades.** Joining social groups helps you do better in your schoolwork. That's because you'll make friends who often become study buddies, provide tips about study skills, and tutor you (if necessary). In addition, taking a break from studying by doing something fun and worthwhile helps you look at the material with a fresh eye when you return to it.

9. **To get the inside scoop.** Which class should you take? Is it true that organic chemistry ("Orgo" to those in the know) is the toughest class in the entire university? Is it true what you heard about Professor Frankenstein? When you meet people through clubs, you'll get the answers to questions like these—and many more.

8. **To become socially savvy.** Some lucky people are born with fabulous social skills. They know what to say and how to say it. The rest of us schlubs have to learn social skills by interacting with others. Joining clubs teaches you how to function in social situations and become more relaxed with acquaintances as well as strangers. Social savvy will prove invaluable later when you enter the wonderful world of work.

7. **To learn valuable skills.** Much of what you learn in college that you need in the real world takes place *outside* the classroom. For example, we joke around the house that my husband majored in yearbook and minored in math and accounting. As the editor-in-chief of the college yearbook for three years, he learned a great deal about printing and publishing that was never taught in his business classes. He used these skills during his 25-year career in publishing.

6. **To improve the world.** Many clubs are more than social groups. Fraternities and sororities, for example, often run charity drives and donate significant amounts of money to the community. Groups tutor young children, hold clothing drives, and even build houses for the under-privileged. You *can* make a very real differ-ence in the community and have fun at the same time. As Kathyrn Werntz from Alfred University (New York) advises, "Volunteer! Whether it's in your major or not, get experi-ence volunteering. You'll be making the world a better place as you ease your transi-tion into the 'real world.'"

Crib Notes

"I believe that the key to getting adjusted to college is fitting in with the right group of people. I'm a jock. I've been at three colleges and have played base-ball at all of them. Every time I switched colleges I joined the team and made some great friends."

—Jimmy Anderson, the State University College of Technology at Farmingdale, New York

5. **To make new friends and network.** If you've selected a large university, you're prob-ably one person out of 20,000 on the campus. When you get into an organization, you be-come 1 out of 100. This is a great way to make a large campus smaller. It's also the best way to make new friends. Never underesti-mate the importance of college friendships. In addition to providing lifelong satisfaction, college friendships are a valuable source of networking later in life.

4. **To overcome shyness.** I can tell you that you've got the rest of your life to hang out with a familiar, safe group. I can tell you that it's hard to not fit in, to feel different. But you know all this. Here's the bottom line: No pain, no gain. The uneasiness you feel meeting new people can help you gain the confidence you need to mature and succeed in the world outside the academic one. Joining a social group now, while you're an undergraduate, can help you conquer bashful-ness.

3. **To be all you can be.** Participating in extracurricular activities helps you be-come a more well-rounded person.

2. **To reduce homesickness.** "Homesickness" is a dirty secret no one wants to talk about. People seem to think that if they ignore it, it will go away. No such luck: Homesickness is like dandruff or that extra 10 pounds—to fight it you need to take stern measures. Many people are homesick when they first start college. Adjusting to college the first semester is especially difficult; in fact, it's when most people I know drop out. Belonging to a club or social group can help lessen the shock of moving to a new place.

Below "C" Level

"When you join a religious group, remember that just because the people share the same faith doesn't mean they share the same beliefs. Diplomacy and compromise are key in organizing religious events. It must be a give-and-take. Plus, the clergy is different from what you are used to and this can be a big adjustment."

—Michelle Stern, Mt. Holyoke College

And the number-one reason for getting involved in college life?

1. **To have fun!** Here's the equation:
   Joining clubs = having fun.

As you make some lifelong friends, learn new skills, and feel better about yourself, you'll discover that college can be enjoyable as well as educational. Don't get me wrong: I've been a professor for more than two decades, and I can say in all modesty that my classes are lively and enjoyable. But what a drag to just sit in class and not play a musical instrument, write for the newspaper, or play on a team. So what are you waiting for? Join up now!

Extra Credit

I'm a practical sort of person, so here's my tip: Joining clubs is also a great way to meet potential love interests. When you're in a club or group doing things you enjoy, you're bound to meet people who share your interests. Friendship provides perhaps the strongest basis for love ... as my own story shows. I met my husband in college while we were both working on the yearbook. Our mutual interest in books and publishing gave us the foundation for a strong friendship. By junior year, we realized that our friendship had blossomed into love. As a result of my own happiness, I tell all my college students to join clubs!

Know Thyself

"Socially, I cannot stress this enough: Join the speech team (also called forensics or the debating club). Cream of the crop in terms of intelligence and drive; traveling across the country, too (depending on your school's interest and budget); scholarships; trophies; and lots of talking. If talking's not your thing, then join a different club. A club or team is the fastest, easiest way to become part of college life."

—Judith Pasko, California State Northridge

Now that I've convinced you to join clubs, sports teams, and service groups, how can you decide where you fit in best? Start by getting a complete list of the activities offered on your campus. You can find these lists in the student handbook, on the university's Web page, through the dean of students office, or from the student activities board. You'll be astonished at the great variety you find.

The offerings can be divided into these main divisions:

➤ Cultural arts groups

➤ Fraternities and sororities

➤ Intramural sports

➤ Minority student groups

➤ Political action groups

➤ Publications

➤ Religious groups

➤ Service groups

➤ Special interests (left-handed scissors users, etc.)

➤ Student government

If you attended a very large high school, perhaps you could choose from 30, 40, or maybe even 50 different clubs. Small high schools might offer only 10 to 15. A large university, in contrast, can offer upward of *300* different clubs, organizations, religious groups, teams, fraternities, sororities, and service groups.

Learn the Lingo

Intramural sports are open to all students, not just athletes. To get involved, you don't have to try out—just sign up.

Crib Notes

"Get involved and be proactive. Don't expect opportunities to drop in your lap automatically."

—Catherine Thomas, University of Maryland (College Park) and Pennsylvania State University

Oklahoma State, for instance, offers over 200 organizations and clubs. The University of Tennessee kicks it up a notch with more than 300 official student organizations. They are either stand-alone groups or local chapters of national organizations, and all these organizations are registered through the dean of students office. The following list is just a sampling. Read and see which groups you'd like to join.

➤ African Student Association
➤ Amnesty International
➤ Bahai Association
➤ Bowling Team
➤ Campus Entertainment Board
➤ Chinese Students Association
➤ Classics Club
➤ College Republicans
➤ Criminal Law Society
➤ Culinary Club
➤ Dance Marathon
➤ Equestrian Team
➤ Film Committee
➤ Gay and Straight Network
➤ Habitat for Humanity
➤ Kundalini Yoga Club
➤ Lacrosse Club

➤ Lambda Legal Society
➤ Law and Medicine Society
➤ Martial Arts Club
➤ Martial Arts Club
➤ Muslim Students Association
➤ Racquet Sports Club
➤ Rugby Club
➤ Sailing Club
➤ Student Bar
➤ Student Government Association
➤ Students for a Free Tibet
➤ Swing Dance Association
➤ Ultimate Frisbee Club
➤ Water Polo Club
➤ Water Ski Club
➤ Weightlifting Club
➤ Wrestling Club

And don't forget the Society for Creative Anachronism, the Student Organization for Deaf Awareness, and the Fencing Club!

Don't Be a Stranger

After you study your college's club offerings, it's time to make your choices. As you think about which activities to investigate, remember the following:

➤ **Consider your interests.** You don't want to become a member of the math club if differential equations give you the dry heaves. Likewise, "Save the Whales" is a poor choice if you really have no interest in freeing Willie. You won't be committed to your organization if you're not interested in what they're trying to accomplish.

➤ **Carefully study the descriptions of the clubs.** Don't forget to check out the Web pages as well as the print descriptions in the student handbook.

➤ Ask your *resident advisor* (*RA*) for additional information about any clubs that appeal to you.

➤ **Talk to club members.** Ask them for details about the club's activities. See if you like the people you talk to. Do you feel an instant bond, or think "No way I fit in here"?

➤ **Stop by the club for a visit.** Most clubs hold an open house at least twice a year, in the fall and spring. Talk to club members and see if you admire them for what they're trying to accomplish, whether it's a rowdy game of rugby or an attempt to master the intricacies of contract bridge.

➤ **Build on interests.** If you already have an interest in a specific activity and enjoyed it in high school, participate in it again. For example, if you enjoy soccer but don't have time to play on a varsity team (or didn't make the cut), join the intramural or club teams. That way, you can still have the fun of participating, make new friends, and keep yourself in shape.

➤ **Try something new.** Pick something new that has always interested you. As Michelle Stern, a freshman at Mt. Holyoke College, advises, "Try new things. Try out new clubs and sports that you never did before. You may end up loving it. You may end up thinking in a totally new way. It's a great experience to open yourself up to something totally new. That's what college is for."

What happens if you think you chose wrong? It's not the end of the world. Give the club at least six months before you decide to bail. It takes time to get used to anything new, so be sure to withhold any decisions for at least a semester.

Extra Credit

My son attends Princeton University, which offers scores of singing groups. He joined one singing group in his freshman year, another in his sophomore year, and adores them both. Nonetheless, he found that Princeton doesn't offer a barbershop quartet—so he's thinking of starting one! Take a tip from my resourceful son; if you can't find the group you want, start it yourself.

Learn the Lingo

Resident advisors (RAs), student advisors (SAs), or **area advisors (AAs)** are upper-class students hired to oversee underclass students. RAs are an invaluable source of information on every aspect of college life, so don't hesitate to go to your RA with questions.

43

So Many Choices, So Little Time!

Deciding on clubs is a little like standing before one of those wall-to-wall Chinese buffets. Should you pile your platter high with moo shu pork or shrimp-and-lobster sauce? What about egg rolls and shrimp toast? And do you have room for won ton soup?

There are so many clubs that it can be equally difficult to decide which ones to select. You can use the following worksheet to help you decide which clubs to join.

1. What do you like to do in your spare time? For instance, do you enjoy athletics, politics, religion, community service? Try to list at least five items.

   _____

   _____

   _____

   _____

   _____

2. Study your list. Arrange the items from most-to-least important to you.

   _____

   _____

   _____

   _____

   _____

3. Now, what are you looking for in a club? For example, are you interested in making new friends, improving the environment, or learning a new skill?

   _____

   _____

   _____

   _____

   _____

4. What activities are you involved in currently? Why do you enjoy these activities?

   _____

   _____

   _____

   _____

   _____

5. What activities would you like to get involved in? Why do you think you would enjoy these activities?

_____

_____

_____

_____

6. Which clubs match your interests? Why?

_____

_____

_____

_____

7. Did you attend the activities fair and open houses to check out the clubs in person?

_____

_____

_____

_____

_____

Are We Having Fun Yet?

You know that getting involved in the social life on campus can help you make lifelong friends, develop your talents, and teach you valuable social skills. Being a part of campus life is a whole lot of fun, too. Joining up can often make the difference between a happy college experience and a miserable one.

That said, here are a few suggestions to consider as you select, join, and participate in campus social life:

1. Joining an activity for the sake of joining can be worse than standing back. It's not enough to sign up for clubs willy-nilly; rather, you have to pick the activities that suit your abilities, interests, and personality.

Crib Notes

You can often tell a great deal about a club by studying its Web page rather than the "official" college print description. That's because the club's Web page is often assembled by club members, not the university staff, so you're getting the members' viewpoint.

Crib Notes

"You'll be very busy, and have many new friends—but even in the midst of many people, it's okay to feel lonely. Finding more about yourself and your values takes both time and personal strength, and you have to do it on your own."

—Terrence McGlynn, Occidental College (undergraduate), the University of Colorado (graduate), the University of San Diego (professor)

2. Be careful not to overload yourself. Remember, organizations are secondary activities to schoolwork. One semester, I was an editor on the yearbook, a writer for the newspaper, and a member of the student judiciary board—while taking 18 credits (and working a part-time job). It's not surprising that I was laid low with pneumonia that semester.

3. Give yourself time to learn the ropes. I've mentioned this before, but it's worth saying again: If you want to be a leader, more power to you—but don't expect to be King or Queen of the Hill overnight. Be prepared to advance through the ranks by dint of hard work, consistency, and reliability.

When you join in campus life, not only do you develop skills you will use throughout your life, you also create a network of people who will help you in your future. You can be taught many things from books; however, you develop leadership only through experience. Best of all, you get to have a lot of fun along the way. It's time to get started!

The Least You Need to Know

➤ You spend only 10 percent of your time in college sitting in the classroom. Use the other 90 percent to get involved in campus life.

➤ Joining extracurricular activities can help you improve your grades, become socially savvy, learn valuable skills, and improve the world.

➤ You'll make new friends, network, overcome shyness, and become a more well-rounded person. You'll also have a blast!

➤ As you choose your activities, consider your interests, talk to your RA and club members, and visit the club during its open house.

➤ Don't join too many clubs. You don't want to spread yourself too thin.

Chapter 5

It's All Greek to Me: Fraternities and Sororities

In This Chapter

➤ The inside scoop on Greek life

➤ Advantages and disadvantages of going Greek

➤ A worksheet to help you decide whether to pledge

➤ National fraternities and sororities

"Why should you pledge [join] a fraternity or sorority? When you do, you automatically have 70 to 90 people on your side. Exciting social outlets and volunteer opportunities will come to you; you don't have to seek them out. The other members of your fraternity or sorority won't all be your closest friends—and they don't have to be—but some will become so. Regardless, they will be on your side."

—Jessica Swantek, The College of William and Mary

Jessica is having a great time as a member of a sorority, but not everyone shares her experience. In this chapter, we'll explore the advantages and disadvantages of joining a special kind of campus club, the fraternity or sorority.

The Glory That Was Greece

Fraternities and sororities are nothing new; they've been associated with colleges and universities since the 1700s. At that time, students established fraternities and sororities to encourage their buddies to participate in activities outside the classroom.

Today, fans of fraternities and sororities argue that the *Greek system* provides students with leadership opportunities as well as lasting friendships. In many cases, this can be true. Unfortunately, some fraternities and sororities have become little more than excuses to get roaring drunk and engage in potentially dangerous pranks. But before we get into the advantages and disadvantages of Greek life, you need to know a little more about these special campus clubs.

A Glossary of Greek Life

As with any organization, fraternities and sororities have their own jargon. While the terms can vary from campus to campus and group to group, the following are standard in United States colleges and universities:

Learn the Lingo

Fraternities and sororities are called the **Greek system.**

Learn the Lingo

Alumni are graduates of a specific school or college. **Alumnus** is the masculine form; **alumni** is plural. **Alumna** is the female form; **alumnae** is plural. It's sexist, but the plural masculine form (alumni) is used to refer to both men and women.

➤ **Active.** A member of a fraternity or sorority who has been fully initiated into the group.

➤ **Bid.** An invitation to join a fraternity or sorority.

➤ **Brothers.** How fraternity members refer to each other.

➤ **Chapter.** An individual franchise of a national Greek-letter fraternity or sorority.

➤ **Fraternity.** A group of male college students united in a special kind of social organization. The bond is supposed to endure for life.

➤ **Hazing.** The practice of subjecting potential members of a fraternity or sorority to various tests of endurance or humiliations. Hazing has been outlawed on many campuses.

➤ **Invitational parties.** Parties to which only certain potential members are invited with the purpose of convincing them to join.

➤ **Legacies.** Close relatives of current or former members of a fraternity or sorority. In nearly all instances, the chapter is obligated to accept these students as members, whether they want to or not.

➤ **Open-house parties.** Brief receptions designed to familiarize potential members with the flavor of the fraternity or sorority.

➤ **Open rush.** An informal, relaxed party held after the main rush is over.

➤ **Pan-Hellenic council.** The group that oversees all fraternities and sororities on a specific campus.

➤ **Pledge.** A person who is not yet fully initiated into the fraternity or sorority.

➤ **Preferential parties.** The final round of parties during the formal rush.

➤ **Rushee.** A student who is going through rush while considering whether to join a fraternity or sorority, or which one to join.

➤ **Rush week.** A brief, stressful time when members of fraternities and sororities recruit new members.

➤ **Sisters.** How sorority members refer to each other.

➤ **Sorority.** A group of female college students united in a special kind of social organization. The bond is supposed to endure for life.

Crib Notes

On every campus, each fraternity and sorority has a reputation—the geek house, the jock house, the culture club, the party girls, and so on. While such reputations are overgeneralizations, they may contain a kernel of truth. Listen to the scuttlebutt and decide how much to believe, based on your personal observations.

The Greek Way

Thanks to the classic John Belushi gross-out film *Animal House,* it's easy to get a one-sided idea of life in a fraternity or sorority. Depending on your viewpoint, the truth is a relief or a disappointment. However, as a result of deaths caused by hazing and accusations of gender bias, today's fraternities and sororities are far tamer than their reputations might suggest.

The adventure starts with rush week, which has been likened to a Darwinian feast of survival of the fittest.

Below "C" Level

Recognize that fraternities and sororities are more popular on some college campuses than others. At Princeton University, for example, membership in an "eating club" such as Campus or Ivy is far more prestigious than membership in a fraternity or sorority.

Hey, Look Me Over

Membership in a fraternity or sorority is obtained through a formal, an informal, or a summer rush process. Formal rush typically occurs before school or at the beginning of the fall or spring semester. Informal rush occurs immediately after the formal rush period. Not surprisingly, summer rush occurs during the summer. It's important to note that every fraternity or sorority can decide whether to participate in a formal, an informal, or a summer rush process.

Crib Notes

Rob Swantek, a member of the Kappa Sigma fraternity at Vanderbilt University, advises: "If your campus offers fraternities/sororities, pledging is much easier to do as a freshman, as opposed to waiting until your sophomore or junior year. This is because the majority of your class will be going through the same pledging process." His sister Jessica, a member of a sorority she wishes to remain unnamed at the College of William and Mary, offers just the opposite advice. Robert pledged as a freshman; Jessica as a sophomore.

Extra Credit

National Lampoon's Animal House (1978) spoofs college life in the early 1960s. The film stars John Belushi, Tim Matheson, Thomas Hulce, Peter Riegert, Stephen Furst, Karen Allen, Kevin Bacon, Mark Metcalf, and Martha Smith. It spawned a number of dreadful imitations and a mercifully short-lived TV series, *Delta House*.

Rush begins with a series of open-house parties. These parties are brief, usually about half an hour each, to give potential members the chance to visit every house in which they are interested. Next comes the invitational parties, which are longer and more elaborate. Finally, there's the last round, the preferential parties. By this time, the fraternities and sororities have narrowed their choices down, just as you have. You'll be invited to the preferential parties only if you're considered a top prospect. If the fraternity or sorority wants you, you'll likely be in for the hard sell.

Rush is about a week long and often highly stressful. The fraternity or sorority is eager to woo the best of the newcomers, while the newbies and upper-class students are anxious to get into the "hot" frat or sorority. The system has some significant drawbacks. In addition to the pressure, it's almost impossible to get to know someone in a week, much less potential "brothers" and "sisters."

Mutual Admiration Society

As you've figured out by now, rush is a process of mutual selection, matching the characteristics and personalities of potential members and the individual fraternity or sorority. Reread the part about "mutual selection" because it's the key to the whole process. The fraternities and sororities are shopping for the right people—but you're shopping, too.

Below "C" Level

"Your mom/dad was a member of [insert sorority/frat here] and really wants you to join to keep up the family tradition. Besides, all your friends are considering pledging. Finally, you know that membership in a national organization would look great on your resume. Beware of pressure to join a fraternity or sorority. Make sure the decision is really yours."

—Christy Wagner, Ball State University (Muncie, Indiana)

If you do decide to rush, your goal is to find the fraternity or sorority that best suits your interests. It's the same process you went through as you selected a college, trying to make the best possible match. Concentrate your efforts on finding the people you want to become close friends with, the ones who share your values and goals.

Two Sides to Every Coin

Now that you know how rush works, let's look at the pros and cons of joining the frat crowd. Then you can decide if it's the right move for you, and if so, when.

Advantages of Going Greek

Here are the main advantages of joining a fraternity or sorority:

➤ **Rush can be exhilarating.** For the social butterflies among us, it's great fun to meet new people and be wined and dined.

➤ **You might get a room with a view.** In some instances, fraternities provide much-needed housing for members. The housing can be better than the dorms, too.

➤ **You gain a group of friends.** This can be a powerful asset, especially at very large universities where you might feel lost at first.

➤ **You gain social skills.** Being a member of a fraternity or sorority teaches you to be at ease in a wide variety of social situations.

➤ **You learn to be a leader.** Leadership opportunities within the fraternity or sorority provide you with valuable chances to organize projects and people.

➤ **You'll form a valuable social network.** There's no denying that frat friends often stay bonded for life.

➤ **You'll forge a sense of identity.** Greek life serves to bond group members together. And being a member of a long-established group (especially a prestigious one) gives you instant recognition on campus.

Crib Notes

News flash: The college Greek world is just like the real world. As you're considered for membership, you'll be judged just as much on your appearance, grooming, and background as on your personality and interests. Maybe more so.

Below "C" Level

Whatever you do, don't take rush week and rejection too seriously. Who you are, what you accomplish, and how you feel about yourself matters a lot more than getting into a fraternity or sorority.

Disadvantages of Going Greek

Here are the main disadvantages of joining a fraternity or sorority:

➤ **Rush can be brutal.** It's not easy putting on a happy face every day for a week in seemingly endless rounds of meet-and-greets. How many more hands can you pump?

➤ **Rejection can be devastating.** Maybe you didn't make it into your first-, second-, or even third-choice college. Now you can't get into the frat or sorority you want? Some people bag the entire process because they don't want to get hosed.

➤ **You might get a room with a view.** If you're living with the same people all the time, you're less likely to widen your circle, learn new things, and become more well-rounded.

➤ **You gain a group of friends.** An instant set of buddies can become a convenient excuse for not extending yourself socially to meet new people.

➤ **You might be wasting your time.** As the months slip by, you may realize that the fraternity or sorority has narrowed rather than widened your horizons and opportunities.

➤ **Your schoolwork might suffer.** It's nearly impossible to keep up with your schoolwork if you're makin' whoopee in the frat or sorority house every night.

➤ **It's costly.** None of this fun stuff comes cheap. There are initiation fees, pledge fees, dues, party costs, gifts, clothing costs, and many other charges. The total bill can easily be several hundred dollars a year and often soars into the thousands.

➤ **There's potential for disaster.** Yes, most fraternities and sororities have cleaned up their act—but not all of them. As I'm writing this, the president of Massachusetts Institute of Technology has just apologized to the parents of a young man who died of alcohol poisoning during a frat rush a year ago.

You Can Work It Out

To join or not to join? In the final analysis, only you can make that decision, but I can help by providing you with some questions to consider. Complete the following worksheet to help you crystallize your thought process.

1. What are the advantages of joining a fraternity or sorority?

   _____

   _____

   _____

2. What are the disadvantages of joining a fraternity or sorority?

   _____

   _____

   _____

3. What pressure is being put on you to join? Perhaps the majority of students in your school are pledging; maybe The Parents have waxed eloquent about their halcyon days in the frat or sorority house.

   _____

   _____

   _____

Crib Notes

Some fraternities and sororities have so many legacies (relatives of former members who they are obligated to accept) that the organization is effectively closed for that year. You might be rushing a house that is already closed.

Below "C" Level

Don't box yourself into a corner with an all-or-nothing choice. Yes, Sorority A might be better for you than Sorority B, but how much better? Remember that houses change every year as seniors come and go. Last year's hot house might be next year's tepid one. Weigh all the options and keep an open mind.

Crib Notes

Relax: Nothing is carved in stone. You can always get out of pledging or even depledge (withdraw your bid for membership) if you find that the fraternity or sorority doesn't suit you after all.

4. What pressure is being put on you not to join? Anti-Greek sentiment can be as powerful as pressure to follow in Mommy's or Daddy's footsteps.

_____

_____

_____

5. In your heart of hearts, how do you feel about joining? Why?

_____

_____

_____

The Least You Need to Know

➤ The Greek system has special terms. Learn them so you're in the know.

➤ Membership in a fraternity or sorority is obtained through either a formal or informal rush process. Consider rush a process of mutual selection.

➤ There are advantages and disadvantages to joining a fraternity or sorority; only you can decide if membership is right for you.

➤ To get as much information about your top choices as possible, access the fraternity's or sorority's Web page.

Chapter 6

When It's Not Smooth Sailing

In This Chapter

➤ Coping with homesickness

➤ Relieving stress

➤ Dealing with depression

➤ Considering whether to transfer

➤ Failing classes

"Being in college is a little scary too. During the first semester, I have seen people drop out, decide that they want to transfer or take a break, attempt suicide, have mental breakdowns, have anxiety attacks (like myself), etc. This just makes you realize how real the world is. I also noticed how living at home sometimes kept me sheltered from the evil in the world. Even though it is scary, knowing about the bad things only makes us wiser and helps us to avoid them."

—Maureen Colson, the State University of New York at Potsdam

Sometimes things don't go exactly as we plan. This is especially true when it comes to big life changes and great expectations. Fortunately, most problems you encounter at college can be eased with a little planning, some common sense, and a dollop of tender loving care.

Below "C" Level

"Missing home, friends, and family can be rough the first few weeks— enough to make some people drop out or seriously consider it. It helps if you know people from your high school at college, but that's not always possible. Get a long-distance calling card, a box of tissues, and tough it out."

–Christy Wagner, Ball State University (Muncie, Indiana)

Crib Notes

When my son started college last year, we got an 800 number that works both ways—we can call him and he can call us for the same surprisingly affordable amount. Since our son is determined to pay all his expenses, we didn't want him to feel that he couldn't call because it would punch a big hole in his budget. Much thanks to my dear friend Angela Swantek for this great idea.

The Ones I Left Behind: Dealing with Homesickness

"I couldn't call home because every time I dialed the number, I started to sob. I missed my family so much! Everyone at home thought I was doing great, but I was miserable."

—Anonymous

Nancy Corbin, director of clinical services for student-counseling services at Iowa State University, says her office is seeing a significant increase in requests for counseling from freshman who are having trouble making the transition to college life. Despite their technical sophistication, Ms. Corbin notes, today's teenagers increasingly lack the skills they need to deal with being on their own. "They have 'point-and-click expectations,'" she says. "And when they get homesick, they have a hard time admitting it."

Sometimes it's the students who least expect it who get slammed with homesickness. Perhaps they were big fish in the little high school pond and find the competition of college life daunting. Or maybe they didn't realize how much they really enjoy being with their family—despite little sister's annoying whine or big brother's bossiness. Whatever the reason, homesickness can strike anyone, so don't think you've got a "get out of jail" pass on this one. If you do feel a little homesick (or a lot), it's natural. You can bet your bottom dollar that nearly all the freshmen are feeling the same way, to varying degrees.

What should you do if homesickness strikes? Try these suggestions:

1. **Acknowledge your feelings.** If you're homesick, there's no reason to be a martyr. You don't have to sob on everyone's shoulder, but neither do you have to pretend you're completely fine.

2. **Join in the fun.** At least for the first few weeks, keep yourself busy with clubs, sports, and other activities. As you get more and more integrated into campus life, you'll find that feelings of homesickness naturally subside.

3. **Call or write home.** You miss them; odds are good that they miss you (even if they *have* given away your room to your younger brother). Keeping in touch can help reassure you that the entire family is going through a period of adjustment; you're not the only one feeling sad.

4. **Talk to your RA.** RAs (resident advisors) are carefully selected to be kind and compassionate. In addition, they are trained to help ease some of your initial homesickness. Your RA can reassure you that you're not a failure because it's taking you a little bit more time than your roommate to adjust to college life.

5. **Go for walks.** With all the classes, homework, and dorm activities, you can lose sight of yourself. One way to combat this is to take a little time out—which is different from hiding—and figure out what you want and where you're going. Look at the beauty around you. Relax and enjoy nature.

6. **Get some counseling.** If your homesickness doesn't start to abate within a few weeks, it's time to take a trip to the campus counseling center and make sure that all you're suffering from is homesickness. (Later in this chapter, I talk about the signs of depression and ways to deal with it.)

Recognize that commuters can feel homesickness, too, but in a slightly different form. "The only kind of homesickness I experienced was the everyone-else-gets-to-go-away-to-college-while-I'm-stuck-at-home," said Barbara Bengels, who commuted to Hofstra University.

Below "C" Level

If you've left a sweetheart back home, realize that the relationship is apt not to last. Maureen Colson, a freshman at Potsdam College, has already realized this: "I've learned that no matter what, 90 percent of the time, long-distance relationships don't really work because they are way too hard to do in college." You might be feeling homesick for your honey, or you might be realizing that the relationship is tanking fast.

Stressed Out

"Watch out for moments of despair caused by too much stress. They creep up and catch you unaware. You may not be viewing your progress from the best perspective. If you need an intellectual treat, audit a course in music appreciation, art history, ceramics, fencing, or social dance. Retreat into your favorite CD, or try a Gregorian chant for a mind release."

—Mary Ellen Snodgrass, University of North Carolina at Greensboro

Remember back in high school when you thought life would be a bowl of cherries if you could just make your own decisions? Well, now you *are* on your own—so why do you sometimes feel like you got stuck with the pits? The answer could be too much stress.

Stress can be caused by ...

➤ **Too much work.** Maybe your classes are more difficult than you anticipated or perhaps you're taking too many credits.

➤ **Too many outside commitments.** Couldn't resist joining the marching band? Just had to play on the intramural ice hockey team? Took an on-campus job and an off-campus one?

➤ **Illness.** Sickness can set you back in studies and cut your play time.

➤ **Bad decisions.** Perhaps you got involved with the wrong person, overspent your money, or have been drinking too much.

High Anxiety

Extreme stress can even lead to panic attacks—terrifying moments that seem like heart attacks. Have you ever experienced these symptoms?

➤ Chest pain or tightness

➤ Choking or smothering sensations

➤ Dizziness

➤ Tingling hands and feet

➤ Sweating and faintness

➤ A sense of disconnection or unreality

➤ Trembling and shaking when you're not cold

➤ Fear of dying or fear that you're going crazy

➤ Doing something uncontrollable or out of character during these attacks

(Symptoms list adapted from the American Psychiatric Association)

If these symptoms describe your experiences, you might have had a panic attack. If you've had several of these symptoms, I strongly suggest you seek help at the campus health clinic and the counseling center.

Extra Credit

According to a study reported in the medical journal *Lancet,* not getting enough sleep can age people prematurely and promote serious illness. Researchers found biological signs of accelerated aging in healthy young men after one week in which they slept four hours a night. According to J. Allan Hobson of Harvard Medical School, these findings suggest that serious sleep loss "might even predispose you to getting diseases that are known to be genetic." "We don't know if it [sleep deprivation] would make life shorter, but it certainly makes for a less healthy aging," says University of Chicago endocrinologist Eve Van Cauter.

Stress Busters

Use the following strategies to reduce stress right now.

1. **Get enough rest.** Most college students sleep four to six hours a night. You need at least eight hours of sleep a night. There's no magical "sleep bank": You can't sleep 12 hours a day on vacations to pay back sleep loss. In fact, sleeping more than eight hours at a time can make you feel more tired.

2. **Eat regularly.** Remember those "three square meals a day"? That advice still holds. Many college students skip breakfast or go all day without eating. When your body is deprived of regular energy, it makes up for it by lowering your metabolism, or energy level. In other words, skipping meals does not help you lose weight or stay awake.

3. **Eat a balanced diet.** Eat veggies, meats, carbs—you know the food pyramid. Limit salty, greasy snack foods; snack on fruit, popcorn, and bagels.

4. **Get regular exercise.** Daily exercise breaks during midterm and finals week are a must, even if you're just taking a walk around campus to get away from the study area for a few minutes.

Crib Notes

College students abuse caffeine, especially around exam time. Downing a pot of coffee and staying up all night to study is commonplace. Did you know that too much caffeine can lead to nervousness and forgetfulness? Clearly, caffeine abuse can add to stress, not relieve it.

59

5. **Don't drink to excess.** If you're old enough to drink, imbibe in moderation. Part 4, "Reality Bites," describes how to deal with drinking and drugs on campus.

6. **Be prepared.** Do your work so you can relax. Read, study, take notes, and attend class. If you're prepared, you've obviously removed a huge source of stress.

The Freshman Blues—or Something More?

"I'd had some trouble coping with pressure in high school, but nothing like this. Suddenly, I'd never felt so alone in my whole life, like I'd fallen into a bottomless black pit. I just wanted the despair to stop—any way at all."

—Anonymous

Extra Credit

If you suffer from depression, you are not alone. Today, nearly 20 million Americans suffer from clinical depression. It is the single most prevalent mood disorder in America today.

What if you're past the usual "I miss Mommy and Daddy and Cubby and Sissy and Kitten?" What if you've lost your appetite, your zest for life, and you're thinking, "I hate my life and want to die"?

You know that being sad when something bad happens is a normal, healthy emotion. Getting a bad grade on a test you really studied for can cause a bout of sadness. So can a breakup, problems with your parents, or the loss of a loved one. Sadness is perfectly healthy when it is appropriate and lasts for a reasonable length of time, such as a few days. Depression, however, is a completely different kettle of fish. Depression is a serious disease.

Some people suffer from a bout of depression after a trauma, such as a major injury. They may be depressed for days or weeks. Other people are affected by chronic depression that lasts for months at a time. It comes and goes.

Major Symptoms of Depression

How can you tell if your sadness is really depression? First, understand that depression is a medical and psychiatric illness that has specific symptoms.

The symptoms of depression vary between individuals. While one person may be too agitated to sleep, another may become lethargic and sleep most of the day. Sometimes it can help to look at changes in thought and behavior for telltale signs of depression. According to the American Psychiatric Association, you may be depressed if at least five of the following symptoms have been present during the same two-week depressed period.

➤ Have you been feeling sad, down in the dumps?

➤ Do you no longer enjoy pleasurable activities, such as sports, hobbies, and class?

➤ Have you withdrawn from social activities?

➤ Do you often feel really tired?

➤ Are you irritable and cranky?

➤ Do you have trouble sleeping or do you sleep too much?

➤ Have you been gaining or losing weight?

➤ Do you often feel down on yourself, that everything is your fault? Do you feel useless or hopeless?

➤ Do you have trouble making decisions or concentrating on your work?

➤ Do you often feel agitated or unable to move?

➤ Do you cry a lot?

➤ Do you ever feel that life isn't worth living?

➤ Do you ever have thoughts about hurting yourself?

Learn the Lingo

According to the American Psychiatric Association, **clinical depression** (or **unipolar depression**) is a mood disorder in which the individual may feel sad, helpless, and hopeless, as if life is overwhelming. The person may also experience decreased interest in activities and little pleasure in anything, including sex.

College and Depression

Depression often runs in families, and you might recognize a similar syndrome in a parent, brother, or sister. However, depression is often unrecognized and seen as a flaw of character. Many mental health professionals believe that stress can set off depression in people who are prone to the condition because of a variety of factors.

Transitioning to college is a prime time for stressful life events. Students move away from home, so the stability of home life is suddenly missing. Further, trying to live on their own and maintain high academic standards presents a much higher level of stress for many students. College is also the first time many teens test major relationships—and if the relationship fails, life can get rough. Parents are beginning to grow older at this point in the student's life, too; the people who were always so strong and supportive are beginning to feel the effects of age and mortality.

Depression can be scary and debilitating. It can make doing even the simplest tasks, like pouring a bowl of cereal or taking a shower, difficult. If you think you might have depression, get to Health Services immediately. Depression is almost always treatable with a combination of medications and therapy. You can manage your condition so it goes away. When you know your vulnerabilities and how to handle them intelligently, depression doesn't have to come back to haunt you.

Crib Notes

"If you have been religious, don't forget the church/synagogue/mosque. Approach it in your own style, as often as you need it. Try on some new faiths for size and texture. Remain anonymous. Don't get pulled in to church choir, volunteer work, etc., if you only want worship and spiritual support."

—Mary Ellen Snodgrass, University of North Carolina at Greensboro

Hello, I Came to Say I Cannot Stay

Odds are good that you'll settle into college life and make some good friends. You'll find some super professors (every campus has a few top-notch ones, I promise), and realize that your college has a lot to offer.

Or maybe not. If you suspect that you've picked a college that's not right for you—or that college isn't for you at this time—here are your options:

1. **Stay where you are and be a grouch.** No one's stopping you, so you can make the worst of a bad situation.

2. **Turn the situation around.** Yes, you don't like the college; you've made that point. Now get with the program. If you make an effort to integrate yourself into college life, you might find that you didn't make the wrong choice after all. And if it still doesn't work, at least you've given it the old college try.

3. **Transfer to another school.** If finances permit, you can skedaddle out of there so fast you leave shine-lines. However, know that if you leave in the middle of a semester, you will forfeit part or all of your tuition, room, and board money. In addition, of course, you won't get any credit for the classes you began. A more intelligent course of action is to stay for at least a year or two and then transfer. That way, more of your credits will be locked in and you'll know that you gave your school a fair shake.

4. **Drop out and get a job.** "Drop out!" you recoil in horror. Yes, drop out, leave school, move on. College isn't for everyone. It may be the wrong choice for you at this time—or ever. Leave school and get a full-time job. Use the time to decide what you really want to do with your life and how you can achieve your goals and make your dreams come true.

Down but Not Out

"If your school has a writing center or a tutoring program and you think you need help, USE IT! That's what it is there for. The people there never tell you that you are stupid. They are so helpful. This also goes for utilizing your advisor's help when you have a problem."

—Michelle Stern, Mt. Holyoke College

If your grades go south, first figure out why. Are you spending too much time partying? Are you anxious, stressed out, or depressed? Are you having trouble understanding the material because you were poorly prepared in high school? After you figure out *why* you're failing, it's time to take appropriate action. Try these ideas:

1. **See the professor.** All faculty members post and keep office hours, and may also be available before or after lectures. Professors can also be contacted via e-mail or telephone. Make an appointment and explain your concerns.

2. **See the teaching assistant.** In large introductory classes, students often meet with *teaching assistants (TAs)* rather than professors. As with professors, TAs also hold office hours to help students.

3. **Get tutoring.** Many departments offer tutoring services. Don't be shy or embarrassed; many people need a little help adjusting to college. All colleges offer tutors and academic advisors. Use them!

4. **Change your study habits.** The work is harder in college, the competition is stiffer, and there are far more distractions. As a

Crib Notes

If you think you're going to transfer (or even suspect it), select your first-, second-, and third-choice colleges. Make sure they will give you full credit for all the classes you take now. Often, you need at least a C average in a class for the credit to transfer.

Learn the Lingo

Teaching assistants (TAs) are graduate students who run small classes and grade papers for large classes.

63

result, you'll almost certainly need to adjust your study habits from high school. (This is covered in Part 2, "A Class Act.")

5. **Do your work.** I'm a full-time English professor in a large state university. Speaking as a professor now, just do the work. Attend class, do your reading, and write your papers. We can't pass you just because we like you; you have to do the work.

The Least You Need to Know

➤ If you feel homesick, acknowledge your feelings, participate more fully in campus life, call home, and talk to your RA. If you don't feel better, get some counseling.

➤ Reduce stress and anxiety by getting enough sleep, eating balanced meals, exercising, cutting back on the booze, and doing your course work.

➤ Recognize the signs of clinical depression and seek help immediately if you suspect that you're depressed.

➤ Think carefully before deciding to transfer or drop out.

➤ If your grades plummet, see the professor or TA, get tutoring, change your study habits, and work harder.

Part 2
A Class Act

"The first two weeks of college were the hardest. The work was a big adjustment. I didn't know that I was going to have to spend about five to six hours a night on homework. I was kinda cranky about that. The workload was a smack in the face for me. I consider high school a breeze now."

—Maureen Colson, the State University of New York at Potsdam

It's not easy to learn how to learn. It requires will and discipline, what the nineteenth-century English biologist Thomas Henry Huxley called "the ability to make yourself do the thing you have to do, when it ought to be done, whether you like it or not."

But just about everyone can do it. In this section of the book, I teach you how to study effectively and manage your time successfully. You'll get the inside scoop on preparing for tests, taking tests, and learning from your test performance. This section concludes with a chapter on the bane of college students: writing research papers.

Chapter 7

You've Got Class

In This Chapter

➤ Class attendance

➤ You and your professors

➤ Class syllabus

➤ Doing well in class

"I had a real problem with the workload my first couple of years. I came out of high school with the thought that college was going to be a huge party (as does everyone) and realized very quickly that studies should not be taken lightly."

—Billy Fields, Indiana University

College isn't the same as high school: If it was, it would be called "More High School." Yes, both high school and college have classes, chairs, and teachers, but that's where the similarities end. College classes and high school classes are very different; ditto on teachers. (The chairs, however, are pretty much the same.)

A Whole New World

In high school, you attended class because it's the law. In college, however, attendance is up to you. If you didn't attend high school classes, a school official would call home or send your parents a registered letter; if the problem persisted, you could even be visited by a truant officer and "escorted" to class. If you don't attend a college class—whether or not attendance is mandatory—no one will come after you. They might not even notice. When it comes to attendance at college classes, you're completely on your own.

Crib Notes

Pay close attention to the way your professors introduce themselves so you know what they prefer to be called. According to Dr. Terry McGlynn of the University of San Diego: "Don't call your professor Mr. or Ms. and definitely not Mrs.—use Dr. or Professor—unless they tell you otherwise. I personally don't care, but many professors do. We don't get the pay we deserve, but we do appreciate the illusion of respect from fawning students yearning to live in a bigger world."

This is both good and bad: It's nice to be treated as an adult, but it can be tempting to take advantage of all this newfound freedom. And if there was ever a chance to blow off class, freshman year is it. You've got lots of new friends and activities; there's a whole campus to explore. Then there's the lure of sleeping late, especially on cold winter mornings when your class is across a snowy campus.

Below "C" Level

Your professor doesn't have to give you any wiggle-room at all. For instance, if you want to leave class early for an appointment, your professor doesn't have to oblige you. The Higher Authorities (administration) will back the professor, not you.

Stand strong: Resist temptation and get your carcass to class each and every day. Here's why:

1. **You'll learn more.** College is fun, but you're really there to learn. Some learning takes place in the form of clubs, social activities, and sports, but the bulk of the information you need is delivered in the time-honored way: in the classroom.

2. **You'll get higher grades.** Your grades matter in the short term (for plum summer jobs and midwinter internships) and the long term (for graduation, graduate school, and high-paying jobs). You will get better grades if you attend class. It's as simple as that.

3. **You'll earn a good reputation.** If you've paid attention in class, contributed to the discussion,

and aced the tests, your professors will be far more willing to write letters of recommendation when you need them—and you will.

4. **You'll pave the way to success.** If you blow off class from the beginning, it's brutally hard to get into the groove later on. Too many students start off on the wrong foot by skipping class and spiral down the drain with alarming rapidity.

Your first week of classes can set the tone for the entire semester, so make the decision to do your work—and do it well. In this resolve, your professors can be strong allies.

Learn the Lingo

All college teachers can be called **professors;** only those with a doctorate (Ph.D.) can be called **Doctor.**

The Power of the Prof

Here's the hierarchy of professors in most colleges and universities:

Top of the Heap	Middle of the Road	Bottom of the Food Chain
Full professor	Assistant professor	Lecturer
Associate professor	Instructor	Adjunct (part-timers)

While you may not have shown your high school teacher much respect as a scholar, your college professors will expect (in some cases, *demand*) such honor and deference. The gulf between you and your college professors is apt to be as wide as the Atlantic Ocean—and most professors like it this way.

Terry McGlynn reminds me that if you're in a large university with graduate student teaching assistants, give them the same respect as your other professors and you will be richly rewarded, if only with good karma.

All colleges and universities have special ranks, such as endowed chairs and visiting professors. Both are usually accorded great prestige. When she was an undergraduate at Fordham College, Sapna Maloor realized how important a professor's status can be when it comes to selecting classes. "Adjuncts [part-time professors] generally tend to be really hard," she notes. "They want to make a good impression, which they won't do if everyone passes with A's or fails with F's."

Learn the Lingo

The phrase "publish or perish" refers to the common practice of retaining and promoting only those professors who publish copious high-quality scholarship.

An Apple for the Teacher

So what are college professors all about? What makes them tick? How can you use this knowledge to do better in college? Following are the most common college professor mindsets and guidelines for dealing with them. (*Note:* A professor can fit into more than one category. For example, a "Dedicated and Determined" professor is also often a "They Take It Personally" professor. Therefore, carefully assess each professor to see what he or she requires of you.)

Below "C" Level

While most professors take their teaching seriously, teaching ability rarely matters when it comes to promotions. Your professor may be a brilliant expatriate who hasn't yet mastered English but has been promoted to the rank of full professor. Unfortunately, it's *your* responsibility to fill in the gaps in understanding.

Crib Notes

Not only can Dedicated and Determined professors teach you a lot, they also usually have valuable connections in the field. Their connections prove very helpful when you're seeking admission to a prestigious graduate school.

Dedicated and Determined

In most cases, Dedicated and Determined profs chose the field as their life's work, their raison d'être. They do independent research and write articles and books on it. They are perfect profs to take whether you're a freshman or an upper-class student because their enthusiasm for the subject is usually contagious. And whether you like the subject or not, you'll get a first-class education from them.

Lee Silverberg, a graduate of Southwestern University, feels so strongly about the value of Dedicated and Determined professors that she advises, "After taking the requirements within your major, pick your classes based on who is the best professor, regardless of the class."

They Take It Personally

Closely allied to the Dedicated and Determined professors are the professors who want you to be just as excited about their subject area as they are, even if the class is "just" a requirement. Showing up for class tells them you care. Staying awake and asking an occasional question doesn't hurt, either. Going to see them during their office hours seals the deal. Never try to blow these professors off because They Take It Personally. (I should know: I'm Dedicated and Determined and I Take It Personally!)

One-Track Minds

These profs focus on the topics they believe are most important. Unfortunately, these subjects may or may not correlate to what is covered in the textbook or what you really need to know. This could present a real problem to a freshman because if you listen to the professor's lectures and don't read the textbook, you're probably not going to get the grounding you need. Clearly, with these professors, you *must* read the book.

Extra Credit

Mike Martin, an adjunct writing professor at LaRoche Community College in Pittsburgh, takes his teaching to heart. Here's Professor Martin's advice: "Class conduct matters: The attitude you portray can change your grade dramatically. Smile in class and appear interested. At least pretend to take notes. I never feel bad about failing students who obviously never write anything down and who seem to think their professors are trying to do something terrible to them. Use your professor's suggestions and expect criticism."

If you're just a lowly freshman taking the class to fulfill a requirement, you may be in over your head with these professors. Pray that you have a good teaching assistant to explain the rest of the information you need.

Well-Meaning but Clueless

These professors really are trying to stay ahead of the curve, only they're not sure where the curve is. While you might not get much out of the class, very often these professors can be sweet, well-meaning, and earnest. If you listen closely, you might get steered in the right direction.

The Empty Suit

They burned out years ago and are just phoning it in. If you get stuck in one of these classes, try your hardest to get out. Fast.

Crib Notes

Many college professors use textbooks they have written themselves. If your professor has written the textbook, he or she will probably emphasize material covered in lectures over the reading from the book.

Grade Grind

"Reconcile yourself to the absolutely certain fact that you won't have the same grades you did in high school. One quarter of the students at my college had a high school GPA of 4.0 or higher. And almost nobody has a 4.0 after they get here. If grades mean everything to you, prepare to be disappointed."

—Terrence McGlynn, the University of San Diego

Learn the Lingo

A **syllabus** is a listing of class activities, requirements, readings, quizzes, essay tests, and exams.

Below "C" Level

"To professors, there is only one kind of stupid question: one that can be answered by reading the syllabus. If you want your professor to like you personally, take the time to read the syllabus."

—Terrence McGlynn, the University of San Diego

Terry is being a bit harsh, but there's more than a grain of truth in his comment. College work *is* hard and you'll be surrounded by a lot of smart, determined people. The slackers get weeded out fast. So how do you get good grades?

Start by knowing each professor's expectations. Fortunately, this is easy: Not only do they announce them, but they also put them in writing and hand them out. This wonderful document is called a *syllabus,* and it's distributed to you the first week of class. Increasingly, many professors post their syllabus on their Web pages so when you crumple yours up in the bottom of your backpack, you can just get another copy online.

The syllabus is a wonderful document. Think of it as a contract, because that's how your professor views it. The syllabus lays out your responsibilities, the professor's expectations, and the general rules for the class. If you stay in the class, the professor is going to assume that you agree to the rules specified in the syllabus and hold you to them.

If you don't like or agree with something in the syllabus, talk to the instructor or transfer to another class. Never assume that a professor will not do something printed in the syllabus. Read and know it.

Following is the syllabus I prepared and used for my English 101 class this semester. At my university, English 101 is basic writing, the class all freshman must take.

Dr. Rozakis   EGL 101   Monday/Wednesday   Fall 2000

Keep this syllabus. Tape it to the inside cover of your notebook. You will use it all semester. You are responsible for all the material listed below. Read and take notes on everything.

1. <u>Preparation.</u> You are expected to come to class prepared. You will have read the work assigned, taken notes, written all papers. Bring notebooks, books, and pens to class. Be sure to have your textbooks and dictionary every day.

2. <u>Attendance.</u> I take attendance at every class and regard it as very important to your progress as students, writers, and thinkers. Attendance and lateness will be factored into your final grade. Leave yourself enough time to get to class. Lateness is distracting and discourteous and you may find yourself inadvertently marked absent. If you do miss a class ...

   Consult your syllabus to see what you have missed.

   Call me at my office to explain the circumstances to me.

   E-mail me to explain the circumstances to me.

If I do not hear from you after two absences, I will assume you have dropped the class.

You are responsible for the work even if you are not in class. This means that "I was not in class" is not an acceptable excuse.

3. <u>Deadlines for Assignments.</u> Work assigned must be completed and submitted on the date specified on the syllabus. If you are absent, you can ...

   Hand your paper in earlier, before the deadline.

   E-mail your paper to me.

   Give your paper to another student to give to me.

   Mail your paper to me. You will get credit if it is postmarked on or before the deadline.

LATE PAPERS WILL *NOT* BE ACCEPTED.

If you miss an in-class test, you will have one week to make it up. You must see me during my office hours for the make-up assignment.

4. <u>Keyboarding.</u> All in-class work will be handwritten. All at-home essays are to be keyboarded. Unless you have a physical disability that prevents you from typing, I will not accept any handwritten essays. Please see me at once if you have a physical disability that prevents you from keyboarding.

Books

The Complete Idiot's Guide to Grammar and Style, Laurie Rozakis (Alpha Books)

The Complete Idiot's Guide to Writing Well, by Laurie Rozakis (Alpha Books)

A decent dictionary, to be brought to class daily

Day	Date	In-Class Work	Homework
W	9/6	Introduction to class	Purchase books; Part 1: No Uncertain Terms
M	9/11	Three-step writing process	*G & S:* Chapters 4–5: Parts of Speech
		Write mock essay; analyze writing process *WW:* Chapter 8	
W	9/13	What makes good writing?	*G & S:* Chapters 6–7: Pronouns
		Mob paper; nanny paper	*WW:* Chapter 2
		Audience, purpose, tone, etc. 5-page essay structure; *WW:* Chapter 3	

continues

continued

Day	Date	In-Class Work	Homework
M	9/18	Four modes of discourse In-class essay: interviews	Complete essay at home
W	9/20	Peer analysis and revision *WW:* Chapters 7, 11	Rewrite essays at home; retype
M	9/25	Narration: structure, openings *WW:* Chapters 10, 13	*G & S:* Chapters 9–10
W	9/27	In-class essay: Fractured Fairy Tales	Rewrite essays at home; retype
M	10/2	*G & S:* Chapter 11: Common Errors	*G & S:* Chapters 12–15
W	10/4	*G & S:* Chapters 12–15: Sentences *WW:* Chapter 6	At-home essay: Sentence variety
M	10/9	School closed; religious holiday	
W	10/11	Sentence combining: ape paper, etc.	*G & S:* Chapter 17: Punctuation
M	10/16	In-class essay	*G & S:* Chapter 18: Capitalization
W	10/18	Peer analysis and revision *WW:* Chapter 9	Rewrite essays *WW:* Chapter 14
M	10/23	Argument: Choosing a topic, audience *WW:* Chapter 14	*G & S:* Chapter 19: Spelling
W	10/25	Guide to research; selecting a topic *WW:* Chapter 17 *WW:* Chapter 17	Three topics due next class
M	10/30	Library orientation—10 biblio. cards *WW:* Chapter 18	15 biblio. cards due next class *WW:* Chapter 19
W	11/1	Library work continued	
M	11/6	Note card lesson; avoiding plagiarism	25 note cards due 11/13
W	11/8	*G & S:* Chapters 20–23: Style	Editing exercise
M	11/13	Brainstorm subtopics/outlines	At-home essay
W	11/15	Internal documentation/endnotes *WW:* Chapter 20	Essay revision; retyped
M	11/20	Chapters 24–25: Letters, resumes *WW:* Chapter 23	Rough draft
W	11/22	Thanksgiving recess	
M	11/27	Works Cited page; sample term papers	Rough draft
W	11/29	Sample term papers	Rough draft
M	12/4	Rough drafts due	Keyboard final copy
W	12/6	Paper presentation	Complete term paper In-class writing seminar
M	12/11	Term paper due; speeches	Resumé; *WW:* Chapter 22
W	12/13	Speeches *WW:* Chapter 24	Revise/correct term papers
M	12/18	Last day of class: final exam	

Crib Notes

Some college professors want to stretch you and get your attention with intense class sessions and incredibly challenging exams. At the end of the semester, however, you will see a tremendous curve on their tests. So stay calm and keep at it. You'll probably end up with a better grade than you thought—especially if the average on the first exam is 50 percent or below!

Stop Up and See Me Sometime: Office Hours

While your professor may seem stern and unapproachable, most professors welcome the chance to answer questions and clarify confusing points. Professors set aside regularly scheduled blocks of time, called *office hours,* to meet with students. Professors announce these times in class and post them on their office doors.

If you're doing well in a class, by all means show up to office hours to visit with the professor. Here are two reasons to hang out with your professor during his or her office hours even if you don't need extra help or have a problem:

➤ The prof could be an interesting person who could teach you a lot.

➤ If the prof gets to know you well, he or she will write you a great letter of recommendation when you need it.

If you're doing badly in a class, before shelling out money to see a tutor, use office hours first because you're already paying for them with your tuition. Further, your professor knows what will be on the exam; the tutor probably won't.

Not Drowning, but Waving

Another great way to do well in class is to participate. This isn't possible in lecture classes larger than the population of your town, but it *is* possible in small seminars and precepts run by teaching assistants. Try these suggestions:

➤ Make intelligent comments that are on the topic.

➤ Don't worry about quantity; we're looking for quality here. One good comment goes a long way.

➤ Use body language to indicate that you're following the conversation. Lean forward to show you're paying attention; nod to show agreement.

➤ Laugh at the professor's jokes. We make no claims to being Letterman or O'Donnell, but we do try our best. *You* try being funny at 8:00 A.M.!

Staying Ahead of the Ball

Stay ahead of your work, at least a few days ahead. How?

➤ Read ahead.

➤ Highlight key material and take notes ahead.

➤ Study ahead of time for tests. Don't cram.

➤ Read your syllabus and know what's happening.

Below "C" Level

You may have some classes in which the professor has put together a "notes packet" that contains copies of all the overheads and notes that will be used. Don't let those notes become an excuse to get lazy. You still have to show up, pay attention, and take notes.

If you can do this for each of your classes at the very beginning of school, you'll be in great shape. People will notice you. Your hair will be thicker, your muscle tone will improve, and you will be at one with the academic universe. Seriously, once you get one day ahead, you can work at the same pace as everyone else but always be ahead.

What if you start falling behind? Get help early. At the first sign of trouble (e.g., low quiz or exam score), go see the professor. Find out why you didn't do so well and learn ways to correct the problem. If you don't, you can spiral down faster than you can imagine. The longer you wait, the more difficult it will be to save yourself.

Go for the Gold

I've given you many ways to maximize your chances for academic success. Here are some contributions from my panel of experts:

1. **Go to class!** "It's hard to pass if you don't go to class." —Doug Hamblin, University of Kentucky

2. **Get a good seat.** "Sit in the middle of the class, toward the front of the room. This assures that the professor will know your face and see that you're in class." —Doug Hamblin, University of Kentucky

3. **Ask questions.** "Most importantly, ASK QUESTIONS. If you're between grades, it is my experience that participation and attendance will get you the higher of the two grades." —Doug Hamblin, University of Kentucky

4. **Be proactive.** "Realize that it's sink-or-swim. You're in for a shock if your high school stressed self-esteem and you're used to having your feelings protected. In college, your professors don't care how you feel about yourself; only achievement matters. You're seen as an adult capable of dealing with the consequences of your actions and the world order." —Val Delaportes, SUNY New Paltz

5. **Be nice to yourself.** "Don't compare yourself to other people. Do the best you can with who you are at any given time." —Catherine Thomas, University of Maryland (College Park) and Pennsylvania State University

---

The Least You Need to Know

➤ Don't make the mistake of thinking that college *is* high school redux. It's an entirely different experience.

➤ Attend all classes.

➤ College professors are scholars who command respect.

➤ To succeed in class, follow the syllabus, attend office hours, participate in class, and work ahead.

➤ Sit where the professor can see you, take responsibility for your work, and do your personal best.

Chapter 8

Time Flies When You're Having Fun

In This Chapter

➤ Track your time

➤ Learn time-management skills

➤ Get organized

➤ Set up a study center

➤ Resist procrastination and time wasters

"One thing that I can tell you is that I think it's stupid how college kids talk about how it's great to be away from home 'cause they have soooooooooooo much freedom. Then when they're done talking about that they talk about how they never have time for anything 'cause they're reading, studying, and writing."

—Nick Monroy, Hofstra University

Star Trek was wrong: The final frontier is not space; it's time. If you can master the way you use time, you're well on your way to college success. How can you make time for eating, sleeping, partying, classes, and studying? That's what you'll learn in this chapter.

World Enough and Time

One of the most wonderful things about college is the sheer amount of time you'll have. No more time frittered away on tedious bus rides to school; no more time slipping away on useless busy work. Even if you take six classes, sign up for training in Underwater Fire Prevention, dance barefoot on aluminum foil, attend all your classes, and even sleep eight hours every night, I guarantee you're going to have a lot of free time.

When it comes to college success, the secret isn't lack of time—it's making the best use of it. Doing well in college has little to do with raw intelligence. Brilliant students can flunk out if they waste their time, while average students can ace their classes by using their time wisely.

Here Today, Gone Tomorrow

Why do you feel so rushed and stressed since you've gotten to campus? Why is it you don't have enough time to study? Many activities make your college life demanding, and there's always something to distract busy college students from their studies. Before you can plan your time, you must first understand how you're spending it.

So where does all that time go? Take the following inventory to find out.

Crib Notes

"In the chaotic whirlwind that is college, don't forget to enjoy what you're doing and who you meet while you're there. Those years go by all too fast."

—Catherine Thomas, University of Maryland (College Park) and Pennsylvania State University

---

Extra Credit

The custom of dividing each day into 24 parts seems to have originated with the ancient Egyptians around 35,000 B.C.E. They divided daylight and darkness into periods of 12 hours each, but that meant the duration of each hour changed during the year as the nights lengthened and shortened. Around 300 B.C.E., the Babylonian astronomers adopted the now-universal practice of making all 24 hours equal in duration, regardless of when the sun rose or set. In Europe, however, equal hours did not become standard until about 1350 C.E., about 70 years after the introduction of mechanical clocks.

Time Worksheet

1. On average, how many hours do you sleep each night?

   Hours per night _____ × 7 = _____

2. On average, how many hours a day do you spend showering, dressing, and grooming? _____ × 7 = _____

3. On average, how many hours a day do you spend eating? (Include cooking, serving, and cleaning up if you cook for yourself.) _____ × 7 = _____

4. On average, how many hours a day do you spend getting to class? (Include the time it takes to walk across campus or commute.) _____ × 7 = _____

5. On average, how many hours a day do you spend doing errands (such as laundry and cleaning)? _____ × 7 = _____

6. On average, how many hours a day do you spend on activities such as clubs, sports, exercise, church, etc.? _____ × 7 = _____

7. On average, how many hours a day do you work at a job? _____ × 7 = _____

8. On average, how many hours a day do you spend with friends, going out, watching TV, partying, drinking, etc.? _____ × 7 = _____

9. On average, how many hours a day do you spend on e-mail or on the phone? _____ × 7 = _____

10. How many hours a day do you spend in class? _____ × 4 = _____

    Total Hours: _____

    Subtract from 168 (number of hours in a week): _____

    Grand Total: _____ **left**

Your grand total is the number of hours you have left for studying, after you've done everything you need to do and everything you want to do. Here's a sample, figured on the high side:

➤ **Sleep**   8 hours × 7 days = 56 hours

➤ **Grooming**   1 hour × 7 days = 7 hours

➤ **Eating**   2 hours × 7 days = 14 hours

➤ **Commuting**   1 hour × 7 days = 7 hours

➤ **Errands**   1 hour × 7 days = 7 hours

➤ **Clubs**   2 hours × 7 days = 14 hours

➤ **Job**   none

➤ **Friends**   2 hours × 7 days = 14 hours

➤ **E-mail/phone**   1 hour × 7 days = 7 hours

➤ **Classes**   3 hours × 4 days = 12

Total hours: 138 hours

168 – 138 = 30 hours

Grand Total = 30 hours left

Thirty hours—that's a lot of hours left just for studying!

Below "C" Level

Only *you* can decide how to spend your time. Don't let friends, roommates, and team members bully you into spending time their way.

Trimming the Fat

Take a look at what you've written in the Time Worksheet. Can you see some major time-wasters in your list? Maybe you spend nine hours a week watching television, playing video games, and styling your hair. This cuts into class time, club time, and study time. Study the list and see what adjustments you can make in the way you spend your time. Then learn how to use your time wisely.

As you've no doubt figured out by now, being an undergraduate is a full-time job, requiring 35 to 40 hours a week, including attendance in class, studying, and course-related work.

Five Easy Pieces

Learning time-management skills is a matter of setting priorities. Start by recognizing that everyone is an individual: What works for one person might not work for another. Your roommate may decide to spend his nights in a drunken stupor, cut class, and cram like mad. The lucky puppy may be able to pull his tail out of the fire this way, but it might not work for you. People like your roomie ruin it for the rest of us because they make time management seem like a snap. It's not. Follow the easy steps in these next sections to learn to use your time well.

Understand Your Personal Style

Some people can stay up until 2:00 A.M. studying; others must hit the pillow by 10:00 P.M. or be useless the next day. Some students work great under pressure; others crumble in a panic. My son can stay up late, but he must eat regular meals or he becomes crabby. My daughter, in contrast, needs a solid eight hours of sleep but can skip meals and still be a sweetheart. Think about the conditions that help you succeed and make them a priority in your college life.

Recognize Your Limitations

We all have limits: Learn yours. Know when you've had enough partying and need to take a break. Know when you're not getting the material in class and need to seek extra help. Know which classes are hardest for you and will require extra effort. Know when you must hit the books or risk failing.

Spend a few days recording exactly how you spend your time. Write down everything, and be honest. When your list is done, look for overall balance. Make sure you're sleeping enough; if you have too little sleep, no amount of study will make it worth it. Also check that you have time set aside for meals, fun, and yourself.

Set Your Priorities

One of the hardest things about planning your time is finding the right balance between doing what you *have* to do and doing what you *want* to do. Setting priorities is the key: If you plan your time, then you have the best chance of being able to fit everything you want and need to do into your college life—especially studying.

Make a Schedule

Making a schedule can help you fit all your activities in so you can achieve your goals. A computer spreadsheet program is great for this, but old-fashioned paper-and-pencil works fine, too. List the days across the top, and the time (in hours or half hours, whichever suits you best) down the left-hand side. Do the following:

➤ First write down essential activities, including sleeping, eating, attending classes, and study time.

➤ Then fill in chores such as laundry, since chores must get done eventually, but can be put off for a while if necessary. Also fill in job time and commuting time, if they apply. Both can be adjusted if your studying is suffering as a result.

➤ Fill in socializing, clubs, sports, and other fun activities. Adjust the schedule as needed. For example, add more study time a week before midterms, finals, and other crucial exams.

Crib Notes

Consider getting an on-campus job if you must work and you're spending too much time commuting to and from your off-campus job.

83

Stick to Your Schedule

A schedule is a waste of time if you don't use it. But be kind to yourself: If you skip an hour of studying this week to party hearty, don't beat yourself up. Instead, cut an hour from somewhere else in your schedule (eat a little faster, leave a meeting early) and make up the time. With a little bit of flexibility and a nip-and-tuck here and there, you'll soon have a schedule that helps you use your college time wisely.

Crib Notes

"Learn to use a day planner before getting to college. I knew how to use one and balance my day way before I got to Mount Holyoke, and my life has been a lot easier for it. I knew how to schedule meetings, clubs, meals, time for myself, study and research time, and anything else that may come up in my day. My friends may make fun of me sometimes for being 'a slave to my dayplanner' but I'm a lot more put together than they are."

—Michelle Stern, Mt. Holyoke College

How Much Is Enough?

Figure that you're going to need at least two hours of studying for each hour you spend in the classroom. Therefore, if you're taking 15 credits (five classes) a week, you're going to need 30 hours of studying on average. You can get by on less if you're a quick study or have already taken a similar course in high school. However, many students need this amount—or more—to do well in college. And don't think you can slack off: Study time actually increases as you move into junior and senior years because the work gets harder.

The following hints can make is easier for you to get the most from your study time:

➤ **Use your free time during the school day.** The hours between classes are perhaps your most valuable study time, but they're often ignored. If you have a break—even a short one—use it toreview the material and edit the notes you just took. Here's what college freshman John

Below "C" Level

Every year, several of my students write their papers and forget to hand them in. They leave them home, in their dorms, or at some party. Don't let this happen to you!

Roach of SUNY Farmingdale said: "I review my notes whenever I have time—between classes, at lunch, waiting for friends to come over."

➤ **Study before and after class.** You'll get the most bang from your study buck by reviewing your notes immediately before and after the class.

➤ **Space study periods.** Figure on spending 50 to 90 minutes of study at a time. Study for more than that and you'll start to burn out; study for less, and you won't have a chance to work up a head of steam. It's more efficient to study hard for a clear-cut period of time and take a break rather than study until you're frazzled.

A Place for Everything and Everything in Its Place

Organization is one of the keys to effective studying and success in general. Now that you're in college sharing a space the size of an average shoebox, start by establishing a study space.

Study somewhere without distractions. The library is ideally suited for this; it's one of the reasons it was created, in fact. Read the story of the Three Little Students:

➤ Student #1 studied in the common room in front of the television. He became an expert on reruns of *The Gong Show,* but he earned C's in class.

➤ Student #2 studied on her bed. She was well rested, but earned C's. (As Cornell student Paul Kangas discovered: "Lying in bed while trying to study is a good antidote for insomnia but not the best way to memorize a list of German vocabulary words.")

➤ Student #3 studied in the library. He earned A's.

Moral of the story: Where there is a TV, there is a show to watch. And where there is a bed, there is sleep to catch up on. Eliminate possible distractions and remove temptations to do something other than study. Here are the ground rules:

➤ You study better in places without distractions.

➤ You usually get your studying done faster.

Make the most of your study time by setting up a study center. A study center helps you concentrate on your work and get into the habit of studying. The following chart shows you which places work well—and which ones don't.

Great Study Areas	Poor Study Areas
In your room at a desk	In front of the television
In a quiet part of the library	In your room on the bed
In a dorm study room	In the cafeteria

85

Crib Notes

If you study at the same time every day, your friends will learn to leave you alone during this time. As a result, you'll get more done.

Your study center should be well lit and quiet. You can't study if music is blaring, if you're talking to friends, or if your roommate is doing the mambo.

If you're lucky enough to have your own computer, it should be a central part of your study center. Computers can help you prepare well-organized notes, make easy-to-read outlines, and write essays and reports. For this reason, you might want to consider purchasing a laptop computer.

And while we're on the topic of organization, pack your backpack every night so you've got everything you need to study and for class the next day. This solves those "Oh-No!-I'm-Late-for-Class-and-Where-Is-My-Paper/Notebook/Report?" morning refrains. Here's a checklist of materials you'll need:

Study Supplies

_____ Assignment pad

_____ Binders or notebooks

_____ Calculator

_____ Completed assignments (papers, reports, etc.)

_____ Dictionary

_____ Paper

_____ Pens

_____ Pencils

_____ Textbooks

_____ Telephone numbers and e-mail addresses of classmates whom you can rely on to know what's happening if you miss a class

_____ Watch

Danger, Will Robinson!

Everyone tells you about the vices you'll be faced with when you go to college: drinking, smoking, drugs, wild sex. There are other vices that are just as insidious, but less well known: procrastination and time-wasting. Procrastination is the bane of many a college student.

Crib Notes

Should you bring a computer to campus? If you already own a computer, by all means bring it. If not, wait until you get on campus. This way, you can see what the university provides or recommends. Most colleges have computing facilities, many open 24 hours a day. If you decide to buy a computer anyway, many universities offer price breaks since they buy computers in bulk.

Tomorrow Is Another Day

Well, yes, Scarlett, but not always when it comes to studying. You shouldn't beat yourself up about slipping from your study schedule here and there, but neither should you take refuge in these old excuses:

➤ "I'll get it done tomorrow."

➤ "I'll study better tomorrow [morning, afternoon, evening]—anytime but today."

➤ "What do you expect? I've always been a procrastinator."

➤ "I truly believe that all deadlines are unreasonable, regardless of the amount of time given."

➤ "I shall never forget that the probability of a miracle, though infinitesimally small, is not exactly zero."

➤ "If at first I don't succeed, there is always next year."

You're in college to get an education. To do so, you have to attend class, pay attention, get your work done, and study. If you tend to procrastinate, now's the time to break the habit.

Come Into My Web, Said the Spider to the Fly

The Internet offers several intriguing ways to waste time. For many college students, Napster is the most treacherous. I have Beth Bolger of Cortland University to thank for this section.

"Let me just download this one song that I *have* to have," you think. But soon that one song isn't enough: You've had a taste, and now you're hooked. You become jealous of your roommate's extensive collection, so you spend hours downloading. Just when you think there isn't another song you could possibly want, at 3:00 A.M. the girls downstairs start blasting "Hotel California." So you spring out of bed, chastising yourself for neglecting that classic (meanwhile, the fact that you also forgot to study for your psych test doesn't faze you).

Then you stare at the window, watching the song download with the speed of a glacier. An hour and twenty minutes later, you have 99 percent of the song when the "Transfer Error" message pops up and you lose the whole thing. Then you start writing a paper (because that's what you swore to your parents the brand-new computer was for), but you can't save it because there's no more room on your hard drive. It's filled with songs.

Then we have instant messages. On the surface, IMs are a great way to keep in touch with family and friends. But IMs can also become a sinister force keeping you from studying or sleeping. You could be studying or reading and you hear the sound of the door opening—the audio signal that a friend is now online—and it sends you hurtling for your computer to see who just signed on. It's nice to chat and keep in touch, but soon instant messages begin to dominate your life. Even during lonely times when no one is signed on or everyone has an "away" message, you can't study. No! You sit and read everyone's away messages. You might stop to read for five minutes, then you get up again to see if anyone's away message changed while you were gone.

You may be laughing, but Napster and Instant Messenger aren't laughing matters. They can suck away valuable study time. Beth isn't the only one who told me about these time-wasters; Kathryn Werntz of Alfred University wrote: "Do not spend more than one hour a day on e-mail. It is addictive. Do not spend more than one hour on the Web—even for research—it is addictive."

Below "C" Level

"Don't get into the immature brag-fest about saving everything to the last minute. If you are investing time and energy in school, make the most of it. Work hard every day. Leave the 'I can't believe how drunk I was' and 'I can't believe how many classes I cut' nonsense to kids whose parents don't mind wasting money and time on frivolities."

—Mary Ellen Snodgrass, the University of North Carolina at Greensboro

The Least You Need to Know

➤ Calculate how you use your time. The time is there—it's up to you to use it as efficiently as possible.

➤ Set priorities by understanding and working within your personal style, making a schedule, and sticking with it.

➤ Make studying a priority.

➤ Get organized by setting up a study center free from distractions and putting all your class materials in your backpack.

➤ Resist time-wasters, especially spending too much time on the Net (Napster and instant messages are especially tempting).

Chapter 9

Study Smarts

In This Chapter

➤ Take a study self-assessment

➤ Get the right attitude

➤ Become a powerful reader

➤ Learn how to take great notes

➤ Master memory tricks

➤ Study in groups

"I soon realized that when my high school teachers told me that college wasn't a piece of cake, they weren't kidding. I couldn't believe the amount of studying I had to do in college."

—Syreeta Owens, the State University College of Technology at Farmingdale

As they begin their freshman year in college, many students don't know how to study—in large part because they haven't been challenged in high school. In high school, self-esteem blossoms as a result of rampant grade point inflation. In college, the bubble bursts with the discovery that grades are based on real achievement. It's always a shock and often a mess.

A Whole New World

"I thought college was like high school. I thought I would pretty much just show up for the test and pass. So I met my friends every morning and went out for breakfast. I rarely went to class and I never studied. I realized it was a mistake when my first semester grade report was all F's."

—Jonathan Hutzel, the State University of New York College of Technology at Farmingdale

Extra Credit

Over 1.6 million college students are enrolled in study skills classes in two- and four-year colleges and universities, according to the National Association for Developmental Education. An additional 900,000 take advantage of tutoring and supplemental instruction, individually or in groups (*The New York Times*, November 12, 2000).

In 1999, the University of California at Los Angeles surveyed over 364,000 students. Researchers discovered that in their senior year of high school, students were studying far less than they had in the past. In 1987, for example, 43.7 percent of all students surveyed studied more than 6 hours a week; by 1999, the figure had dropped to 31.5 percent.

Nearly 20 percent of the students surveyed admitted that they studied less than an hour *a week*. College professors recommend that for every hour of class time you study two hours *a day*.

It's not going to come as a shock, then, to learn that a significant number of college freshmen who insist they know the material thoroughly are astonished when they bomb their first tests. The number-one hint for studying smart is easy: Put in the time. Recognize that studying must be your priority and set aside time for it—at least twice the amount of time you spend in class.

The Moment of Truth

Have you ever used these excuses to get out of doing your schoolwork?

➤ "I'm just not smart enough to pass this class."

➤ "The professor isn't any good, so I'll never be able to learn."

➤ "I'm just not meant for college. They let me in by mistake."

If you talk yourself into failing, you probably will fail. But if you talk yourself into success, you have a good chance of doing well. Study smart by having a positive attitude about school and yourself.

Start by ...

➤ Being enthusiastic about learning.

➤ Deciding that you *can* do well on tests and papers.

➤ Having discipline and using your time wisely.

➤ Persisting and not quitting.

➤ Having self-respect.

➤ Making friends with people who support your hopes and dreams.

Below "C" Level

Never skip classes near an exam—you may miss a review session and other crucial information.

The Journey of a Lifetime Begins with a Single Step

Studying in college *can* seem overwhelming. Stop, drop, and roll. Take a deep breath. Now take control. Here's how to do it:

➤ List all the things you have to do in order from most important to least important.

➤ Break your workload down into manageable chunks. You can study math for 1 hour, not 10. Likewise, you can study French for 45 minutes, not 100.

➤ Schedule your time realistically. Begin studying early and slowly build as the exam approaches.

➤ Use all your time. For example, use the hour between classes to review notes.

➤ Be sure to build in study breaks. You'll study more effectively if you take brief breaks, about 15 minutes each.

As you study, follow these steps:

➤ Preview by surveying your syllabus, reading material, and notes.

➤ Identify the most important topics emphasized and any areas you still don't understand.

➤ Spend the most time on the information the professor has stressed in class.

Be an Active Reader

It's no secret that being a good reader makes your college work easier—especially studying and taking tests.

Happily, reading doesn't have to be a chore. Try each of the following methods for making reading easier and more fun and decide which ones work best for you.

Preview the Text

Before you read or study, preview by examining the different parts of the text: the cover, table of contents, art (pictures, illustrations, photographs, charts, maps), art captions, subtitles. As you preview, ask yourself these questions:

➤ What will this reading teach me?

➤ What main topics does this text cover?

➤ How are the topics arranged? What will I read first, second, and so on?

Crib Notes

"Never let studying keep you up late, because you retain information better with a full night's sleep (according to a new study just published in *Nature*). If you're anxious about an exam, sleeping the whole night will give you a better grade than cramming the whole night."

—Terrence McGlynn, Occidental College (undergraduate), the University of Colorado (graduate), the University of San Diego (professor)

Make Predictions

When you *make predictions,* you make educated guesses about what's to come. The process looks like this:

What I Know + Story Clues = Prediction

As you read, your brain tries to figure out what's coming next in the story. As a result, you make predictions *before* you read and *while* you read. Once you find out what's coming next, you confirm or change your predictions. If you're reading a novel or story, you ask yourself:

➤ "Based on what I know and clues in the story, what do I think will happen next?"

➤ "How accurate were my predictions?"

➤ "What new predictions can I make using the facts I just read?"

Set a Purpose for Reading

Here are some of the main purposes you have for reading college-level texts:

➤ To learn new information
➤ To review notes
➤ To confirm a belief
➤ To discover opinions
➤ To get facts
➤ To get instructions

Your purpose for reading shapes the way you read. For example, when you study, you read slowly so you understand and remember the material. You don't want to miss any facts or details that could be important. You also take notes to record key words, dates, and facts. If you're reading to be entertained, however, you read more quickly.

Bridge Information

Connecting new facts with your prior knowledge helps you remember new information when you study it. After you preview, predict, and set a purpose for reading, take a few minutes to jot down notes on what you already know about the passage. Ask yourself "What do I know about this subject?" Decide what you want to find out, too. After you finish reading, you can complete your chart by writing down what you learned.

You can arrange your ideas on a chart like this one:

What I Know → What I Want to Find Out → What I Learned

Skim the Text

When you want to get a general idea about a text, you skim it. *Skimming* is a fast method of reading in which you glance at a passage to get its main idea or to find a key point. Skimming makes reading easier because it helps you focus on the important parts of the text.

Learn the Lingo

Skimming a text is scanning the words to get the general idea or find an important fact.

To skim a text …

➤ Preview the text, make predictions, and set a purpose for reading.

➤ Run your eyes across the page. Try to read as fast as you can.

➤ Focus on the key words, which are nouns and verbs.

➤ Look for the facts you need. They are often in the first and last sentences of the passage. Read these facts more slowly.

➤ Pause at the end of every page or passage to restate the meaning in your own words.

Below "C" Level

Skimming isn't a substitute for a complete reading. Skim *before* you read the text—not *instead* of reading it.

Find the Main Idea

A *main idea* is the most important point that a speaker or writer is making. The main idea tells what the whole passage is about. Every *detail*, or small piece of information in the passage, gives information to support or explain the main idea. When you find the main idea, you know the author's point. This helps you understand the whole passage more clearly. In some cases, the main idea is directly stated in a passage. In other cases, you have to figure out the main idea from clues in the passage.

To find the stated main idea in a passage, follow these steps:

➤ Find the *topic* or subject of the passage.

➤ Look for a sentence that gives an overview of the topic. It explains what the entire passage is about.

➤ Check to see if the sentence tells what the passage is about.

Learn the Lingo

When you make an **inference,** you "read between the lines" to find the information or opinion the author does not directly state.

Below "C" Level

Don't confuse summaries and paraphrases. Both restate information in your own words, but summaries are shorter than the original text; paraphrases can be the same length or longer.

To find the unstated main idea in a passage, you have to make *inferences,* or educated guesses. Follow these steps:

➤ Find the topic or subject of the passage.

➤ Look for details that relate to the topic.

➤ Make an inference about the main idea from the details.

Summarize What You Read

To *summarize,* find the most important information and restate it in your own words. Summarize every time you study to help you understand and remember what you read. To be sure you have included all the important details in your summary, make sure it answers these questions: *Who? What? When? Where? Why?* and *How?*

To summarize a passage …

➤ Preview the passage, make predictions, and read the passage.

➤ Find the main idea and important details. Explain them in your own words.

➤ Skim the passage again to make sure you have included all the important points.

➤ Begin your summary by stating the main idea. Then summarize the key details.

Monitor Comprehension

Pause if you're getting a little confused. Ask yourself, "What am I having trouble understanding?" Once you know, try some of these strategies to get back on track:

➤ Read more slowly.

➤ Reread any parts that confuse you.

➤ Use the details to visualize or imagine the scene you're reading.

➤ Restate what you've read in your own words.

Get Help

At the first sign of trouble, speak to the professor or teaching assistant during office hours. Go to the tutoring center or get private tutoring from an upper-class student. Many departments offer tutoring services, too. Make use of study resources on campus. Find out about and use labs, tutors, videos, computer programs, and alternative texts. Sign up for an orientation session in the campus library and computer facilities.

Note This

When you took the self-assessment at the beginning of this chapter, maybe you checked "My class notes are a mess, so I don't use them." Perhaps you just throw up your hands in despair and don't take notes at all. That's a big boo-boo. Taking super notes reinforces what you learned as well as helps you remember what you heard. Good notes also serve as a study guide that helps you get top grades on tests. Here's how to take useful notes.

1. **Write only the key information.** When you're listening in class or reading on your own, write down the main points—and just the main points. They include …

   ➤ The main idea.

   ➤ Important names, dates, numbers.

   ➤ Key details.

   ➤ Any questions you have about the material.

To find the key information, listen or read for word clues, such as *the most important reason, the main point,* or *this will be on the test.* Professors and writers often repeat vital facts in different ways, so also watch for repetition.

Below "C" Level

If you checked "I go to class most of the time, but I usually zone out," you need to get more sleep, eat right, and get regular exercise. If the condition continues, it's time to see a doctor for a check-up. (Or transfer classes, if the professor is that dull!)

Crib Notes

ALWAYS copy down everything a professor writes on the board. If it's on the board, you can assume it's important.

2. **Outline and highlight.** When you're taking notes from a textbook, arrange your notes in an outline. Follow the book's organization. Then go back over your outline and highlight the most important information. You can also highlight the key facts in any notes you take in class.

Below "C" Level

If you usually study while listening to music or watching TV, turn off the music and the TV. Trust me here; all the research backs up the importance of concentration while studying.

3. **Keep it brief!** To help you keep up with a lecture, develop a system of abbreviations. For example:

   ➤ + or & = "and"
   ➤ b/c = "because"
   ➤ w/ = "with"

4. **Organize your notes.** Keep your notes in a binder, organized by topic. Also keep any handouts the professor gives. When you study, you'll have all your notes in one place.

5. **Write clearly.** Your notes will be useless unless you can read them! If you take messy notes, rewrite them after class when your memory is fresh.

Study to the Max

"I took a Shakespeare course where, on a play exam, the professor made us identify the act from which individual quotes came. I discovered an interesting mnemonic device: I would read Act I in my dorm room, Act II in the cafeteria, Act III in the library, Act IV in the bathroom, and Act V in the park. Then, on the exam, seeing each quote, somehow I was able to remember where I was sitting when I first read it. So all I really had to do was memorize the place where I read each act of the play."

—Meish Goldish, Case Western Reserve

Meish is on to something important: Context. You'll remember more when you can key the study context (physical location, as well as mental, emotional, and physical state) to the test context.

Now, let's say you really *are* putting in the time but you just don't seem to get the grades you deserve. Tests determine how much you remember and understand, so getting more mileage from your memory can help you make better use of your time—just as Meish did. Studying in groups can also help you learn more and remember it longer.

Try the following ideas for beefing up your memory.

1. **Link it.** Connect new ideas to what you already know. For example, if you know that *either* is spelled *ei* rather than *ie,* you can use this to learn that *neither* is spelled with the same pattern.

2. **Repeat it.** Repetition helps fix information in your mind, so recite facts aloud or write them down.

3. **Play with it.** Use *mnemonics,* memory tricks that jog your mind. For example, if you want to remember the order of the planets, try learning this saying: *My Very Educated Mother Just Served Us Nine Pizzas.* The first letter of each word reveals the order of the planets: Mercury, Venus, Earth, Mars, Jupiter, Saturn, Uranus, Neptune, Pluto.

Learn the Lingo

Mnemonics are memory aids.

4. **Write it down.** Write important information on index cards. Use these flash cards often to help you remember historic dates, definitions, foreign language vocabulary, math formulas, and other facts and ideas.

5. **Sing it.** Songs stick in our mind because of their strong rhythm. Set important facts such as state capitals, presidents, and science facts to songs to help fix them in your mind.

6. **Visualize it.** As you study, form a mental picture of a person, place, thing, or idea. Do this by imagining how it looks, smells, sounds, tastes, or feels.

Study with Your Buddies

"Studying well is more important than studying heavily. If you want to spend less time on classes and more time having fun, study with people who get better grades than you."

—Terrence McGlynn, Occidental College (undergraduate), the University of Colorado (graduate), the University of San Diego (professor)

Studying with classmates can help you in many ways. Group members can take turns summarizing the material aloud or quizzing each other on important topics. Some group members ask questions to help clarify confusing points while other group members provide the answers. Group members can pass around their notes, too, which helps fill in gaps in everyone's notes—especially if you've missed some classes and don't understand all the information. Since everyone looks at a topic in his or her unique way, group members can help you analyze the readings and class notes from different angles.

Avoid group work if you find it hard to stay on track in groups or realize that your friends don't do their share of the work. In addition, group study might not work for you if you often measure your progress against others and find yourself coming up short.

Extra Credit

"Studying in college is much more work than high school, but if you have good study habits it's not a problem. Try studying with other people; as a freshman, some people in your hall will probably be in most of your classes. In college, every test counts, and there are almost no make–ups. So if you do nothing else, study for the major tests!"

—Jonathan Kadishson, Lehigh University

Crib Notes

Study groups are most effective when they're small, no more than three to five students.

Ants in the Pants

Now, this section is for all you college kids who checked "I can't sit and study for long periods of time without becoming tired or distracted." Welcome to the club. Here's how to handle a short attention span:

➤ Do difficult tasks first to get them out of the way.

➤ Study your most difficult material first, when you're least tired.

➤ Do as much of your studying in the daytime as you can. What takes you an hour to do during the day may take you an hour and a half at night, when you're tired.

➤ Use brief intervals of time for rote memorization, review, and self-testing.

➤ Use spare moments for recall/review.

➤ Do rote memory tasks and review, especially details, just before you fall asleep.

➤ If you get tired or bored, switch task/activity, subject, or environment. Stop studying when you feel like you're losing it.

Studying brings short-term and long-term rewards. Right now, good study habits help you learn more in college and remember it better. Your self-confidence will soar as people praise your achievements. Studying more effectively also leaves you more time for sports, clubs, jobs, and partying. Later on, those same good study habits help you do well in your job. You'll find it easier to make smart life choices, too. Start studying smart by getting the right attitude.

The Least You Need to Know

➤ Have a positive attitude about yourself and college.

➤ Be an active reader by previewing, making predictions, setting a purpose for reading, bridging information, skimming, finding the main idea, summarizing, using SQ3R, monitoring comprehension, and getting help if you need it.

➤ Take useful notes by writing down key information, outlining, highlighting, keeping it brief, organizing, and writing clearly.

➤ Use mnemonics (memory tricks) and consider studying in groups.

Chapter 10

Test Time

In This Chapter

➤ College tests vs. high school tests

➤ Preparing for tests

➤ Taking tests

➤ After the test

➤ Dealing with difficult professors

"College exams are going to be a breeze, I thought. After all, I aced all my tests in high school without breaking a sweat. When I got back my first round of midterms, I nearly fell off my chair: How could *I* get D's?"

—An anonymous freshman

As this poor rookie discovered, college tests are not like high school tests at all. They differ in frequency as well as difficulty. This chapter guides you through the test-taking process.

What Fresh Hell Is This?

How often will you be descending into the ring of hell that contains college exams? College professors are free to test whenever they feel the need. I test the students in my short-story class every meeting, administering a brief quiz to make sure they actually read the story. My writing students, in contrast, get a test once a week; the students in my "Women in Literature" class have a midterm, a final, and three major essays.

The number, frequency, and length of exams varies from college to college as well as professor to professor. Jonathan Kadishson, a student at Lehigh University, told me that most professors at Lehigh give two sets of large tests (called *4 o'clocks*) during the semester, and then the finals. In calculus, for example, the grades break down this way:

Task	Credit
Homework/attendance/miscellaneous	20 percent of final grade
The two 4 o'clocks	40 percent of final grade
Final exam	40 percent of final grade

This system is clearly different from high school, where one bad grade doesn't mean that much and you can make everything up. In college, every test counts, and there are almost no make-ups. Jonathan advises, "If you do nothing else, study for major tests!"

Getting a Running Start

Before you can prepare for a college test, you have to know what you're preparing *for*. That's because each test is different. Knowing what to expect helps reduce test jitters, too. Here are some issues to consider:

➤ What is the test format—true/false, multiple-choice, fill-in, essay, or some combination of the above?

➤ What information will be tested? What content do you need to know?

➤ How much of the test is based on your notes, how much on the textbook, and how much on class work?

➤ How long will the test be? An hour? Two hours?

You can often get the answers to these questions from reading the syllabus, checking the professor's Web site, and listening carefully in class. If you don't get the information you need, ask the professor or TA for clarification.

Pay attention to the questions that other students ask, too, and the answers they receive. After class, talk to classmates and your study group. See how they interpret the instructions the professor has given. This is a good way to check your comprehension, too.

One of the most effective ways to prepare for an exam is to study exams from previous years. Reviewing old exams helps you become familiar with the format of the test (the sections, the number of questions, which questions are mandatory and which are a matter of choice). You can also make sure you understand the way the exam questions are worded, and get some practice at writing proper answers. Sometimes old exams might give you a clue to content, as some topics are tested every year, some only every two or three years.

Where can you get old exams? Try these sources:

➤ The university library

➤ Your teacher or tutor

➤ Students who have taken the class before you

➤ Fraternity brothers, sorority sisters, and other club friends

Okay. Now it's time to learn *how* to take college tests.

Before the Test

Whether you're taking an objective test or writing an essay test, the following suggestions will help you do your best.

1. Arrive Early

Get to the classroom with time to spare. Allow yourself enough time to settle in to your seat, lay out your pens and pencils, and relax. If you're sitting in your chair early with everything set to go, you'll have time to calm down and focus on the task at hand.

Below "C" Level

Some professors (including yours truly) lock their doors and turn away latecomers. Get to the test early enough so you're not locked out!

2. Choose Your Seat Carefully

Sitting near friends during a test can be distracting. If you see your friends handing in their papers early, you may feel pressured to do the same, even if you're not finished. Choose a seat that will best help you focus on taking the test and reduce any distractions.

3. Be Prepared

Be sure to have everything you need for the test: pens, pencils, erasers, calculators, rulers, and so on. Since you put all these materials in your backpack the night before (as I advised you in Chapter 8, "Time Flies When You're Having Fun"), you should be well-prepared on the day of the test.

Crib Notes

Always carry extra batteries for your calculator. Calculators (and other battery-operated study aids, such as electronic spell-checkers) have a nasty habit of running out of battery power just when you need them the most.

4. Read the Directions Carefully

As you read the directions, pay close attention to what you must do. Ask yourself these questions as you read:

➤ "How many questions do I have to answer?" On some tests you have to answer all the questions; on other tests, only a few—any five out of seven, for example. Answer what you're required to: no more, no less.

➤ "Where do I have to write my answers?" You might have a special answer sheet, a *blue book,* or your own paper.

➤ "How much information do I have to include?" You might have to show every step in a math problem, for example, or include a set number of paragraphs in your essay.

5. Budget Your Time for Short-Answer Tests

Before you start working on the test, figure out how much each part of the test counts toward your test grade. On some tests, every question is worth the same number of points. On other tests, however, some sections may be weighted differently.

Here's the rule: Spend the most time on the sections that count the most. Spend the least time on sections that count the least.

If you don't finish a question in the time you've allotted, leave it and move on. You can return to the question if you have time at the end of the test. If you do skip a question, be careful to mark your answer sheet correctly so you aren't "one off."

Learn the Lingo

Most colleges require students to write their test responses in standardized booklets. Since these booklets have blue covers, they're called **blue books.**

6. Budget Your Time for Essay Tests

Decide how much time you can spend planning, drafting, and revising. Don't make yourself nuts trying to stick to your schedule, but *do* keep an eye on the time and try to stay on track. For a 1-hour writing exam, for instance, you can spend about 5 minutes planning what you're going to write, 30 minutes writing, 20 minutes revising and editing, and 5 minutes proofreading.

If you have time left over, spend it proofreading your essay for errors in grammar, usage, and punctuation and recopying messy parts of your essays.

During the Test

It's the moment of truth. Here's what to do when you're face-to-face with the test questions and the clock is ticking.

1. Write Your Name

"Oh, Dr. Rozakis, you are so silly," you scoff. Stop scoffing—it's astonishing how many test papers get turned in without names on them. Let this not happen to you.

> **Below "C" Level**
>
> Speaking as an English professor: NEVER leave an essay test early. I don't care if you *are* a budding Hemingway—use all your time and always check your writing for errors in logic, organization, and skills.

2. Skim the Entire Test Before You Start Answering Questions

Here's what to look for:

➤ Question types (short answer, true/false, etc.)

➤ Question content (what, specifically, the questions are testing you on)

➤ Question difficulty (which ones look easy and which ones look hard)

Knowing what's on the test helps you develop a test strategy (see the following "Choose a Test Strategy" section). It also reassures you that you studied the right material and are well-prepared.

3. Jot Down Notes and Key Facts

Write down any important details or facts while they're fresh in your memory. These notes may help you answer questions later. In addition, having some notes reduces test anxiety because it reminds you that you have learned a lot.

> **Crib Notes**
>
> Write your notes on scrap paper, inside the test booklet, or in the test margins. Always make sure you can write in these places before you do. After all, you don't want your notes being counted as an answer!

4. Choose a Test Strategy

There are three ways you can approach any test:

➤ **Method #1:** Work from beginning to end, answering every question in order—even if you have to guess.

➤ **Method #2:** Answer the easy questions first and then go back and work on the harder questions.

➤ **Method #3:** Answer the hardest questions first, and then go back and answer the easy ones.

None of these test-taking methods is right or wrong, but for most people, Method #2 works best. This strategy helps you use your time well by getting the greatest number of correct answers down fast. Further, as you work through the test, you often think of clues that help you answer the more difficult questions. In addition, you may find the correct answer to a hard question revealed in an easier one.

Questions can be easy or hard based on two factors: their *content* (subject) and their *form* (type of question, such as true/false). Use the following chart to determine the level of difficulty based on the question's form.

Question Form and Level of Difficulty

Easier	More Difficult	Most Difficult
true/false	fill-in-the-blank	essays
multiple-choice	sentence completion	
matching		

Therefore, answer all the true/false, multiple-choice, and matching questions you can before you move on to fill-in-the-blank, sentence completion, and short-answer questions. Leave the essay questions for last. Of course, you've already allocated your time, so you know how much to spend on each question.

Below "C" Level

Don't get bogged down on one or two questions, especially if they're not worth big points. Keep moving so you stay within the time limit.

5. Read All the Answer Choices

Even if you think you've spotted the correct answer immediately, don't pounce on it. Instead, read every answer to make sure you're correct. People tend to see what they expect to see, not what's really on the page. This is especially true in high-pressure situations such as tests.

6. Don't Second-Guess Yourself

"The multiple-choice answer pattern really matters," some students claim. "You can never have two C's (or A's, B's, and so on) in a row," you may have heard. Not true! The pattern of letters on the answer sheet doesn't matter at all.

If you do see a pattern, don't be fooled into changing your answers. Your grade will always be higher if you answer questions based on what you know rather than the pattern of the letters on the page.

7. Pace Yourself to Avoid Making Careless Errors

You want to work quickly, but not so quickly that you throw away points through carelessness. It's an awful feeling to lose points on questions that you really could have answered.

Be sure to read the questions at least twice. When you're working on math problems, check that your answers make sense. Are they logical? Finally, after you fill in your answers, check that you have marked the correct answer on your answer sheet.

8. Check and Double-Check Your Work

When you finish the test, always check your work. Even if you've got just a minute, use it to look over your paper.

Ask yourself these questions as you check your exam:

➤ Have I included all necessary words? People often omit words when they're in a hurry.

➤ Have I misspelled anything? Check easy words as well as harder ones.

➤ Have I checked for errors in punctuation, grammar, and usage?

➤ Can my writing be read easily?

Your Guess Is as Good as Mine

Should you guess? If there's *no* penalty for guessing, fill in every single answer—even if you have to guess. After all, you have nothing to lose and everything to gain.

If there *is* a penalty for guessing, try to reduce the odds. For example, if every multiple-choice question gives you four possible answers, you have a 25 percent chance of being right (and a 75 percent chance of being wrong) each time you have to guess. But if you can eliminate a single answer, your chances of being correct rise to 33 percent. And if you can get your choices down to two answers, you have a 50 percent chance of being right. Even if there is a penalty for guessing, pick one

Below "C" Level

If you decide to pull an all-nighter, stay away from "uppers" such as caffeine pills. Staying awake is one thing; getting higher than a kite is quite another.

answer if you can reduce your choices to two. Fifty percent odds are good enough to chance a guess.

Pushing the Panic Button

Panic is a natural reaction to a pressure situation. Nonetheless, panic can prevent you from doing your best on tests, so let's reduce or banish it. Here are some techniques that can help you deal with panic:

Don't panic if ...

1. **Some questions seem much harder than others.** They probably are. That's the way the test was designed. Accept this and do the best you can.

2. **Other students are writing and you're not.** They could be working on another part of the test or not have given a question enough thought. By thinking longer before you answer, you might do better than someone who plunges right in.

3. **Other students finish before you do.** Finishing early doesn't guarantee the best grade. Usually the better papers are handed in by students who have spent more time thinking about their answers and checking their papers.

4. **You're stumped on an answer.** Skip the question and move on. If you have enough time, you can return to it later. If you run out of time before you can return to it, you were still better off skipping it in favor of answering a greater number of questions.

5. **You run out of time.** Your professor might allow you to stay a little later to finish. If not, be confident that you studied, prepared, and did your best.

6. **You blow the test all out of proportion.** It is true that some tests *are* more important than others, especially midterms and finals. But any test is only one factor in your overall education. Remind yourself that you've been working hard in class and keeping up with your assignments. How you do on one test won't affect your entire college career.

7. **You freeze and just can't go on.** If this happens, remind yourself that you're well prepared. Remember that every question you've already answered is worth points. Finally, reassure yourself that you're doing just fine. Stop working

Crib Notes

By and large, high school requires memorization and spitting it back. College involves thinking. You have to understand a concept well enough to see how it can be applied to something you've never discussed in class. That's where most college students bomb out.

and close your eyes. Take two or three deep breaths. Breathe in and out to the count of five. Then go on with the test.

After the Test

After you finish the test, use it to improve for next time. If you got an A, congratulations! If you didn't do as well as you expected, don't despair. Instead, focus on the things you did well to prepare and take the test. Remind yourself that next time you'll do better.

Here are some ways to get the most from your test-taking experience.

Evaluate What You Did Right and What You Can Do Better

With each test you take, you can become a better test-taker if you analyze your strengths and weaknesses. Ask yourself these questions:

➤ What was my biggest problem on this test? Look for a pattern of errors in the questions you missed.

➤ What caused my mistakes? For example, did I run out of time? Did I misread questions? Be honest with yourself; take responsibility for your actions.

➤ How can I overcome this problem? Perhaps you decide to work with a study group to make sure you cover all the important information you might be missing on your own.

Check for Grading Errors

Professors and TAs sometimes make mistakes when they grade tests. There might even be a poorly designed question that has two valid answers.

Don't nag the prof to get points that you really don't deserve, but do talk to the professor if you think your test may have been misgraded. You might be able to get a higher score if you can show that your answer is correct or even reasonable.

Crib Notes

Get a good night's sleep. Yes, I know you've heard it before, but it really works. A solid eight hours of zzzz's can recharge your batteries and give you the winning edge on *any* test. Also be sure to eat a nourishing breakfast.

Extra Credit

Most colleges grade on a four-point scale. To figure out your GPA (grade point average), first assign points to each of your grades as follows:

A   =   4 points
B   =   3 points
C   =   2 points
D   =   1 point
F   =   0 points

Multiply the points for each grade by the number of credit hours the class is worth. For example, if you got a C in a 3-credit English class, you'd do this math: 2 (the C) × 3 (the credit hours) = 6. To get your GPA, divide your total points for all classes by your total number of credit hours.

Study Smarter

Adjust your study methods based on your self-assessment, your test score, and your professor's advice. For example, if you find that your notes were weak, you might want to take notes in a different way. You can also photocopy your textbook and then highlight key points. Write comments in the margins, too.

Get Some Help

> "I had to get a math tutor. And I went for extra help every day that my professor had office hours. I had to swallow my pride in order to do well."
>
> —Robyn Smith, Syracuse University

In high school, you might have gotten by just fine studying on your own. In college, however, you might find that your math grade is in the basement because you don't understand the material. I've said it before, and I'll say it again: If you've had the professor explain it during office hours and you're still confused, check out the college's tutoring service.

Decide to Do Better Next Time

Right now, you might feel like crumpling the test paper and throwing it into the garbage. Even though you're frustrated, don't give up. Think of the test in a positive way and you'll get more from the experience. Use what you learned to be the best student you can be. It takes courage to learn from a painful experience, but you've come this far already. With more effort, you can raise your grade.

Extra Credit

"This platitude is really true: Don't let grades get in the way of learning. This semester I had a lucky student who was offered a free trip to China for a week and a half, but it was leaving in a few days. This meant she would miss an exam in my class for 15 percent of her grade, and probably would miss things in other courses too. The decision was a no-brainer. She won't get an A in my lab now, but who cares? She got to go to China!"

—Terrence McGlynn, Occidental College (undergraduate), the University of Colorado (graduate), the University of San Diego (professor)

That Prof Just Doesn't Like Me

"The professor/teaching assistant doesn't like me," you say. Actually, you may be right. Professors are human, like you. They tend to judge students by the way they act.

When you treat your professors with respect, they will treat you with respect. If you do your work to the best of your ability and take school seriously, your teacher will respond. Get with the program by taking an active and positive role in the classroom. Do the following:

➤ Come to every class.

➤ Be prepared. Bring your books, notebooks, and homework.

➤ Sit in the front of the room or toward the front. This reduces distractions and shows the professor that you're serious about learning.

➤ Pay close attention in class.

➤ Take good notes.

➤ Participate in class.

➤ Ask intelligent questions when you're confused.

➤ Resist peer pressure to misbehave.

➤ Treat your teachers with courtesy.

The Least You Need to Know

➤ College tests aren't like high school tests at all. The number, frequency, and length of exams varies from college to college as well as professor to professor.

➤ Make sure you know what form the test will take and what you are expected to know.

➤ Arrive at the test early, choose your seat carefully, be prepared, relax, read the directions carefully, budget your time, and stay focused.

➤ Write your name on the test booklet, skim the test before you start answering questions, jot down notes, choose a test strategy, read all the answer choices, don't second-guess yourself, pace yourself, and double-check your work.

➤ After the test, evaluate your performance and learn from it.

➤ Treat your professors with respect and they'll like you better.

Chapter 11

Master of Your Domain

In This Chapter

➤ Overview of objective tests

➤ True/false, multiple-choice, matching, and fill-in-the blank tests

➤ Hints for scoring high on math tests

➤ Writing considerations: topic, audience, purpose, and parameters

➤ Recall, analysis, evaluation, and synthesis essay tests

➤ The writing process

"We all do dumb things in college. Failing tests doesn't have to be one of them."

—John Hauff, the State University of New York College of Technology at Farmingdale

Chapter 10, "Test Time," gave you an overview for taking college tests. In this chapter, you'll learn the details of mastering college tests in all subjects.

Mama Said There'd Be Days Like This: Taking Objective Tests

Objective tests, like pit bulls, look harmless—but watch that bite! You'd think objective tests would be easier than essays (which most people fear more than deep water, heights, and spiders), but just the opposite can be true. *Objective tests* can be especially painful when the questions have neither an obvious answer nor any answer choices that seem to make sense. Nonetheless, I can teach you ways to approach these tests to maximize your chances of letting your brilliance shine through.

Truth or Consequences: True/False Questions

True/false questions require you to recognize a fact or idea. They also check your reading comprehension. As a result, you have to read them carefully and closely.

➤ **Pay close attention to absolute words.** Absolute words are all positive or all negative—for example, *always, all, all the time, constantly, everyone, never, none, not at all, no one, absolutely not.* If the test item contains an absolute word, the answer will probably be false.

➤ **Look for qualifiers.** Words such as *usually, many, most, rarely, sometimes, generally,* and *frequently* usually make a statement true since they aren't absolutes.

➤ **Study sentence length.** For a sentence to be true, all parts of it must be true. If even one small part is false, the entire sentence is false. Therefore, the longer a sentence, the more likely it is to be false.

➤ **Watch for false logic.** Two sentences can be true but be connected by a word that makes them false. For example: *President Abraham Lincoln is famous because he was assassinated by John Wilkes Booth.* Lincoln is famous and he was assassinated by Booth—but being assassinated by Booth is not what made Lincoln famous.

➤ **Consider guessing.** Since you have a 50 percent chance of getting the answer right, guess on all true/false questions you aren't sure about (unless there's a penalty for guessing).

Learn the Lingo

Objective tests include true/false, matching, multiple-choice, identification, and sentence completion. These tests are objective in that they have one correct, factual answer.

Below "C" Level

An answer can be true and still be wrong. The correct choice is the one that *best* answers the question, not the one that is necessarily true.

All of the Above? Multiple-Choice Questions

Multiple-choice tests require you to choose correctly from several options. You may have three, four, or five choices. Multiple-choice tests are most difficult if the choices are very close in meaning.

➤ **Beware of opposites.** Multiple-choice questions can snare you on the words *not, except,* or *best* because you're being asked to choose an answer that's the opposite of what you expect. For example:

Which is NOT an example of ...

All the following choices are correct EXCEPT ...

The BEST answer is ...

➤ **Watch the *all of the above* choice.** For the answer to be *all of the above*, every part of every choice has to be correct. Verify the truth of every part of every choice before you select "all of the above."

A Lid for Every Pot: Matching Questions

Matching tests assess your ability to see which things go together. Thinking of these tests as puzzles will help you match the correct pieces and eliminate choices as you go. Also try these hints:

➤ **Read the answers first.** The questions will be listed on the left; the answers on the right. Read the answers first. Knowing the answers can prevent you from choosing the first or second choice because it seems right, when the real answer is farther down the list.

➤ **Cross off items as you use them.** This helps you limit your choices and increase your chances of getting every answer correct.

Blanking Out: Fill-in-the-Blank Questions

You may or may not have answer choices with fill-in-the-blank questions. If you don't, you'll have to recall the correct answer from the material you studied. If you do have answer choices, you'll have to eliminate and choose the best choice. Here are a few tips:

➤ **Look for links in ideas.** As you read the sentence, substitute a word that makes sense for the blank. This helps you figure out what is missing and how the sentence makes sense when complete.

➤ **Predict answers.** If you've been given answer choices, try to predict the answer without looking at the choices. Then look at the choices to find the one that best matches your prediction.

➤ **Look for context clues.** Introductory words and *conjunctions* often show how the parts of

Learn the Lingo

Conjunctions link words, phrases, and sentences. There are three types of conjunctions: *coordinating* (and, but, so, or, for, yet); *subordinate* (if, when, because, etc.); and *correlative* (not only ... but also, etc.).

117

the sentence are linked. Also watch carefully for negatives, such as *not, never, no,* and *none.*

➤ **Match the grammatical form of the question and answer.** If the verb is singular, the subject or answer must be singular. If the verb is plural, the subject or answer must be plural.

Math Maven Alert!

Even though I'm an English professor, I acknowledge that some of you will be taking math classes in college. (Of course, you always sign up for English classes first because they're so much more fun!) Here are some suggestions for doing your best on college math tests.

Crib Notes

A minor case of the nerves can actually help you when you write an essay test because it keeps you alert and focused.

Crib Notes

As you write a response on an essay test, always add some insight of your own, no matter how small. This not only shows that you've done some serious thinking about the issues, but also sets your essay (and you!) apart from the teeming multitudes.

➤ **Try to predict the answer as you work through the problem.** Then look at the choices to see which one most closely matches your prediction. Solve the problem again, checking your work.

➤ **Draw diagrams to help you think out problems.** Diagrams and pictures are especially helpful for math problems that involve shapes, lengths, distances, and sizes.

➤ **Rephrase word problems.** Restating word problems in your own words helps you understand the problem and its different parts.

➤ **Make links.** Relate each new word problem to others you have done. This will help you see similar solutions.

➤ **Form matters.** Be sure to show the answer in the correct mathematical form. Even if your answer is correct, it will likely be marked wrong if it's in the wrong form, such as decimals instead of fractions.

➤ **Show all your work.** You can sometimes get partial credit for incorrect work if your reasoning was sound but you made a computational error.

➤ **Check your answers.** Even if you're dead sure you got the correct answer and you have hot concert tickets burning a hole in your pocket, stay and check your work. This can help you catch errors in counting, plus/minus signs, and logic.

➤ **Use your noodle.** If an answer doesn't seem right even if you found a matching answer choice, trust your instincts. Recalculate the problem to see where the error occurred.

Extra Credit

In 1580, Montaigne first used the word *essay* to refer to a literary work. Montaigne himself had resigned from his judgeship to devote himself to writing his *Essays*, reflections about himself and humanity in general. In 1597, Francis Bacon was writing his *Essays* "as counsels for the successful conduct of life and the management of men." Since the 1600s, essayists around the world have found appreciative audiences.

Write This Way

Studies have shown that following a specific method for writing—the *writing process*—can produce better essays. Following the steps in the writing process helps you get your message across, include important details, and follow a logical order. When you feel in control, you're less likely to lose it and run screaming from the room, too. Best of all, you can follow the steps in the writing process not only for essay tests, but for any document.

There are three main steps in the writing process:

➤ Planning

➤ Drafting

➤ Revising/editing

Let's look at each step in the process in more detail.

1. Planning involves

➤ Prewriting by listing ideas, making charts and diagrams, and asking yourself the five Ws and H (Who? What? When? Where? Why? and How?).

➤ Choosing which ideas to include and which ones to ditch.

➤ Arranging your ideas logically.

Learn the Lingo

The **writing process** is a series of activities that start when a writer begins thinking about the topic and ends when the writer completes the last draft.

119

2. Drafting involves
   - ➤ Writing your first copy.
   - ➤ Writing all subsequent copies, except the final one.
3. Revising/editing involves
   - ➤ Adding details to make your point.
   - ➤ Deleting information that's off the topic.
   - ➤ Rearranging information so the essay is more logical and unified.
   - ➤ Correcting errors in skills (spelling, punctuation, capitalization, grammar, and usage).
   - ➤ Writing the final copy.

Below "C" Level

No one expects a *perfect* paper in a pressure-writing situation, but sloppy errors undercut your thinking and can sink even the best work.

As a long-time college professor, I strongly suggest that you follow the steps in the order given as you learn how to write under pressure. As you become comfortable with the process, follow the steps in the way that works for you, given your topic, audience, purpose, and parameters.

Write Angles

Earning a high score on essay tests isn't difficult if you prepare, practice, and learn some test-taking strategies. Start by determining your parameters.

Crib Notes

If you run out of time before you finish writing your essay, jot down what you were going to say in a few complete sentences. Your teacher may be able to give you some extra credit even through you didn't finish writing the entire essay.

1. Understand Your Parameters

Here's what you want to know before you start writing:

- ➤ **Topic:** What am I writing about?
- ➤ **Audience:** Who will be reading my writing? What do they expect from me?
- ➤ **Purpose:** Why am I writing? Nearly all college writing tests ask you to write *persuasive* or *expository* essays.
- ➤ **Length and Time:** How long must my essay be? How much time do I have?

2. Answer the Exam Question

When you're writing under pressure, it's tempting to remake the question into something you feel more comfortable answering. Stand tough and resist temptation. Be sure you're answering the question you've been asked, not the one you misread or made up.

3. Use Specific Details

Details take the form of facts, examples, statistics, reasons, definitions, and descriptions. Use details to convince your reader that you know the subject. Details also make your writing vivid and specific.

4. Link Ideas with Transitions

Learn the Lingo

Transitions are words and phrases that signal connections between and among ideas.

Connect related ideas with *transitions* that tie your ideas together and create logic. The following chart shows some of the most useful transitions. The meaning is listed on the right, the transitions on the left.

Transitions	Meaning
Also, and, besides, in addition, further, moreover, too	Addition
Next, then	Order
For example, for instance	Example
Namely, specifically	Explanation
But, in contrast, however, nevertheless, nonetheless, on the other hand, still, yet	Contrast
Likewise, in comparison	Comparison
In the same way, similarly	Similarity
Certainly, granted, naturally, of course, to be sure	Concession
Adjacent, at the side, here, there, in the back, in the front, in the distance, nearby, next to	Place
Accordingly, as a result, consequently, so, therefore	Result
As a result, finally, hence, in conclusion, in short	Summary
First (second, third, fourth, etc.), next, before, afterward, at length, currently, during, eventually, finally, in the future, immediately, later, meanwhile, now, soon, subsequently, then	Time, order

Crib Notes

"It is a great thing to have a computer in your room, if possible. If not, the college should provide computers for you to use. Don't go to college knowing nothing about computers, because they are becoming more and more essential in school. Many of my classes require using the Internet for at least part of the class, and homework. But don't try to master all the various programs and stuff; if you need to learn, you can."

—Jonathan Kadishson, Lehigh University

5. Write Clearly, Concisely, Carefully

The most successful essays always fulfill their purpose, address their audience, and have a logical organization. This is true whether the essay is written at home or during a test.

But if your essay can't be read, it can't be graded. Be kind to overworked and underpaid professors and TAs. Make sure you write neatly. If you're a budding healthcare provider, why not give us a break and print?

Below "C" Level

Never try to snow your reader. If you don't know the answer, don't make one up. You're not writing fiction, ladies and gentlemen; you're writing fact.

6. Budget Your Time

As you write, try not to get bogged down in rough patches. If you do get stuck, leave some space and keep writing. With pressure-writing situations, time is key.

Pace yourself by taking a deep breath every ten to fifteen minutes, putting down your pen for a moment, and stretching. You want to work at a controlled, steady pace.

Glossary of Test Terms

Here are the most common terms you'll encounter on short-answer and essay tests. Study this list so you're sure what you're being asked to do on a test.

Term	Meaning
account for	Explain the causes of
analyze	Divide into parts and describe each part
assess	Decide how important something is, and give your reasons
classify	Arrange into categories or groups
comment on	Explain why something is important
compare	Describe the similarities between two things
concise	In short, briefly
contrast	Describe the differences between two things
criteria	The rules or requirements that apply to something
deduction	The conclusion you come to after looking at all the facts
discuss	Give both sides of an argument and then give your own opinion
evaluate	Explain how important something is
factors	The facts or circumstances that contribute to a result
function	What something does: its purpose or role
give an account of	Describe
identify	Point out and describe; name
illustrate	Give examples (or diagrams) that prove your answer is correct
implications	Why something is important; long-term effects or results
in relation to	Refer to a specific aspect of something
indicate	Show, demonstrate
limitations	Explain where something is not useful or not relevant
scope	The extent or influence of something
significance	The consequence of something
summarize	Give the main points
to what extent	Explain in what ways something is true and in what ways it isn't
validity, valid	Evidence to prove the statement

Test-taking and studying are skills that can be learned. It takes time and effort to do your best on college tests, but your investment will pay off now and in the future.

The Least You Need to Know

➤ When you take true/false tests, zero in on absolute words, look for qualifiers, study sentence length, and watch for false logic.

➤ When you take multiple-choice tests, beware of opposites and watch the *all of the above* choice.

➤ When you take matching tests, read the answers first and cross off items as you use them.

➤ When you take fill-in-the-blank tests, look for links in ideas, predict answers, look for context clues, and match the grammatical forms.

➤ On math tests, try to predict answers, draw diagrams, rephrase word problems, watch the form of the answer, and show all your work.

➤ On essay tests, use the writing process: planning, drafting, and revising/editing.

➤ As you write, answer the exam question, use specific details, link ideas with transitions, write clearly, and budget your time.

Chapter 12

Writing Research Papers

In This Chapter

➤ Selecting and narrowing a topic

➤ Writing the thesis statement and researching

➤ Evaluating sources, taking notes, and outlining

➤ Drafting, documenting sources, and keyboarding

➤ Revising, editing, and proofreading

➤ Dealing with catastrophes

Knowing how to write good research papers is an essential skill for success in college. In this chapter, I'll take you through the process step by step—as only a Professor of English can do!

Research Papers vs. Term Papers

Although the terms "research paper" and "term paper" are often used interchangeably, the two are not the same.

A *research paper* presents and argues a thesis—the writer's hypothesis, theory, or opinion. Therefore, a research paper is an analytical or persuasive essay that evaluates a position. When you write a research paper, you use outside evidence to persuade your readers that your argument is valid or at least deserves serious consideration.

A *term paper* doesn't argue a point or try to convince readers to think or act a certain way. Rather, a term paper is a summary of information from one or more sources.

Nearly all major papers you write in college are research papers because they require analytical thinking and original thought. However, always make sure you fully understand whether you're writing a research paper or a term paper before you begin doing any work at all.

Cheaper by the Dozen

Here are the basic steps you'll complete as you write a research paper:

1. Select and narrow a topic
2. Write the thesis statement
3. Research
4. Evaluate sources
5. Take notes
6. Outline
7. Draft rough copies
8. Find more sources, if necessary
9. Document sources
10. Keyboard
11. Revise, edit, proofread
12. Deal with catastrophes

Let's look at each one in detail.

Crib Notes

If you've been assigned a topic you detest, see if you can find an aspect of the topic you like. Nearly all topics can be tweaked a bit here and there. Of course, always clear those "tweaks" with your professor or TA.

Select and Narrow a Topic

If your professor gives you the topic of your research paper, you're all set. However, professors often make selecting and narrowing a topic part of the assignment, especially in introductory writing classes.

Understand that nearly every topic *can* be researched, but not every topic *should* be researched. Give yourself (and your readers) a break by starting with an original topic or an original way of looking at an old topic. Also, never select a topic that condescends to your readers, offends them, or panders to them. Don't try to shock them, either—it *always* backfires. Select topics that suit your audience, purpose, and parameters (length of paper, time limitations).

To get that beast of a topic tailored to an appropriate size, phrase it as a question. Here are some examples for a research paper five to seven pages in length:

➤ Is workfare working?

➤ Is intelligence determined by nature or nurture?

➤ Are antidepressants being overprescribed?

Write the Thesis Statement

Once you've narrowed your topic, it's time to turn your attention to your *thesis statement*—what you're proving in your research paper.

An effective thesis statement states your main idea, reveals your purpose, and shows how your argument will be structured. Research may lead you to revise your thesis, even disprove it, but framing it at the very beginning will focus your thinking. Here are three models:

➤ Much of the conflict between men and women results from their different ways of using language.

➤ The computer revolution has done more harm than good.

➤ Everyone wins with a flat tax: government, business, accountants, and even consumers.

Below "C" Level

Beware of hot topics—very timely, popular issues—because the books, articles, and interviews on such subjects have often been produced in great haste. As a result, they're not carefully fact-checked.

Learn the Lingo

The **thesis statement** is the central point you're proving in your research paper.

Research

Before you even thumb through the card catalog or turn your computer on, try the following ideas to make your search as easy and enjoyable as possible.

1. **Brainstorm key words.** List the key words for your topic, using the title, author, and subject to direct your thinking. For example, key words for a research paper on the poem "Howl" might include …

   ➤ Title: "Howl"

   ➤ Author: Allen Ginsberg

   ➤ Subject: The Beats

Learn the Lingo

Primary sources, such as auto-biographies, diaries, eyewitness accounts, and interviews, are created by direct observation. **Secondary sources,** such as bi-ographies, almanacs, encyclope-dias, and textbooks, were written by people with indirect knowl-edge. Effective research papers often use a mix of both primary and secondary sources.

2. **Include related words.** Brainstorm synonyms to expand or narrow your search. For example, if you're writing on overcrowding in national parks, here are some possible synonyms:

➤ Environmentalism   ➤ Wilderness

➤ National monuments   ➤ Conservation

➤ Federal lands   ➤ Government lands

3. **Learn the terminology.** Nearly every research tool has an abbreviation or two. For print sources, check the introduction or index for information on abbreviations and terminology used. For on-line sources, check the Help screen.

4. **Know your library.** Take a tour of the university library to familiarize yourself with its contents and arrangement.

5. **Consult reference librarians.** Don't be afraid to ask these marvelous experts for help; that's their job.

Book Learning

Since a university library can have over a million volumes, *classification systems* were created to track the volumes. Knowing how these systems work can help you find the books you need to complete your research.

Books are divided into two classes: *fiction* and *nonfiction*. Fiction is catalogued under the author's last name. Nonfiction books, however, are classified in two different ways: the *Dewey Decimal* classification system (used in community and public school libraries) and the *Library of Congress* classification system (used in college and university libraries). We're going to focus on the Library of Congress system, since that's what you need.

The Library of Congress classification system has 20 classes., Here's a typical Library of Congress call number: PS3523.046S43. (It's for Jack London's *The Sea Wolf*.)

Mags and Rags

For more timely information, check out periodicals, material that is published on a regular schedule, such as weekly, biweekly, monthly, bimonthly, quarterly, and so on. Periodicals include newspapers, magazines, and journals.

University libraries index periodicals on computerized databases. Each entry provides the title, author, and sometimes a summary. You can read the entire article from the screen, print it, or e-mail it to your home computer.

Every library has different periodical databases. Here are some of the best:

➤ DataTimes is an online index to local newspapers.

➤ DIALOG is an extensive, well-regarded database.

➤ ERIC (Educational Resources Information Center) and Education Index are the places to be for information in education.

➤ InfoTrak lists more than 1,000 business, tech, and general periodicals, including *The New York Times* and *The Wall Street Journal.*

➤ LEXIS/NEXIS affords access to thousands of full-text articles. It's great for information on legal cases.

➤ MEDLINE is a well-respected source for information on medical topics.

➤ MILCS is a database of all the holdings of academic and public libraries in specific regions.

➤ OCLC First Search lists all the periodicals, media, and books in the United States and Canada. It has many indexes.

➤ PAIS, the Public Affairs Informational Service, is great for economics. Ditto on EconLit.

➤ ATLA Religion Database covers religion.

➤ VU/TEXT is a newspaper database.

➤ WILSONSEARCH is an online information system containing the Wilson databases not on CD-ROM, such as the Education Index and the Index to Legal Periodicals.

Using the Internet

Use *search engines,* which work with *keywords,* to help you locate Web sites. Here are some of the most popular search engines and their Internet addresses:

➤ AltaVista   www.altavista.com

➤ Cyberhound   www.thomson.com/cyberhound/

➤ Excite   www.excite.com

➤ HotBot   www.hotbot.lycos.com

➤ Lycos   www.lycos.com

➤ WebCrawler   webcrawler.com

➤ Yahoo!   www.yahoo.com

Since not all search engines lead to the same sources, you should use more than one. Use bookmarks or hot lists to mark sources so you can return to them later.

Additional Research Treasures

There are lots of other useful reference sources. For example:

➤ **Interviews.** Discussing your subject with an expert adds credibility and immediacy to your report.

➤ **Surveys.** Surveys can help you assess how a large group feels about your topic or a significant aspect of it.

➤ **Audiovisual materials.** These sources include records, audiocassettes, videotapes, slides, and photographs.

➤ **Government documents.** The government publishes *tons* of pamphlets, reports, catalogs, and newsletters on most issues of national concern.

➤ **Special collections.** Many libraries also have restricted collections of rare books, manuscripts, newspapers, magazines, photographs, maps, and so on.

Evaluate Sources

Just because a source appears in print, in the media, or online doesn't mean it's valid. Before you decide to use *any* source, you have to judge its reliability, credibility, and appropriateness. Use the following criteria as you determine whether a source is valid for inclusion in your research paper:

Crib Notes

There are a growing number of review tools to help you assess online materials. Among the best are Webcrawler's *Best of the Net*, Lycos *Top 5%*, and Gale's *Cyberhound Guide*.

➤ **Authority.** Some sources *are* more reliable than others. As a result, they help you make your point in your research paper. Check the author's credentials and the sources the author cites.

➤ **Source.** The most reliable sources are written by experts and have been reviewed by equally reputable readers. Consider where the source comes from—its writer, sponsoring agency, publisher, and so on.

➤ **Timeliness.** Include both classic and recent reference materials. This combination helps balance your outlook, tempering the current with the traditional.

➤ **Bias.** Every source is biased because every source has a point of view. Bias is not necessarily bad, as long as you recognize it as such and take it into account as you evaluate and use the source. Select reference materials that reflect opinions from across the spectrum.

➤ **Appropriateness.** Every source must fit with your audience, purpose, and tone. Make sure that you understand the material in the source, that it's written at a level appropriate to your readers, and that it contains the information you need.

Create a Working Bibliography

Next, create a *working bibliography,* a systematic way to organize all the material that looks promising. For each source, write all the bibliographic material on a 3×5 index card. Here's what you should include on the card:

➤ Author's complete name

➤ Title of source

➤ If you're citing printed matter: publisher, place of publication, date of publication, page numbers (for magazines and journals)

➤ If you're citing a Web site: URL, date you accessed the page

If a catalog or index doesn't provide complete bibliographic information, leave blanks you can fill in later.

There are several different methods of documentation. For example, research papers in the humanities often use the Modern Language Association (MLA) style, while papers in social sciences use the American Psychological Association (APA) style. As you write your bibliography cards, follow the documentary style preferred by the discipline in which you're writing.

Take Notes

Now it's time to fit everything in place. Here's how to do it:

1. Skim the sources and arrange them according to difficulty, from easiest to most difficult.

2. Read the general, introductory sources first. You'll use them to lay the foundation for the more specialized and technical material you'll need later.

3. Decide how each source fits with the other sources you've gathered.

4. Take notes on the source, using summaries, paraphrases, and direct quotations. Rephrase as you read to make sure you understand the source fully.

5. Position the source in your paper by deciding where it fits in the overall thesis and paper organization.

Below "C" Level

Don't rely too heavily on any one source—no matter how good it looks. First, this can lead to bias. Second, what happens if the source turns out to be invalid or dated? Your argument can collapse.

Extra Credit

Although it might seem you spend most of your time drafting, studies have shown that only about one third of your time is actually spent at this stage.

6. Connect the source to what you've already written. Correlate all the information to see what you've already discovered and what you still have to find.

Outline Your Paper

Effective research papers (as with all effective writing) present ideas in an organized, logical manner. Follow these steps to organize your paper:

➤ **Group related ideas.** Sort your research into two categories: *general* and *specific*. Then place all the specific ideas under the general ones.

➤ **Eliminate nonessential ideas.** If an idea doesn't fit, set it aside. You can return to it later if you change your mind.

➤ **Arrange ideas in a logical order.** Decide what information to present first, second, third, and so on.

As you research, you'll discover that you're automatically changing the structure of your paper to accommodate what you're finding. Usually the changes are minor, but you may find yourself designing a radically new organization to fit the focal points and supporting details. Once you think you've found the right direction to go in, make a working outline to show the structure of your paper.

Add as many main ideas as you need to prove your thesis, satisfy your audience (the professor), and fulfill your task.

Draft Rough Copies

Use your notes and outline as a framework for your first draft. Start at the beginning and work through everything. Try to write at a steady pace until you reach a natural breaking point, such as the end of a section.

Find More Sources, If Necessary

As you draft, you may have to get additional facts to plug holes in your paper. You can stop writing to research, or continue drafting and fill in the missing material later. I favor the last approach because it helps you maintain the writing momentum you've built up. Just leave some space for the missing material, clearly label it ("insert quote from expert"), and fill it in later. This is especially easy to do if you're drafting on a computer.

Document Sources

As you write, integrate the most convincing outside proofs with your own words. Present material logically, deal with opposing arguments, add examples to support generalizations, and address your readers intelligently. Document your sources to credit their contribution.

It's not enough just to slap the information into your paper, even if you *do* surround any exact quotes with quotation marks. The material must be smoothly blended in and used to make a specific point. For example, here's the opening from a research paper I wrote on Nathaniel Hawthorne's *The Scarlet Letter.*

Another Possible Source of Hawthorne's Hester Prynne

It was near that old and sunken grave ... on this simple slab of slate—as that curious investigator may still discern, ... there appeared ... a herald's wording of which might serve for a motto and brief description of our now concluded legend; so somber is it, and relieved only by one ever-glowing point of light gloomier than the shadow: "ON A FIELD, SABLE, THE LETTER A, GULES." (The Scarlet Letter, 264).

So ends Nathaniel Hawthorne's *The Scarlet Letter,* and so begins the search for Hester Prynne's grave. Hester's grave is more often inquired after by visitors to the King's Chapel Burial Grounds than any other, claims the custodian of that historic enclosure in a 1999 interview. Her grave is apparently sought there because Hawthorne's skillful intermingling of real and fictional people and places has led readers to believe that *The Scarlet Letter* is based on a true story. In his essay titled "The New England Sources *for The Scarlet Letter,*" scholar Charles Ryskamp establishes the fact that the supporting characters in *The Scarlet Letter*—other than Hester, Pearl, Dimmesdale, and Chillingworth, for whom we can find no real historical basis—were actual figures (258). According to Ryskamp, Hawthorne used the most credible history of Boston available to him, Caleb Snow's *History of Boston. ...*

I started by citing a primary source, *The Scarlet Letter.* This shows that I know the necessary basis for the discussion. I integrated the name of a secondary source directly into the body of the paper ("scholar Charles Ryskamp"), used cue words to show how he stood behind his work ("establishes the fact that ..."), and gave credit to my source in parentheses (Nobel, 113).

The Name Game

When you cite material from a well-respected source, put the author's name directly in the body of your text to get more mileage from it. Readers are impressed—and rightly so—when you cite a recognized authority. Placing the person's name in the text shows that you've done your homework and you understand who to line up behind your argument.

Learn the Lingo

Parenthetical documentation, footnotes, and **endnotes** are ways of giving credit to sources you used in your paper.

Below "C" Level

Never omit material from a quotation to change its meaning. Also, if you do excerpt a quotation, always be sure it makes grammatical sense after you've cut it. Use ellipses (...) to indicate omitted material when you're deleting text not germane to your paper.

Credit Given Here

As you weave in expert opinions, facts, examples, and statistics, provide enough information so your readers can easily trace every source. In addition to citing the name of the source and integrating the source, you can add the *parenthetical documentation, footnotes,* or *endnotes*. Documentation the most important way of all because it provides complete information.

Again, there are a number of formats you can choose from as you document your sources, and each discipline favors a specific style. Always ask the professor what form of documentation he or she prefers.

Avoid Plagiarism

As you write, you honor your moral responsibility to use someone else's ideas ethically and make it easy for readers to check your claims. Give a source for everything that's not common knowledge, the information an educated person is expected to know. If you fail to give adequate credit, you can be charged with *plagiarism,* or representing someone else's words or ideas as your own. The consequences of plagiarism are stiff: failure and perhaps even expulsion.

Works Cited or Bibliography Page

A *Works Cited* page provides a complete citation for every work you *cited* in your research paper. A *bibliography* (or *Works Consulted* list), in contrast, provides a full citation for every work you *consulted* as you wrote your paper. Bibliographies are, therefore, usually much longer than Works Cited pages.

In most cases, you need just a Works Cited page. However, you may be asked to prepare a bibliography as well. Be sure to check with your professor so you know which format to follow.

In either case, entries are arranged in alphabetical order according to the author's last name. If the entry doesn't have an author (such as a Web page, encyclopedia entry, or editorial), alphabetize it according to the first word of the title.

Keyboarding

Keyboard your paper in standard 10- or 12-point fonts, such as Times Roman, Courier, or Helvetica. Avoid fancy, elaborate fonts, since they're a pain in the neck to read. Double-space the text and, unless specifically requested to do so, don't right-justify (align) your paper. The right margins should be ragged, like the margins on this page.

Revise, Edit, Proofread

Follow these steps as you revise:

1. Let your draft "cool off"—that is, allow at least a day between drafting and revising. This break helps you see where you need to make changes.

2. Read your draft once all the way through.

3. Decide whether you want to revise this draft or start again.

4. If you revise, focus on one issue at a time. For example, first read for organization, next for details, and so on.

Learn the Lingo

Plagiarism is using someone else's words without giving him or her adequate credit.

Crib Notes

When you shop for feedback, look for readers who can be both objective and ruthless. For example, tutors at college writing centers are brilliant editors because they're not afraid to tell the truth.

Get someone to help. Select readers whose opinions you value and tell them exactly what you want them to look for in your document. For example, if you're seeking feedback on a first draft, you'll most likely want comments about organization and tone. By the second draft, however, you'll probably be looking for feedback on style rather than content. Try not to be defensive. If the feedback is negative, don't take it personally.

When you proofread your writing, look for errors in spelling, punctuation, grammar, and usage. We're creatures of habit, so we're most likely to make the same writing mistakes over and over.

Below "C" Level

"Don't be afraid to change. If you're like me, you probably don't like being told to do things a certain way. You want to do them the way you are comfortable with. That attitude won't get you anywhere in college. If your professor wants your work a certain way, do it! This is really true with research papers."

—Danielle Bobb, the State University of New York College of Technology at Farmingdale

Deal with Catastrophes

ALWAYS build in some time to deal with disasters: the computer crashes and you lose a week's work, you get the flu and can't work for a week, your roommate has a meltdown and you spend two days talking her off the roof. Far too many of my students write their research papers the day before they are due—and their haste really shows. The papers are riddled with careless errors, lapses in logic, and gaps in information. Don't let this happen to you.

The Least You Need to Know

➤ Select topics that suit your audience, purpose, and parameters (length of paper, time limitations).

➤ An effective thesis statement states your main idea, reveals your purpose, and shows how your argument will be structured.

➤ Carefully evaluate all your sources, take accurate notes, and outline your paper.

➤ As you write, integrate the most convincing outside proofs with your own words.

➤ Avoid plagiarism (literary theft).

➤ Revise, edit, and proofread your paper; be sure to allow time to deal with disasters.

Part 3

Money Matters

"If you need the money, getting a job won't hurt your grades, and won't cramp your social life. You'll organize your time more efficiently if you have a job."

—Terrence McGlynn, University of San Diego

In this part of the book, you'll learn how to manage your money; juggle college classes, clubs, and jobs; and negotiate with financial aid about your loans. With the tab at some elite colleges topping $35,000 a year, this chapter is a must!

Chapter 13

It's All About the Benjamins: Managing Your Money

In This Chapter

➤ Making a budget

➤ Opening and using a checking account

➤ Balancing your checkbook

➤ Using ATM machines

"I've experienced, like most college students do, that no matter what, you never have any money. We're all poor! A common quote on my campus is 'I can't go unless we take BearExpress.' BearExpress is a cash account that you can only use on campus."

—Maureen Colson, Potsdam University

It's late at night and you've been hitting the books hard. Wouldn't a pizza with extra cheese taste great around now? Call the local pizzeria and ka-ching! It's yours. Or it's Saturday night and everyone's going to the movies in town. Buy the ticket, a tub of popcorn, and a large soda. Ka-ching! How about this: It's the end of the month and your phone bill comes in. It's a monster alright, about the size of the gross national debt of a small banana republic. Ka-ching! Ka-ching! Ka-ching! You're flat broke.

College students *do* have a lot of expenses, but with a little guidance, you can learn to handle your money wisely. That's what this chapter is all about.

Financial Wizard

"The thing I found most odd about my first weeks at college was the freedom … and the responsibility I never was prepared for. You are entirely on your own, so you must figure out what your expenses will be and make a budget. Stick to it and leave yourself an emergency stash—not for midnight beer runs but the unexpected phone bill that may be double your budget."

—Bob Greenberger, SUNY Binghamton

The first step to attaining fiscal responsibility is establishing a *budget,* which is simply a written plan for managing your money. You can write your budget on a piece of paper or set up a more formal worksheet on your computer. There are several easy spreadsheet programs for this purpose, such as Excel or Quicken.

The formula behind an effective budget is simple:

Good budget = Money coming in > Money going out

Bad budget = Money coming in < Money going out

Budget Format

Following is a model budget form for a student whose parents pay her tuition, food, and housing. Adjust this form to match your fixed and variable expenses. For example, if you're a commuter, add money for gas and car insurance; if you're not on a meal plan, add money for food. Subtract your total expenses from your total income to discover how much money you have left over at the end of every month—or how much money you're short.

Monthly Budget

Income

    Take-home pay from job $_____

    Loan income $_____

    Parental contribution $_____

        Total $_____

Fixed Expenses (expenses that do not change)

    Laundry $_____

    Personal supplies $_____

Variable Expenses (expenses that change). Enter an estimated amount, since these expenses change.

    Telephone $_____

    Snacks $_____

    Movies, shows, concerts, CDs, etc. $_____

    School supplies $_____

    Transportation $_____

    Clothing $_____

        Total $_____

        Total income $_____

                                               −

        Total expenses $_____

                                               =

        Amount left over (or short) $_____

Hints for Avoiding the Budget Blues

As a college student, one of the most important tasks you face is learning how to manage your money. It's not as hard as it sounds. Try these ideas:

➤ **Earn more.** If you're not working, consider taking a part-time job. If you *are* working, think about increasing your hours or getting a job that pays more. (This is covered in detail in Chapter 16, "Working Stiff.")

➤ **Spend less.** If you're not willing to work more, you're going to have to spend less. Set yourself limits, something like $15 a week for incidentals.

Below "C" Level

Don't beat yourself up if you overspend one month; everyone slips up now and again. Instead, cut back the next month to balance your budget.

➤ **Don't let bills slide.** If you don't pay your bills on time, you'll get slapped with late fees.

➤ **Watch credit.** Don't spend more on credit than you can afford to pay off. (This is covered in detail in Chapter 14, "A Crash Course in Credit.")

➤ **Don't loan too much money to your friends.** A small loan here and there is kindness; a large loan here and there is foolishness. You're likely to lose both your money and your friend.

➤ **Track your money.** "Keep receipts if there's a chance you need to return the clothes or books you just bought. Save the phone bills so when you reforecast your budget you can see a more realistic usage history," advises Bob Greenberger, SUNY Binghamton.

Check It Out

"When I was in college, I had a friend who thought as long as he had a checkbook with checks in it, he could write checks. You can't, which he found out fast."

—Anonymous

Having a checking account solves the thorny problem of carrying or mailing cash. You don't want to be running around campus with your pockets bulging with bills; neither do you want to be stuffing cash into an envelope and dropping it into the mailbox.

I feel that checks are the single best way for college students to keep track of their money and avoid overspending because ...

➤ You know exactly how much money you have at all times.

➤ Writing a check is less convenient than spending cash, so you're less likely to make impulse purchases.

➤ Every month, you can look back at your checks and see just how you spent your money.

➤ It's too easy to overspend on your credit cards (as you'll learn in Chapter 14).

➤ It can be tricky remembering how much money you've withdrawn through ATMs, even with those cute little receipts.

Therefore, checks are especially useful for college students. When you open a checking account in a bank, you make a deposit. The bank issues you a book of checks. Instead of carrying cash, you carry the book of checks and write checks to pay for what you purchase. If a check is lost or stolen, you can call the bank and ask to stop payment. (There is a fee for this service, usually $7 to $20, depending on your bank.)

When you write a check, you're empowering the bank to pay a specific amount of money from your checking account to the person (or company) whose name you write on the check. The person brings the check to the bank to *cash* it—exchange it for money. After the bank pays the check, it's returned to you in the mail stamped "paid." The amount is deducted from your checking account. The stamped check is your receipt.

Getting Checks

Local merchants rarely cash out-of-town checks, so when you get to campus, open an account at a local bank. Try to open the account in the summer because the local banks will be mobbed the first week of school. Then you'll be all set when you get to campus in the late summer or early fall.

Look for a bank that has an office in your hometown as well as one in your college town. This enables you to use the campus ATM without having to pay a fee. It also allows your rich uncle to deposit money in your home bank and have it credited to your school account.

Follow these guidelines as you set up your checking account:

➤ Have your checks printed with your campus address, whether dorm or apartment. Most stores and companies won't accept checks that don't have an address printed on them.

➤ Banks charge for printing checks. You can often get printed checks more cheaply through a mail-order company rather than through the bank. These companies advertise in coupon sections of the Sunday newspapers.

Learn the Lingo

Cashing a check is exchanging it at the bank for money.

Crib Notes

All bank fees are negotiable, even though the bank doesn't want you to know that. People with the most money on deposit have the leverage to negotiate the smallest fees; those with the least amount of money (like college students) often pay the stiffest fees. Nonetheless, don't be afraid to shop around to find the cheapest bank fees.

➤ Fancy checks cost more than plain ones. Get the simplest checks you can, without pictures of your dog or car.

➤ Since you'll be changing dorm rooms or apartments every year, order the minimum number of checks.

➤ DON'T throw away the check register that comes with your checks. It looks like a little ledger. You'll need it to keep track of your account.

Using Checks

Here are some hints to help you use checks properly:

➤ Always write your checks in pen, never in pencil.

➤ You can write checks only for the amount of money you have in your account.

➤ If you accidentally exceed the amount you have in your account, your check will not be honored because you have insufficient funds. In the vernacular, this is called *bouncing a check*. It's a serious no-no because you're not only getting assessed a hefty penalty but also damaging your credit rating.

➤ Banks can issue you overdraft privileges, meaning they will honor your checks if they bounce. There may be a stiff fee for this service, however.

➤ When you write a check to pay for an item in a store, you need proof of identity. Use a driver's license, school ID, or credit card. Some merchants require you to have a check-cashing card, issued by your bank. Ask the store for its check-cashing policy if you're interested in buying something.

➤ Nowadays, few banks charge a fee for writing checks. If your bank does charge a fee, shop around for one that doesn't.

Extra Credit

Money orders, available from the post office or bank, are used like checks. You can get a money order for any amount up to $1,000, and you have to pay a fee to use one—from around 75¢ for a $50 money order to around $1 for a $500 one. Always immediately fill in the person or company to whom you're sending the money order; a blank money order is the same as cash. Save your receipt so you have proof that you bought the money order, if it is lost or stolen.

Making Deposits

You can deposit money to your checking account in two ways: by transferring money electronically through the ATM or by giving a deposit and deposit slip to a real live bank teller.

Deposit slips come preprinted with the same information that appears on your check; you can find them in the back of each package of checks. You can fill one out at the bank if you happen to be without one. Check out the words that appear under the date: "DEPOSITS MAY NOT BE AVAILABLE FOR IMMEDIATE WITHDRAWAL." If you deposit cash, it should be available almost at once, but if you deposit a check, the bank can hold the funds up to a week until they release the money. That means you don't have access to the money for a week. If you try to write a check using that money, the check will bounce. Since you don't want to bounce checks, always leave ample time for deposits to clear.

Balancing Your Checkbook

Balancing your checkbook means reconciling all your checks and deposits. It's actually easy, just basic addition and subtraction—not even any multiplication or division.

Balance your checking account in your check register, that handy little ledger that came for free with your checks.

As you balance your checkbook, follow these suggestions:

➤ Log each check in your check register *as you make it out.* Immediately subtract the check amount from your check register balance. This way, you'll have a running tab of how much money is in your checking account.

➤ Do your math carefully to avoid nasty surprises. If you're as math-impaired as I am, use a calculator. (I won't tell if you won't.)

➤ If you're a techie, you can use one of the wonderful computer programs such as Quicken to balance your checkbook. Just type in the checks and the amounts, and Quicken does all the math for you.

Learn the Lingo

Balancing your checkbook is doing the math to make sure your balance matches the bank's balance.

Below "C" Level

You can use your VISA, Master-Card, and similar cards to get a cash advance from an ATM. But beware: Many credit companies charge stiff fees for this service. Reserve this option for an emergency.

➤ Your bank issues a monthly statement that lists all the deposits you made, all your checks the bank paid, and your balance. Make sure your balance matches the bank's balance. If it doesn't, determine who made the error at once. If it's a bank error, call the bank as soon as possible to have it corrected. NEVER assume that the bank's statement is correct.

➤ Balance your checkbook once a month. Like studying, the longer you let it go, the harder it is to do—and the more likely you are to bounce a check.

Which Way to the ATM?

Many colleges have ATMs (automated teller machines) on campus or close by. These machines allow you to withdraw money from your checking and savings accounts virtually any time, day or night. ATMs have both advantages and disadvantages, as the following chart shows:

Advantages of ATMs	Disadvantages of ATMs
Get cash on demand.	Must carry around cash.
Can avoid opening a checking account.	Service charges per withdrawal.
Fast and easy	To avoid service charges, people withdraw more money than they need, leading to over-spending.

If you decide to open an ATM account—and nearly all college students do—don't make the numerical password something obvious, like your birth date. Instead, make the password something like your gym locker combination, your grandmother's birthday, or your high school student ID number.

The Least You Need to Know

➤ Become fiscally responsible by making a budget and sticking to it.

➤ To balance your budget, you may have to earn more or spend less.

➤ Open a checking account and keep it balanced.

➤ ATMs are a handy way to withdraw money from your account—but keep track of your balance.

Chapter 14

A Crash Course in Credit

In This Chapter

➤ Definition of credit

➤ Types of credit cards

➤ Terms you need to know

➤ Applying for credit

➤ Using credit wisely

"College is totally expensive—not only tuition, but also food, living, books, lab fees, etc. Plan on spending a whole lot more than you think."

—Danielle Guarracino, Cornell University

Danielle is right: College is costly, even if you attend one of the least expensive schools. As a result, many college students use credit to bridge the gap between checks from parents, earnings from jobs, or loans. Credit *is* a useful tool—but only when used properly. In this chapter, you'll learn how to use credit intelligently.

Credit Concerns

Steven Shaw, a student at Washington College, has resisted the lure of easy credit. He says, "Credit cards are particularly insidious for students who make impulsive purchases, or those who don't understand that paying the minimum balance each month gets you deeper in debt. A lot of my friends who have graduated are still facing years of credit card debt they accumulated in college." His advice? Pay cash. And if you can't afford it, don't buy it.

Below "C" Level

Think long term: For many college students, credit card debt is just another nail in the coffin. Unless you have a rich uncle, a fat trust fund, or a full scholarship, you're going to have to pay off loans after graduation. Do you really need hefty credit card bills as well?

Learn the Lingo

Credit is deferred payment.

Learn the Lingo

Interest or **finance charges** are the fees you pay for the privilege of using credit.

Like Steven, some students avoid credit as they would the dreaded 8:00 A.M. class. Other students, in contrast, embrace credit—perhaps a little too enthusiastically. Then we have the students who use credit wisely, which is where you'll fit by the end of the chapter. When used judiciously, credit can help you get what you need when you need it. Let's start by learning what credit is—and isn't.

Credit Is ...

Credit enables you to buy something now and pay for it later. As a result, credit can help you when you're short of cash. Further, carrying a credit card can be a lot safer than carrying cash. Cash can be lost or stolen. Credit can be traced so that you're protected against theft or loss.

Further, credit enables you to buy things when they're on sale or when you need them, even if you don't have the cash at that moment. For example, you need your books at the beginning of the semester, whether your student loan has come through or not. You can buy online with a credit card, too.

Most important, using a credit card helps establish your credit history, which is essential for the big-ticket items you'll purchase after graduation: cars, apartments, houses.

Credit Is Not ...

Credit is not free money. Every dollar you charge you'll have to pay back. As you think how great that DVD player you're about to charge will look in your dorm room, think about how many hours you'll have to work to pay it off.

The privilege of using credit cards comes with a price, however—literally. How high the price is depends on how you manage your credit. Pay your balance in full, and on time, each month, and the cost is zero. Make partial payments, or late payments, and the cost can be steep. The penalty for making partial payments rather than paying in full is called *interest* or *finance charges*. Interest makes up a large part of the total cost of using credit. Keep the following facts about interest in mind:

➤ If you charge a purchase to your credit card and don't pay it off until the end of the grace period, that charge will start collecting interest. (The *grace period* is the extra time you have before the payment is due.)

➤ The longer you put off paying for that purchase, the more interest it collects—and the more money you owe.

➤ Certain types of charges, such as cash advances, can carry additional charges such as transaction fees and even higher interest rates than charges for purchases. Late fees and over-the-limit fees can also increase your balance.

In addition to interest and finance charges, some companies charge a yearly fee for their credit cards. This fee usually ranges from $25 up.

Types of Credit Cards

There are several different types of credit cards: bank cards, store cards, gasoline cards, and secured cards. Let's look at each one in detail so you can decide which ones—if any—are right for you.

➤ **Bank credit cards.** Companies such as Visa, MasterCard, American Express, and Capital One offer their own credit cards. These cards can be used in a wide variety of stores and restaurants, and can even be used overseas. You may want to get a card from one of these companies because they can be used for nearly all your purchases.

➤ **Store credit cards.** Every major department store issues its own credit card. For example, Macy's, J.C. Penney, and Wal-Mart have their own store credit cards. Store cards can be used only in the stores that issue them. As a result, these cards are not really necessary for college students. You can always use a bank card such as a Visa or MasterCard if you want to buy something in a store.

➤ **Gasoline credit cards.** Oil companies such as Shell, Exxon, and Mobile also issue credit

Below "C" Level

Interest piles up fast if you're not careful. For example, if you charge a stereo for $235 and pay for it over time, in a year you will owe an extra $40 in interest alone!

Crib Notes

To see if you can use your credit card in a specific store or restaurant, look for your card's logo in the window or by the cash register.

149

cards to customers. You can use a gas credit card to pay for gas and service at the company's gas stations. While this is handy, especially for college students who commute, gas companies often charge more for gas paid for by credit. They give cash-paying customers a lower price. Wouldn't you rather have the savings? (Save even more by pumping your own gas.)

➤ **Secured credit cards.** If you've had credit problems in the past or have reason to believe you'll have trouble handling credit responsibly, consider getting a secured credit card. You place money in the bank as security against default. Therefore, your credit limit is defined by the amount of money you placed in security. This type of card can help you reestablish your credit and provide you with identification as you write checks.

Typically, you deposit $100 to $500 in an interest-bearing account, and the bank sends you a credit card with at least the same credit limit as your deposit. If you don't pay on time, your account is tapped for the sum you owe. Secured cards charge 16 to 20 percent on unpaid balances and annual fees in the $20 to $40 range.

Learn the Lingo

A **debit card,** like a check, withdraws money from your account. A debit card *is not* a credit card—even if it has a credit card logo on it.

Don't confuse a credit card with a *debit card*. A credit card enables you to use someone else's money and pay it back at a later time. With a debit card, in contrast, you use your own money. A debit card works like a check, as you withdraw money from your own account.

Debit cards are easier to use than checks because you don't need identification to get money; however, it's easier to keep track of your balance with a checking account.

Plastic Pursuits

Should *you* get a credit card? Consider getting a credit card if ...

➤ You can handle money responsibly.

➤ You're good at budgeting your money.

➤ You have gaps between checks and loan payments that must be bridged with credit.

➤ You're ready to establish your credit history.

➤ You have genuine school-related expenses that can only be covered by a credit card.

➤ You commute to college. (Credit cards are useful when you're on the road and emergencies occur.)

Don't get a credit card if ...

➤ You know you have a tendency to overspend.

➤ You haven't yet learned to budget money well.

➤ You don't need or want a credit history yet.

➤ You have cash for your college needs.

➤ You really don't need a credit card.

Stephanie Muntone of Oberlin College offers this advice:

> "It's good to have a credit card in case of an emergency. We were once stuck late at night because the car broke down on the way back to Oberlin from a dinner excursion. Because someone had a credit card, we were able to pay for a tow and a ride home. But there's a bad side of credit cards: Don't allow yourself to buy anything you can't pay for at the end of the month when the bill comes. You can easily run up a huge debt and be paying off interest throughout your 20s. Many of my friends fell into this trap."

Crib Notes

Some credit cards require payment in full each month; you can't spread out your payments over several months. These cards are good if you want the discipline of paying off your debt each month. They tend to have a higher yearly fee, but don't add a finance charge.

Credit Spoken Here

Credit, as with any other field, has its own terms. Here are the terms you should know before you sign on the dotted line:

➤ **Annual membership or fee.** This is the amount you're charged every year ("annually") for having a credit card. It's charged whether you use the card or not.

➤ **Cap.** A limit on how much a variable (changing) interest rate can increase or decrease during a set length of time.

➤ **Credit limit.** The maximum amount you can borrow under the agreement of your credit account.

➤ **Index.** An economic indicator on which your interest for a variable rate loan is based.

Below "C" Level

"Don't apply for credit cards while in school. They're too easy to use and too hard to pay off. College loans are hard enough to pay back without paying off credit card debt on top of that."

—Lori Marlar, Murray State University

151

➤ **Minimum payment.** The minimum amount you must pay (usually monthly) on your account.

➤ **Transaction fee.** The fee charged each time you draw on your credit line.

➤ **Variable rate.** An interest rate that changes periodically in relation to an index. Payments may increase or decrease accordingly.

Extra Credit

Your card's **APR** (**annual percentage rate**) is used to determine your daily periodic rate. The higher your card's APR, the more interest you pay. Variable rate cards are based on inflation and are guided by a financial index (such as the Prime Rate). When the index goes down, so does the interest rate on your card. Fixed rate cards keep the same rate of interest, regardless of inflation.

Below "C" Level

"Freshmen probably shouldn't have credit cards because credit is hard to handle. Freshmen who get credit cards from their parents as 'emergency' money often misuse them. All freshmen should have checking accounts for emergencies."

—Nathan Buxhoeveden, Virginia Military Institute

Applying for Credit

If you decide to get a credit card, follow these steps:

1. Carefully research the different credit card offers. You can do this most easily online. Find the credit card that's right for your needs.

2. Select a card that offers low interest and no yearly fee. But watch out: With some credit card companies, the trade-off for having no annual fee is the absence of a grace period before the interest starts piling up.

3. Fill out the application form carefully. Read the entire form and make sure you understand how much you will be paying for the convenience of using credit. Be especially alert for "low introductory rates" that later go up.

Credit Maven

"Credit cards are good for emergencies, but not on a daily basis. For daily money, get an account with a bank in town and an ATM card. This helps keep spending in check."

—Chris Seifert, University of Illinois

So your shiny new credit card arrived in the mail today. Before you start using it, read these suggestions:

1. Sign the back of a new card immediately. If you don't, a thief could sign it for you and begin using it.

2. Record your credit card number, expiration date, and the company's toll-free phone number in a secure place. The easiest way to do this is to photocopy the front and back of all your cards. Also save all the information that came with your cards. You'll need this information if you lose your card or it gets stolen.

3. Before you use your card, set up a filing system. Keep all your receipts so you can compare them to the statement when it comes in at the end of every month. Mistakes happen, and it's a lot easier to prove misbillings if you have your receipts.

4. Don't insure your credit card. It's a waste of money because your credit liability is only $50 anyway.

5. Don't give anyone your card number or expiration date over the phone unless you started the transaction. NEVER give your credit card information to strangers who call you.

6. When using your credit cards, don't give out your birth date or Social Security number more often than necessary. Thieves use this information to steal your credit history.

7. Watch for identity theft. If your wallet is stolen, be aware that a driver's license and a major credit card are all a thief needs to open

Crib Notes

If your credit cards are lost or stolen, contact the companies that issued them as soon as possible. According to federal law, the most you can be held liable for is $50 worth of purchases. Liability will be less than $50 if you notify the card issuer before the unauthorized user incurs $50 worth of charges.

Grade: **D⁻** (!)

Below "C" Level

NEVER co-sign a credit card for a friend. When you co-sign for a credit card (or a loan), you assume responsibility if the person defaults (fails to pay what he or she owes). If your friend needs you to cosign, it means he or she has a troubled credit history and is likely to default. Run, run, run!

charge accounts in your name. Ask the credit reporting agencies (listed later in this chapter) to place a "fraud alert" on your account. Then you'll have to confirm any future credit applications over the phone.

8. Think twice about getting more than one card. You probably need only one general card, such as a VISA or MasterCard. Every time you apply for a card, it shows up on your credit card history—whether you get the card or not. Having too many cards, even if you don't use them, might make it more difficult for you to qualify for a mortgage or car loan because creditors may feel you're overextended.

Ready, Set, Charge

Question: How do you stop a charging elephant?

Answer: Take away his credit card.

It's an old joke, but it's still accurate: You can stop a stampede by not having a credit card in the first place. But as you've learned, credit is an important tool for college students—when used wisely. Following are some of the most common questions college freshmen ask about using credit. Study these questions and answers to learn what you need to know about being a smart credit consumer.

Question: How can I avoid large debt?

Answer: Learning to spend money wisely is the first step. Budget your credit card spending, charging only what you can afford to pay off at the end of each month or what you intend to pay over time.

Crib Notes

To get a handle on overspending, keep a spending diary to see what you're spending and why. Record every single purchase, no matter how small.

Question: What should I do if I can't control my charging?

Answer: Cut up your cards and get some credit counseling. Look in the telephone book for these services. They're often free or very low cost.

Question: What should I do if I can't make a payment?

Answer: Contact the creditor immediately. In most cases, they will work with you. Creditors usually prefer getting smaller payments than none at all.

Question: What should I do if I've been denied credit?

Answer: Get a copy of your credit report and find out why. You can get a copy by contacting one of the following three national credit reporting agencies:

➤ Experian Consumer Assistance (formerly known as TRW) at 1-888-397-3742

➤ Equifax at 1-800-685-1111

➤ Trans Union at 1-800-888-4213

Question: What should I do if I suspect there's a mistake on my credit card bill?

Answer: Promptly write a letter to the credit card company. Include your name, address, account number, the amount of the suspected error, a description of the error, and an explanation of why you believe the charge is an error. Keep a hard copy of the letter.

Question: What should I do if I suspect there's a mistake in my credit history?

Answer: Contact one of the three national credit reporting agencies given earlier and get a copy of your report. If you do find an error, be sure to contact all three credit reporting agencies to have it corrected.

Question: How can I improve my credit standing?

Answer: Make sure you pay everything you owe as soon as you can. Deal with credit problems promptly; ignoring them won't make them go away.

The Least You Need to Know

➤ Credit is deferred payment, not free money. You borrow, you have to pay back.

➤ Banks, stores, and gas stations offer charge cards; select the one(s) you need.

➤ Carefully consider whether you really need a credit card. If you decide to get one, clearly understand how credit works. Choose the card carefully and keep it safe.

➤ Use your card wisely. Don't get into debt.

Chapter 15

About That Student Loan ...

In This Chapter

➤ Cost of a college education

➤ Understanding the college financial aid package

➤ Educational grants

➤ Types of college loans

➤ Paying back your college loan

"If you take out tens of thousands of dollars in student loans, they will haunt you for the rest of your life. I wish someone had told me that. I still have $12,000 I owe more than 10 years after I graduated. It's really sick and it never goes away. It seems like it's easy to live on borrowed money, but you pay for it later. I would have gone to a much cheaper school if I had realized how loans work. I would have gotten the same or better education."

—Susan Wright, New York University

Financing your college education through student loans doesn't have to be a bitter experience, as it was for Susan. In some cases, you have no choice: no loan = no college. You might be tempted to opt for the less-expensive state school over the elite private school. Or you might decide to go the elite route after all and deal with the loans later. It's your choice, so it's important to have the facts. This chapter gives you the information you need so you can figure out how you're going to pay the tab for your education.

Dollars and Sense

Since nearly everyone pretends that a big old tuition bill isn't going to slap them in the face when Junior turns 18, few people have a plan for paying the educational piper.

Learn the Lingo

The **Ivy League** is the popular name for the eight most prestigious universities in the United States: Brown, Columbia, Cornell, Dartmouth, Harvard, Princeton, University of Pennsylvania, and Yale. The name comes from the schools' membership in an athletic conference for intercollegiate sports.

Below "C" Level

Some schools offer "need-blind" admissions—i.e., a student's financial need has no influence on acceptance. Other schools factor need into the acceptance process. If you're determined to attend a specific school and money is tight, check their financial aid policy well *before* you apply.

Even more astonishing, few families understand how much a college education really does cost. The first step in financial planning is to realistically estimate the total cost of attending college. Looking at the range of college costs will help you understand that a good college education is often surprisingly affordable.

Let's start with the financial worst-case scenario: an *Ivy League* education. The eight schools in the Ivy League—Brown, Columbia, Cornell, Dartmouth, Harvard, Princeton, University of Pennsylvania, and Yale—are the most competitive and prestigious universities in America. As a result, their fees are the highest.

For example, here are the fees and expenses for Princeton University for the 2000–2001 academic year:

> Comprehensive fee (tuition): $25,430
> Room charge: $3,425
> Board rate: $3,781
> Estimated miscellaneous expenses: $2,684
> Estimated total: $35,320

Because the cost of goods and services continues to rise, charges for 2001–2002 will be somewhat higher. The increase is expected to be in the 3 to 4 percent range.

Now that you've caught your breath and recovered from sticker shock, recognize that many excellent colleges and universities charge far less than the Ivies—and still deliver a superb education.

The average private university charges $22,000 per academic year; the average public (state) university, about $10,500. The State University of New York at Farmingdale, for example, charges the following fees to New York state residents:

Comprehensive fee (tuition): $3,200*
Room and board rate: $6,114
Fees: $675
Estimated miscellaneous expenses: $2,500
Estimated total: $12,489

Tuition for out-of-state residents is $8,300.

Moving to the middle of the country, Danville Area Community College in Illinois (a two-year college) charges $1,440 for tuition; Eastern Illinois University charges $4,872; Southern Illinois University charges $8,075; Western Illinois University charges $8,111; Illinois State University charges $8,213; and the University of Illinois charges $10,306. Indiana State comes in at $6,146 for the 2001–2002 year, Purdue University at $9,224, Indiana University at $9,736, and Butler University at $21,166.

As you can see from this small sampling, there's a college for nearly every budget. Carefully consider your pocketbook as well as your desires and needs when you pick a college.

Crib Notes

Note to parents of pre-college kids: Now is the time to help your children prepare for college. The earlier kids start working on their grades, activities, and study skills, the easier it will be for them to get into the school they want and get the financial aid they need.

Please, Sir, May I Have Some More Money?

Colleges offer three main types of financial aid:

➤ **Scholarships/grants:** money you're given outright
➤ **Loans:** money you must pay back after you graduate
➤ **Jobs:** money you must earn through your labor

How can you find out which type(s) of financial aid you're entitled to receive—if any? As you learned earlier in this chapter, check out each college's financial aid policy *before* you apply. If you haven't done this research, don't despair.

When you get that beautiful acceptance letter from the college, set up an appointment with the financial aid office to discuss aid packages. If you have your heart set on one college, you need to meet only with them. If you've been accepted to several colleges, meet with representatives from each one. Try the following tips as you investigate financial aid:

➤ **Lay the family's cards on the table.** Sit down with your parents and discuss how much *they* can afford to pay and how much *you* can afford to pay. Discuss ways to make up the difference. Make sure you all clearly understand how much college really costs, including tuition, room, board, books, entertainment, travel, club dues, clothing, phone bills, and incidental expenses. You can get this information from the schools. Sharing financial information from the get-go helps prevent misunderstandings and shattered college dreams down the line.

➤ **Understand how financial aid is awarded.** Financial aid is given on the basis of *merit* and *need*. Today, most colleges award the bulk of their scholarships on the basis of need, not merit. To earn a merit award, you had to do something extraordinary in high school, like teach sign language to penguins. Few students fall into that category. As a result, most students are given need-based packages. This means your family's income will be scrutinized.

Below "C" Level

It has been my experience that companies that promise to get you hefty financial aid packages are just doing the legwork you can do yourself—without the expense. A number of scholarship search programs are available on the Web at www.finaid.org.

Crib Notes

This is your life, so take charge. Yes, your parents will have to provide their financial information, but you should be running the show.

➤ **Find out how much aid the school offers.** The parents' contribution, the student's summer earnings, and a portion of the student's own savings are used to determine whether the applicant needs financial assistance. Not all schools can meet 100 percent of need.

➤ **Find out what impact outside scholarships have on your aid package.** Will you be allowed to keep the award or will it be deducted from your aid package?

➤ **Obtain the forms.** Find out what applications you must file to qualify for consideration. All financial aid applicants must file the Free Application for Federal Student Aid (FAFSA) to be considered for all types of college aid. The FAFSA is available in high school guidance offices or at the FAFSA Web site (www.fafsa.ed.gov). Your specific school might require additional applications. Make sure you get the forms you need and fill them out correctly.

➤ **Meet all deadlines.** The financial aid pie is finite. If you file late, you're not going to get your share.

➤ **Get it together.** Organize your financial aid forms and keep photocopies of any you send out. If you're applying for aid to more than one school, set up one folder for each school. Since you have to reapply for aid every year, having copies of the forms in one place will save you lots of time next year.

➤ **Consider bargaining.** Savvy students with sterling high school transcripts investigate the aid offered by all the colleges that accept them. Then, all other things being equal, they accept the highest bid. I confess I did just this by bargaining my way to a full tuition/fees scholarship for my B.A. I loved my college and received a great education. However, my satisfaction was clearly influenced by the fact that I graduated free and clear, while my friends carried stiff loans for years.

➤ **See what strings are attached.** Often, you must remain in good academic standing to keep your financial aid. Also, if family circumstances change, the aid package may be adjusted accordingly.

➤ **Be nice.** "Financial aid offices can be scary places. ALWAYS be friendly to them, and get to know one counselor well. They make many subjective decisions that can save you lots of money, and they'll be in your favor if they personally know you and like you," advises Terrence McGlynn (the University of San Diego).

➤ **Understand the payment plan.** Find out if you can pay tuition in installments or if you have to pony up the full amount every semester. Schools often provide an installment plan (but charge interest for the privilege).

➤ **Be creative and flexible.** If you can't get the money you need from the colleges that have accepted you, don't despair. There are many other sources of college money, if you're willing to do some research and think outside the box. For example, look for specialized scholarships such as awards from service groups like Rotary International and alumni. There are relatively few of these awards, but if you match the requirements, you can hit gold. Find information in the reference section of your high school or community library and on the Internet. In addition, the Reserve Officer Training Corps (ROTC) sponsors an extensive scholarship program on nearly all college campuses. You might decide to enlist in exchange for financial support.

Below "C" Level

Never be ashamed to seek financial aid. The money is there to help *all* students get an education.

Educational Grants

Colleges can also assign grants from a variety of sources: endowments, general revenues, yearly gifts from alumni and friends, and federal programs. As with scholarships, grants are gifts: They do not have to be repaid.

Nearly all grants are awarded on the basis of financial need. Some require recipients to meet geographic, academic, career, or other kinds of restrictions. For example, graduates of New Jersey public high schools who are eligible for need-based grant aid receive their awards from the Cane Fund. Cane recipients are not required to work (including both term-time and summer employment) and therefore receive a larger portion of grant aid in their award.

Colleges can also award Federal Supplemental Educational Opportunity Grants (FSEOGs). Preference in awarding FSEOGs is given to students with the lowest expected family contributions.

The Loan Arranger

Currently, there are two special government need-based loan programs for students: *Perkins loans* and *Stafford loans*. In addition, many colleges offer their own loan program to students who demonstrate financial need.

Federal Perkins Loans

Preference in awarding Perkins loans is given to students with high need. These loans have an interest rate of 5 percent once the repayment period starts. The Perkins limit is $12,000 for undergraduate studies, with a maximum of $4,000 per academic year.

Repayment of both principal and interest begins 9 months after the borrower leaves school and can extend for 10 years. Repayment may be deferred for certain circumstances, including periods of disability and service in the armed forces or public service organizations. Cancellation of part of the loan principal is possible for borrowers who teach in schools serving low-income or handicapped students or who work in law enforcement.

Crib Notes

Most students receive at least a portion of their financial aid from federal funds: Work-Study, FSEOGs, Pell grants, Perkins loans, and Stafford loans.

Federal Stafford Loans

Stafford loans have a $2,625 yearly limit for freshmen, $3,500 for sophomores, and $5,500 for juniors and seniors. Students may borrow as much as $23,000 during a 5-year period, with a $65,500 ceiling on total borrowing for undergraduate and graduate education.

The variable interest rate is paid by the federal government while the student is in college. The interest rate in repayment is currently 8.19 percent. Repayment of principal and interest begins 6 months after enrollment ceases and may extend for 10 years. The options for deferring repayment are similar to those for the Perkins loan.

Other Loans

Many colleges award interest-subsidized loans as part of a financial aid award because they believe that a student should be willing to invest in his or her future. A typical loan, for example, has a 7 percent interest rate, charged annually, and a $4,500 yearly limit. Students have 10 years to repay the loan after college. There are no application fees for these loans.

Some families also take out regular consumer bank loans, including home equity loans and commercial-insured tuition plans. After you and your family take a careful look at interest rates, administrative fees, tax advantages, and other terms, decide whether these kinds of loans are in your future.

Payback Time

> "When you get a loan, keep in mind that you have to pay it back."

—Kelly Betts, C.W. Post College, Greenvale, New York

It's crucial that you understand the responsibility you assume when you accept a loan. Most important is the obligation to pay a combination of principal and interest after graduation until the loan is repaid. You'll get further information about the rights and responsibilities related to awards when the loan is approved. Read the information carefully and make sure you understand exactly what you're signing.

Here are some suggestions to consider when you take out college loans:

➤ Borrow only what you need for your education.

➤ Take the loan agreement seriously. Defaulting on a college loan can have a negative effect on your credit history for years to come.

➤ Before you or your parents sign the loan agreement, check it over for errors. Even a small error can have a major impact on the loan.

➤ If you don't get the loan, you have a legal right to find out why. You can also get a copy of your credit report and see if it is accurate.

➤ Keep track of each loan. Know when you must start repaying each loan and how much you must pay.

Below "C" Level

Juniors and seniors can defray their room charges by serving as RAs (resident advisors). RAs work very hard and must have a patient nature, however, so carefully consider whether you're cut out for the job.

The Least You Need to Know

➤ Understand how much college costs.

➤ Understand how financial aid is awarded and how much aid the college offers. Apply on time.

➤ Be creative and flexible in seeking funding sources.

➤ Grants and scholarships don't have to be repaid; loans do.

➤ If you qualify, you can fund your education through loans offered by the federal government (Perkins loans, Stafford loans), the college, and private banks.

Chapter 16

Working Stiff

> ### In This Chapter
>
> ➤ Pros and cons of working while in college
>
> ➤ Questions to ask yourself
>
> ➤ Working during summer vacation and long breaks
>
> ➤ On-campus jobs and work study
>
> ➤ Creating your own part-time jobs

"Working while you're in school is a good way not to make you or your parents go broke. I worked 8 to 13 hours a week and had no trouble earning good grades as a computer science/math major."

—Chris Seifert, University of Illinois

Should you work while in college? There's no simple answer to this question, but I *can* give you the information to help you make a more informed decision.

Working Nine to Nine

"If you need the money, getting a job won't hurt your grades, and won't cramp your social life. You'll organize your time more efficiently if you have a job."

—Terrence McGlynn, the University of San Diego

Terrence McGlynn clearly favors combining work with school, but not everyone agrees. If money is tight, you may not have a choice: no work = no school. Or perhaps you can float tuition, room, and board, but not books and incidental expenses. If that's the case, your main task is figuring out how to balance classes, studying, and a job. We'll deal with that later in this chapter. Right now, let's explore the pros and cons of working while in school.

Below "C" Level

Remember that college "incidental expenses" aren't incidental at all—they run about $2,000 to $3,000 per year on average.

Crib Notes

Line up your summer job well before school ends so you don't get closed out in the rush of college kids returning to town.

The upside to working while in school:

➤ **More money.** You'll have the cash to buy what you need.

➤ **Better skills.** You'll learn some bankable skills, such as interpersonal communication and time management.

➤ **Preparation for the future.** Work builds your resumé. You might even make connections that lead to full-time employment after graduation.

➤ **Perspective.** You'll get a breather from campus life, intense relationships, and dorm politics. This helps you realize that there's life after college.

➤ **Self-awareness.** If you're working in your field of study, you might decide that your major isn't right for you after all.

➤ **Maturity.** You'll find the transition from school to work easier if you've got prior work experience.

The downside to working while in school:

➤ **School woes.** Your grades might suffer if you're working too many hours. Earning money for your books won't do you any good if you never have time to open them.

➤ **Graduation problems.** If you're working a lot, you might have to take fewer credits. As a result, you may not graduate with your class.

➤ **Treading water.** If you're in a menial job, you might not be learning any useful skills.

➤ **Wasting money.** Paradoxically, earning more money might make it more difficult for you to manage your funds. You might find yourself letting the money slip through your fingers rather than using it for things you need.

➤ **Reduced social life.** You might not be able to jet down to Ft. Lauderdale during spring break with your frat buddies because you have to work.

➤ **Less family time.** You might have to stay on campus during vacations to meet your job commitments. As a result, you may not be able to get home as often as you'd like.

Overworked and Underpaid

As you're trying to decide whether to work, ask yourself these questions:

1. Do I really need the money? Will you be working to pay for things you *need,* such as textbooks and computer supplies, or for things you *want,* such as CDs and concert tickets? If you're working for extras, you might be better off tightening your belt and forgoing the job. Instead, concentrate on your studies.

2. How much time can I spare to work? Keep in mind that being a full-time student is a full-time endeavor. A full load of 12 to 18 credits requires about 36 to 54 hours per week in class work and homework.

   The more outside work you have, the less time you'll have available for academic study.

3. Can I realistically balance school and work? Know your limits. Some people are really good at multitasking; others are not.

4. Will my health suffer if I work? To do well in course work requires getting plenty of rest and being alert and receptive during class. If you're working too much or find that you can't balance school and work, you might get sick more often than usual.

5. Will the pay be enough to make it worth my time? Before you take a job, make sure you're going to earn enough money. Say you've been offered a sales job in a store. If you have to pay for transportation and buy dressy clothes rather than wear your usual college sweats, you may clear only pennies. You might even end up losing money on the deal!

Below "C" Level

Working "off the books" is swell—unless you have an accident and aren't covered for worker's comp, or until the IRS catches you. Always work within the law.

Crib Notes

You can often find jobs through alumni as well as fraternity brothers and sorority sisters.

Hard Day's Night

If you *do* have the luxury of postponing work for a while, I strongly recommend that you wait until sophomore year or the second semester of freshman year before taking a job. Here are some other options:

Crib Notes

"Make friends with the people in charge of registration. They will often bend rules to help you out if you run into problems, especially if you have money troubles. Of course, working in the registrar's office or in financial aid is the best of all."

—Dan Vayda, Washington College

➤ **Work during the summer.** It's tempting to take the summer off after a hard year at school, but forgo beach blanket bingo and sleeping late in those hazy, lazy days of summer. Instead, work your little fingers to the bone so you have some breathing space during the school year.

➤ **Work during school breaks.** Most college kids get a long winter break, up to 6 weeks. Use that time to put in 40+ hours a week. My son works as a cashier in a supermarket every intercession to fill his wallet for the spring term.

➤ **Cut back.** Austerity is painful, but it might be preferable to working, at least at first. Pass on the evening out; say no to the off-campus concert. Consider postponing going Greek until you have the money for the initiation fees. It's better than adding more debt by borrowing.

Getting the Home Court Advantage

"Working on campus is better than working off campus because they work around your schedule on campus. At my college, the max number of hours is 10 to 20 hours a week. Don't work more than 10 a week, at least freshman year. I work four hours one day, but I'm an RA and a double-major."

—Kelly Betts, C.W. Post College, Greenvale, New York

If you decide that working while you attend college is right for you, working on campus has a number of irresistible advantages. For example …

➤ You don't need transportation to get to the job.

➤ As you work, you hobnob with support staff, administrators, and professors who can help you.

➤ Since you're right on campus, you meet potential dates and love interests.

➤ Working on campus helps you get integrated into the school community. This is especially important if you're dealing with homesickness or having trouble making friends.

Work-Study Programs

"As far as financial aid, my parents took out student loans through the local credit union. I worked on campus through the work-study program. I worked as a secretary for a professor for a few years and then moved on to bigger and better places ... the library! What a great place to meet people."

—Marie Lilly, Clarion College, Pennsylvania

Colleges often build on-campus jobs right into financial aid packages. Most of these jobs require an average of 9 hours a week for 30 weeks. A standard 9-hour-a-week job provides a freshman with approximately $2,200 a year.

If you haven't already been offered an on-campus job as part of your aid package, get over to the Dean's office and ask for information on your college's *work-study program*. Here's what another member of my panel of experts said about work study:

"What got me through college financially was work study. Granted, it meant I had to spend my first two years scrubbing pots, but it also meant a smaller loan for me to repay, plus enough spending money that I never had to write to my mom for cash. It also injected a bit of realism into the rarefied and sheltered world of the college undergrad—a foretaste of what having to work for a living will be like.

—Shanti

Usually, work-study jobs are nothing demanding or especially thrilling. For example, I worked at the Student Service desk making IDs and answering the phones. A close friend was a go-fer for the Dean of Health Sciences, while another buddy cleaned tables in the cafeteria. Routine work is good at first, because the last thing you need your freshman year is a job as a rocket scientist or brain surgeon.

Here are some typical work-study jobs:

➤ Working in the dining halls

➤ Being a research assistant

➤ Joining the residence life staff (Resident Advisors, etc.)

➤ Working in the bookstore

➤ Being a lab assistant

➤ Working in the library

➤ Being a tech assistant in the computing center

➤ Tutoring in the Writing Center

➤ Grading papers for professors

➤ Working in academic offices

Learn the Lingo

Work-study programs offer students on-campus jobs, often as part of their financial aid package.

Some colleges also provide off-campus jobs as part of their work-study program. Colleges often help students work in community service areas such as social services, transportation, public safety, crime prevention, recreation, youth service, and other activities specified in the Community Service Act under the Federal Work-Study Program. More information about these job opportunities is available from your college's Student Employment Office.

Getting a Leg Up on the Competition

After your freshman and sophomore years, consider tying work to academic study through an internship or a co-op. This is usually far more possible than you might think. Here's how former science major/current science professor Terrence McGlynn put it:

Below "C" Level

On some campuses, working menial on-campus jobs is looked down on. There's nothing demeaning about honest work. The people who degrade jobs are snobs not worthy of your consideration.

"Most science majors don't realize how much they can get out of doing research until it's too late. If you're thinking of grad school or med school, talking to professors about research as a frosh or sophomore is important. You probably won't be approached, but doing research (for credit or money) is easy at most colleges if you find the right professors."

In this instance, you're working for the experience more than the money. Never discount the importance of working for excellent experience. Making the right connections while you're in college can help you find and fine-tune your major, get into a good grad school, and even get a job.

Be assertive and go after what you want. No one reads minds, so be sure to ask the professors you'd like to work with if they need any help. Before you call up and ask, however, find out from your advisor, the campus newspaper, or published journal articles what research is being conducted in the various labs around campus. Not only will you stand a better chance of getting the job because you're clearly more prepared, but you'll also line up the positions that suit your interests and abilities.

Crib Notes

If your campus doesn't have any active laboratories or current openings for assistants, check out hospitals and universities in the area.

Talk to other students to see which professors are looking for assistants. Chris Seifert, a student at the University of Illinois, offered this advice:

"Do your best in class. Professors are always looking for graders. They approach the

top-scoring students in each class. The money is often significantly above minimum wage and the work is easy. If the professors like your work, they will often
write you glowing letters of recommendation for graduate school."

In Chapter 22, "I Get Around," I'll show you how to kick the job search up a notch
and apply for internships in your field of interest.

Do-It-Yourself Jobs

You don't have a work-study job and you want to work on campus—or as close to
campus as you can get. What to do?

You're a college kid, which means you're as sharp as the point on your brand-new
pencil. Use your noggin to create the job that suits your interests, abilities, and time
limitations. Here are some ideas to get you started:

➤ **Do manual labor.** Clean garages, shovel snow. Mow lawns, rake leaves. Clean
houses and run errands. Speaking as a homeowner, I can guarantee that the
chores just keep on coming.

Put an ad in the local newspaper, tack ads up on telephone poles, and post fly-
ers in the local supermarket. If you're hard-working, honest, and pleasant, you'll
soon have more work than you can handle.

➤ **Bartend or wait tables.** I know college kids who clean up working one or two
black-tie events a month.

➤ **Tutor.** Many colleges have tutoring services
and will match you with clients, or you can
arrange tutoring gigs on your own.

➤ **Baby-sit.** Don't sneer: I made piles of money
this way. Best of all, once I had the rugrats
safely tucked into bed, I had plenty of time to
get my schoolwork done. Yes, I had to give
up some Saturday night social time, but my
sweetie and I just made dates during the week.

➤ **Keyboard papers.** You'd be surprised how
many people can't type or are too lazy to type
their own papers. There's lots of money to be
made here.

Crib Notes

Foreign students often look for
English-language tutors. Contact
the ESL (English as a Second
Language) office or foreign-
language department for potential jobs. If you speak a foreign
language well, you'll be in
greater demand.

Still stumped? Tap into your area of expertise. My
students and their friends have created lucrative
part-time jobs from their talents and hobbies. These
jobs include ...

➤ Videotaping weddings, bar mitzvahs, and birthday parties.

➤ Installing computer software.

➤ Teaching people how to use their computers.

➤ Creating Web pages.

➤ Writing movie reviews for the local newspaper.

➤ Covering college and high school sports for the community newspaper.

➤ Walking dogs and grooming pets.

➤ House-sitting for people on vacations and professors on sabbaticals.

➤ Starting your own business, such as selling handmade earrings, chocolate chip cookies, and so on.

Extra Credit

Some colleges have an agency system in which students operate their own businesses. Some of these businesses include appliance rentals (mini-refrigerators, microwaves, water coolers, etc.), furniture rentals (futons, etc.), food delivery, and computer installation, repair, and general assistance. Why not start your own on-campus business?

Working while you're in school can offer you more than a paycheck. Jobs help you meet people, teach you valuable new skills, and help you manage your time more effectively. College jobs also help you explore different career paths so you can determine whether you're majoring in the right field. Working also builds pride and self-esteem as it helps you prepare for graduation. Best of all, down the road, you can tell your kids how you walked 10 miles (uphill) in a blizzard to work while you attended college.

The Least You Need to Know

➤ Carefully consider the advantages and disadvantages of working while you're in college.

➤ Decide whether you need the money and can spare the time. See if you'll make enough money for the job to be worth your time.

➤ Consider working summers and during long school breaks, instead of during the school term.

➤ Working on campus has many advantages; campus work-study programs are tailored to a student's needs.

➤ Create your own job, such as manual labor, bartending, waiting tables, tutoring, and baby-sitting.

Part 4

Reality Bites

"In the chaotic whirlwind that is college, don't forget to enjoy what you're doing and who you meet while you're there. Those years go by all too fast."

—Catherine Thomas, University of Maryland (College Park) and Pennsylvania State University

Here you'll learn about coping with all the stuff that keeps parents up nights gnawing their fingernails: dating, sex, drinking, and drugs. College can be the best of times or the worst of times—depending on how well you balance these issues. I'll help you learn to balance the urge to party hearty with your responsibilities and health.

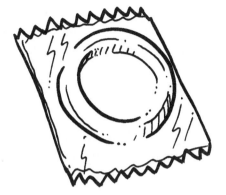

Chapter 17

Sex 101

In This Chapter

➤ Long-distance romances

➤ The virginity issue

➤ Birth control

➤ Sexually transmitted diseases

➤ Sexual etiquette

➤ Rape and campus security

Don't know much about history
Don't know much biology
Don't know much about a science book
Don't know much about the French I took
But I do know that I love you
And I know that if you love me too
What a wonderful world this would be.

"(What a) Wonderful World" by Sam Cooke (1959, ABKCO Music, Inc.)

You know all the clichés: Love makes the world go 'round, love makes the world look brighter, yadda yadda yadda. As someone who met the world's most wonderful man in college, I'd be the last person to advise you to steer clear of love on campus. However, love and sex are two very different things. In this chapter, we'll explore your sexual choices and their ramifications.

Life in the Fast Lane

> "Don't hold on to boyfriends or girlfriends you were dating in high school, especially if they are not in college yet. One grows a great deal in a short time in college and instead of growing with the other person, you grow apart. Don't hold yourself back from growing into the best adult you can be. Friendships are great to hold onto, not intimate relationships."
>
> —Michelle Stern, Mt. Holyoke

Long-distance relationships rarely last. As Terrence McGlynn of the University of San Diego advises, "Dump your boyfriend or girlfriend before you go away to college. At least from everyone I have met, less than .01 percent of high school couples last in college. I know of hundreds upon hundreds of high school couples that broke up on Christmas break of freshman year. This way, you won't feel guilty when you're inevitably creating a closer bond with someone new." Mary Buell Nemerov from the University of California at Berkeley is even more adamant: "Always, always break up with your high school boyfriend/girlfriend before moving to college," she advises.

What's Love Got to Do with It?

Sex. Just say the word and people start paying attention. Sex sells everything from soap to snack food, cars to cappuccino. Let's not forget the obvious links between sex and alcohol, cigarettes, and perfume—virtually every consumer good is sold through sex appeal.

Therefore, if you're an average college freshman, you're apt to think that everyone is doing it, has done it, and knows just how to do it. Everyone but you, that is. Nothing could be further from the truth, as Stephanie Muntone of Oberlin College confirms:

> "Many of your fellow freshmen will be every bit as nervous and inexperienced as you are about sex. Don't feel like you are the only virgin in the incoming class. Boys are just as likely to be inexperienced as girls are."

What I Did for Love

The decision whether to have sex is one of the most personal choices you'll ever make. As when making any key life decision, you must consider it carefully. As you decide whether to become sexually active, consider these points:

➤ Never assume you're the only virgin you know. The biggest talkers are often the least inexperienced between the sheets.

➤ Don't do anything until you're ready. Really ready.

➤ Only *you* can decide when you're ready. Not your roommate, your boyfriend/girlfriend, or your frat or sorority friends.

➤ You don't have to prove anything to anyone, not your roommate, your sweetheart, or yourself.

➤ You can't make someone love you by using sex. Neither can you keep their love by putting out.

➤ If your significant other tells you it's time to "prove your love" or "put up or shut up," show them the door. Then lock it.

➤ *No* means no. It doesn't mean *maybe, perhaps,* or *why not try a little harder to seduce me.* If you refuse to take *no* for an answer, you can be charged with rape—as you should be.

➤ If you do decide to do the wild thing, make sure you use birth control.

Below "C" Level

Ladies, you can get pregnant the first time and any time you have sex. Douching with Coca-Cola, Drano, and other chemicals won't abort a fetus, but they can seriously harm your reproductive organs and perhaps even kill you. Guys, you can't get pregnant, but you can become a father—and pay child support for many years.

Better Safe Than Sorry

If you're having sex, the rule is simple: Use condoms, the first time and every time. They're cheap, portable, and easy to use. In addition to preventing pregnancy, condoms protect you against sexually transmitted diseases. Used alone, condoms have a success rate of 90 to 98 percent; used with spermicide, their success rate is close to 100 percent. Latex condoms are the most reliable kind.

Maybe you're thinking, "But if I whip out a condom, won't he or she think I was planning this seduction? Doesn't that take all the mystery and wonder and glory out of sex?" Perhaps planning does destroy the marvel of the moment, but nothing takes the fun out of sex faster than death. And you're risking death if you have intercourse without using a condom.

Crib Notes

If you're short of cash or a cheapskate, check out your college infirmary. Virtually all college infirmaries give out free condoms.

Sexually Transmitted Diseases

In addition to making the earth move, sex can cause a surprisingly wide variety of illnesses called *sexually transmitted diseases,* or *STDs* for short. Untreated, some STDs can lead to genital cancer or worse; even when properly treated, STDs can seriously incapacitate you for a long time. Unlike a scorned lover, STDs don't go away if you ignore them.

According to the Alan Guttmacher Institute, an estimated 12 million people contract STDs every year. Two thirds of them are college-aged men and women. Extrapolating these numbers, the institute estimates that 1 in 4 people under the age of 25 will contract an STD at some point in their life.

You should know about these STDs:

➤ **AIDS (Acquired Immune Deficiency Syndrome).** Caused by the HIV virus, AIDS is a virus that knocks out the body's ability to fight infections. While some treatments can prolong life, AIDS is fatal.

Learn the Lingo

Sexually transmitted diseases (STDs) are illnesses that are passed through intercourse or other sexual acts. STDs include AIDS, chlamydia, gonorrhea, and herpes.

Extra Credit

Researchers at the Minnesota Hospitals and Clinics discovered that most college-aged students know about STDs, especially AIDS, but still refuse to use condoms. More than 60 percent of the 240 male college students surveyed participated in potentially life-threatening sexual behavior that placed them at "extreme risk" for exposure to HIV, the virus that causes AIDS.

➤ **Chlamydia.** Chlamydia causes urethral infections and painful vaginal and rectal discharges. If untreated, chlamydia can damage a woman's reproductive organs and lead to sterility.

➤ **Gonorrhea.** Gonorrhea causes burning urination and discharges from the sex organs. Untreated, it can cause pelvic inflammatory disease in women, infertility, cervical infection, and blood infection.

➤ **Hepatitis B.** This STD causes major liver problems and can be fatal. Fortunately, there is a vaccine. If you're sexually active or expect to be, get the shot.

➤ **Herpes.** Herpes causes weepy sores on the genitals, fever, and headaches. It can also cause eye infections, cervical cancer, and problems in pregnancy. The herpes sores go away (even though they can reappear periodically), but you carry the virus for life.

➤ **Human papilloma virus (HPV).** This virus, which usually emerges as genital warts, can lead to cervical cancer in women.

➤ **Pelvic inflammatory disease.** It causes fever and pain in a woman's abdominal region and pelvic organs. Untreated, it can cause sterility.

➤ **Syphilis.** Syphilis causes rashes and sores at body openings. Untreated, it can cause blindness, chest pain, difficulty breathing, and insanity.

➤ **Trichomoniasis.** In men, this STD results in painful infections in the urethra and prostate gland.

It Only Takes One Slip

Using condoms can greatly reduce your chances of contacting an STD or getting pregnant, but there's only one completely reliable way of preventing pregnancy or STDs: abstinence. If you do decide to become sexually active, you should know these facts:

➤ Condoms can break or leak. They can be put on wrong and slip off.

➤ Even if your partner swears that he or she has been tested and is not infected with AIDS, people lie.

➤ Even if your partner is telling the truth, he or she may still be infected and not yet know it. It can take time for the HIV virus to show up through testing, which is why sexually active people should have AIDS tests every six months.

Since you can't be sure, be safe. Here's how:

➤ Don't take IV (intravenous) drugs.

➤ I've said it before but I'll say it again: Always wear a condom or make sure your partner does.

➤ Don't reuse condoms. Use a new condom for each sex act.

➤ Be sure that you and your partner are using the condom correctly.

Below "C" Level

If a sexual partner tests positive for HIV or you have had unprotected sex, get an HIV test immediately. If you test positive, see a doctor immediately and don't pass on the virus. For more information, call 1–800–342–AIDS.

I Get Around

Earlier in this book I encouraged you to get involved, but I was talking about joining clubs and sports, not racking up notches on your belt. Promiscuity is bad for a lot of reasons, not the least of which is an increased chance of contracting an STD. When you have sexual intercourse with someone, you're having sex with everyone he or she has ever slept with before. Their bad decisions can become your nightmares.

Sexual Manners

Speaking as a grouch now, there's been a general breakdown of good manners in the world. I don't much care when someone knocks me down to get to a taxi in a hurricane or neglects to send a

Crib Notes

Remember that all colleges provide health care, so don't be afraid to seek help and advice on sexual matters.

thank-you note for my generous birthday gift, but no one can endure rude lovers. Follow these guidelines when dealing with your lovers (and friends) in college as well as in life.

1. **Don't kiss and tell.** Don't brag about your or your sweetheart's sexual skills. We don't want to hear the intimate details of your bedroom acrobatics. Whatever you're doing, keep it between the two of you.

Below "C" Level

The "morning after" pill has recently been approved for use. If you find yourself pregnant and consider this option for terminating the pregnancy, you must be under a doctor's care. Morning after doesn't equal "do-it-yourself."

Crib Notes

What can you do if your buddies won't stop pawing each other? Reassure the hot-to-trot couple that you understand how their lovers might find them hard to resist, but you would feel more comfortable if they would kick it down a notch in front of you.

2. **Be considerate.** I'm always amazed when I hear tales of Roommate A having fun with his girlfriend in Roommate B's bed. Why? He didn't want to get his Own bed messy. Piggy, piggy, piggy. Use your own bed or get a motel.

3. **And while we're on considerate …** Yes, it's your room, but it's also your roommate's room. Work out mutually agreeable private time or take cold showers until you can get a single. It's rude and inconsiderate to keep kicking your roommate out so you can get a little action.

4. **Don't move your significant other into the room.** Yes, people really do this. You're sharing your room with your roommate, not your honey. As Michelle Stern of Mt. Holyoke College says, "Remember that you and your roommate are living together, and therefore you'll both have to make some sacrifices to accommodate the other. You don't eat peanuts after midnight; he or she doesn't bring their significant other over to move in."

5. **And don't play room games.** Be very sure of what you're doing before you move in with your sweetie, because if you break up, one of you will have to find another place to live.

6. **No public displays of affection.** If you're prone to public displays of affection, consider what you're trying to prove with your blatant sexual behavior. Perhaps you're trying to show everyone that you're desirable, attractive, and loved. Whatever scars your inner child suffered at the junior high holiday dance, we realize that you're hot now, so chill out in public.

7. **Remember that you're in college to learn.** (I know, I sure can spoil a party.) You decided to go to college to learn skills you need to be a self-supporting adult. Never let your love life interfere with your studies.

8. **Don't be a sore loser.** Breaking up is hard to do, but don't make it worse by being a jerk. Break off relationships cleanly and quickly. None of this dragging-it-out-for-months nonsense and lame excuses.

A little respect goes a long way to establishing good relations with your roommates, classmates, and fellow students, especially when it comes to sex.

Crib Notes

Recognize that attitudes toward sex are culturally based. The Japanese people, for example, do not approve of public body contact. Kissing in public is considered extremely offensive.

When Sex Turns Ugly: Rape

"Women have very good reasons to be terrified of men in college. The number of reported date and acquaintance rapes are far lower than the actual numbers. I'm a man myself, and I recognize that stepping into a fraternity house is inherently dangerous."

—Terrence McGlynn, the University of San Diego

Did you know …

➤ Every 41 seconds an adult woman is raped in America.

➤ Fifty percent of all victims are 12 to 24 years of age.

➤ One in six college women is raped.

➤ Rape is the fastest-growing crime of violence in the United States. If the current increase in rape cases continues, the FBI estimates that one of every four women will be the victim of a sexual assault in her life.

➤ From 80 percent to 95 percent of the rapes that occur on college campuses are committed by someone known to the victim.

➤ One in 10 men is raped in his lifetime.

➤ Rape is not motivated by lust or sexual desire. Rape is an expression of power or anger.

Source: The FBI Uniform Crime Report, 1997; National Crime Victimization's Survey, 1996

What Is Rape?

The definition of rape varies from state to state. In all states, if a man forcibly subjects a woman who is not his wife to sexual intercourse against her will, he has committed the crime of rape. Recently, an increasing number of states have extended the definition of rape to include certain nonconsensual incidents of intercourse—even if force was not involved. In other states, rape remains narrowly defined as forcible sexual intercourse, but separate statutes address other forms of sexual assault, including nonconsensual (but unforced) sexual intercourse and unwanted sexual activity.

Fear and Loathing

Rape and sexual assault are devastating. Victims often experience paralyzing fear, depression, and self-loathing. Their ability to be physically and emotionally intimate with others may be permanently shattered. For male victims, the problems are compounded by taboo, disbelief, and homophobia.

In addition, rape victims can become infected with sexually transmitted diseases, including AIDS. Female rape victims can become pregnant. Moreover, rape victims aren't the only ones harmed. The shock waves emanating from such violent experiences rattle the lives of parents, roommates, friends, professors, and college staff.

Learn the Lingo

Rape is any sexual act by one person upon another without consent, or by using alcohol, drugs, force, fear, threat of injury, or kidnapping.

Below "C" Level

The more the victim or perpetrator drinks, the greater the rate of serious injuries associated with dating violence.

Start with Safety

"Campus security is your friend. Take the opportunity to learn about them and what they do during your first few weeks on campus. They are people whose job it is to protect you. The easier you make it on them, the less hassle it will be for them to do so, and the less annoying it will seem the next time you need to flash your school I.D. to get into a particular building."

—David Pucik, Columbia University

Your college has a vested interest in keeping you safe, but that doesn't mean they can police you all the time. Follow the suggestions below to help keep yourself safe from sexual predators (as well as ordinary creeps):

➤ **Don't deny the problem.** You learned earlier in this chapter that rape can happen to anyone. Even you.

➤ **Use campus security.** Dave is right: Campus security is there to help you. In addition, many colleges offer security guards or student volunteers to walk women home at night. If these services are available at your campus, use them. If they're not, start them.

➤ **Travel in pairs.** Don't go strolling through dark or poorly lit areas alone at night. Always have at least one friend with you.

➤ **Never hitchhike.** Ever.

➤ **Trust your instincts.** If a party doesn't seem safe, leave. If an area scares you, get to a safer place. If your date is getting drunk and out of hand, get out.

➤ **Watch the booze.** Don't drink to excess, and don't let your date get drunk. Alcohol increases the chances of rape, especially "date rape." Stay sober.

➤ **Lock your doors.** In your dorm and in your car, keep your doors locked.

➤ **Don't fumble for your car keys.** If you're getting into your car, even in daylight, have your keys in your hand well before you approach your vehicle.

➤ **Make sure people know where you are.** Let a roommate, a friend, or your RA know where you're going and when you're coming back.

The Least You Need to Know

➤ Long-distance relationships rarely last.

➤ Carefully consider whether you're ready to become sexually active. If you decide to do the wild thing, make sure you use birth control to prevent pregnancy and sexually transmitted diseases.

➤ Be considerate with friends and lovers: Keep your sex life private and stay focused on your studies.

➤ One in six college women is raped. Protect yourself by using common sense and campus security.

Chapter 18

Dealing with Diversity

In This Chapter

➤ America's changing face

➤ Terms used to discuss diversity

➤ Sexual harassment and discrimination

➤ Dealing with homophobia

➤ Expressing yourself freely

Each to his own taste, said the cannibal to the missionary. The problem? Not everyone has gotten the message. As a result, they may have some difficulty dealing with difference.

Tolerance poses challenges under any circumstances, but it can be even more difficult when you—or your roommate, friend, RA, or professor—is different in race, religious beliefs, culture, or sexual orientation. Jumping into any new environment is hard, especially when the environment is radically different from what you've come to expect. Add major differences in orientation and beliefs, and you have a potentially explosive mix. Sometimes this simmering brew boils over into bigotry and outright discrimination.

In this chapter, we'll explore America's increasing diversity and ways to increase tolerance on campus and in the "real world."

Welcome to the Global Village

If we could shrink the Earth's population to a village of precisely 100 people with all existing human ratios remaining the same, it would look like this:

➤ There would be 57 Asians, 21 Europeans, 14 from the Western Hemisphere (North and South), and 8 Africans.

➤ 51 would be female; 49 would be male.

➤ 70 would be nonwhite; 30 white.

➤ 70 would be non-Christian; 30 Christian.

➤ 50 percent of the entire world's wealth would be in the hands of only 6 people, all citizens of the United States.

➤ 80 would live in substandard housing.

➤ 70 would be unable to read.

➤ 50 would suffer from malnutrition.

➤ 1 would be near death; 1 would be near birth.

➤ No one would own a computer.

➤ Only one would have a college education.

When you consider our world from such a compressed perspective, the need for tolerance and understanding becomes glaringly apparent. Easier said than done, unfortunately. Let's focus our sights on your little corner of the world—America—to explore its diversity.

Extra Credit

More than 25 percent of America's immigrants—6.7 million—were born in Mexico. Other common immigrant homelands include the Philippines (1.2 million Americans hail from there), China/Taiwan (816,000), Cuba (797,000), Canada (695,000), El Salvador (650,000), Great Britain (617,000), Germany (598,000), Poland (538,000), Jamaica (531,000), and the Dominican Republic (509,000). (Source: *World Almanac*.)

Born in the USA

Who is the "typical" American today? According to the most recent census (2000), an estimated 270.3 million people live in the United States. Nearly a third of all Americans chose to identify themselves as minorities. Here's how we describe ourselves:

➤ 223.2 million (82.5 percent) of us are white.

➤ 34.4 million (12.7 percent) of us are black.

➤ 2.3 million (0.9 percent) of us are Native American.

➤ 10.5 million (3.9 percent) of us are Asian and Pacific Islanders.

➤ 30.2 million (11.2 percent) of us are Hispanic.

Since the last census (1980), the sharpest increase in population has occurred in the Asian population: 30.77 percent. The Hispanic population increased 26.1 percent in the same time; the black population, 12.91 percent. White Americans saw their numbers swell by 10.46 percent. (Source: *The New York Times 2000 Almanac*.)

America's Glorious Mosaic

Just how diverse are we? Here are some statistics that underscore the diversity of America today.

➤ More than 100 languages are spoken in the school systems of New York City, Chicago, Los Angeles, and Fairfax County (Virginia).

➤ More than 30 million people speak English as a second language, which means that the 140 different languages spoken in America are spoken by roughly 14 percent of the population.

➤ More than 40 percent of the people living in California are black, Hispanic, or Asian.

➤ There are over 2,000 Hmong from Laos living in Wisconsin alone.

A Peek into America's Bedroom

Pollsters scrutinize every angle of American life, including what goes on behind bedroom doors. According to a study conducted by the National Opinion Research Center in 1998, 3.3 percent of American men and 2.3 percent of American women identify themselves as homosexual. Among college-aged people (18 to 25), the numbers are a bit higher for men, 3.5 percent.

Nearly all experts believe the real number is significantly higher, around 10 percent of the population. Interestingly, men who attend church regularly were 3 percent more likely to have a same-sex partner than those who attend church occasionally or rarely.

Crib Notes

If you're interested in the issues discussed in this chapter, you might want to take some classes in sociology. The subject is rarely offered in high school, so you're not likely to have any prior in-depth exposure to these topics.

Lingua Franca

Before we can explore the issue of diversity in depth, it's important that we all speak the same language. Here are the terms most commonly used to discuss the issue of diversity:

➤ **Class.** An individual's economic ranking based on wealth and the sources of wealth.

➤ **Culture.** A community's behavior patterns, beliefs, and values that are socially transmitted to individuals and to which individuals are expected to conform.

➤ **Gender.** The psychological makeup of an individual based on cultural perceptions of femaleness and maleness (such as femininity, masculinity, androgyny).

➤ **Homophobia.** An intense, irrational fear of same-sex relationships.

➤ **Power.** The ability to influence and enforce decisions in a community; control of valued resources.

➤ **Prejudice.** An unfavorable preconceived idea, judgment, or belief directed toward a racial, religious, cultural, or ethnic group.

➤ **Race/ethnicity.** People grouped according to a common racial, national, religious, or cultural origin.

➤ **Racism.** An assumption that there is inherent purity and superiority of certain races and inferiority of others.

➤ **Sexism.** An assumption that there is inherent purity and superiority of one sex.

➤ **Sexual harassment.** Discriminating against a person based on his or her gender or sexual orientation.

➤ **Status.** The respect a person commands in a community.

Sexual Harassment and Discrimination

"Some schools are more queer-friendly than others. My school is very queer-friendly, but I still find homophobes on campus. Be ready to face all kinds of queer people at college. If you identify yourself as a member of the queer community, try networking. One is able to find role models within the queer community when they are immersed in it, unlike outside the college world, which is heavily heterosexist. But if you are straight, be ready to be open-minded and accepting. People are very open about relationships and themselves at college and if you are not ready for that, consider the community you plan on entering."

—Michelle Stern, Mt. Holyoke College

Like many other minority groups who are perceived to be "different," lesbian women and gay men experience misunderstanding and prejudice. Name-calling, harassment, physical violence, and discrimination are a few of the ways in which lesbians and gays are mistreated. In a study of self-identified gay youth in New York City, 41 percent reported suffering violence from their families, peers, or strangers. Of the violent incidents, 46 percent were directly gay-related.

Some of My Best Friends Are Gay

Homophobia reveals itself in many ways, such as …

➤ Thinking you can identify a gay person based on appearance or behavior.

➤ Expecting gay or lesbian people to change their public identity to fit in with the mainstream.

➤ Worrying about the effect a gay or lesbian volunteer will have on your programs.

➤ Thinking that if gays or lesbians touch you, they are making sexual advances.

➤ Feeling repulsed by public displays of affection between gays, but accepting the same affectionate displays between heterosexuals as "normal."

➤ Feeling that gay people are too outspoken about gay rights.

➤ Not confronting a heterosexist remark for fear of being identified as gay or lesbian.

Below "C" Level

Gay youth are two to three times more likely to attempt suicide than heterosexual young people. It is estimated that up to 30 percent of youth suicides are committed by gay youth annually. In a study of 137 gay and bisexual males, 29 percent had attempted suicide. Almost half the respondents reported multiple attempts.

Extra Credit

Some scientists believe that sexual orientation is determined prenatally. Another theory is that it is determined after birth by environmental factors. In any case, it's generally accepted today that sexual orientation is established early on. Many gays sensed something different about themselves as early as age four or five. The age at which most acknowledge their homosexuality is between 14 and 16 years for males and between 16 and 19 years for females.

Learn the Lingo

Sexual harassment is any action or comment that creates a hostile environment. Sexual harassment in the workplace is forbidden by the Civil Rights Act.

Test Yourself

"Oberlin had a very large gay community. For students who were closeted through high school, college can be very liberating because so many students are out."

—Stephanie Muntone, Oberlin College

Some people are fortunate to land in the right college for them, either intentionally or accidentally. However, sexual harassment and discrimination can be present in even the most accepting colleges, much less those that are less tolerant of diversity. Take the following quiz to see how much you know about sexual harassment and discrimination.

Put a check next to the incidents you consider sexual harassment or discrimination.

_____ 1. Your professor calls on the male members of the class, ignoring the female members (or vice versa).

_____ 2. The textbook implies that men aren't as good at parenting as women.

_____ 3. Your male professor calls you "honey," "sweetheart," "babe," and "bimbo."

_____ 4. All the reading material in the class was written by women—and you're not taking "Women in Literature."

_____ 5. Your professor pressures you to socialize with him or her and you don't want to get involved.

_____ 6. Your professor constantly compliments your appearance, which makes you uncomfortable. Even when you mention your discomfort, the professor continues.

_____ 7. The other students catcall when a pretty woman walks into the room, and the professor doesn't comment on their behavior.

_____ 8. You feel that you're not getting a fair shot at the financial aid pot because of your gender.

_____ 9. All the guys have a drink in the bar after class, and you're excluded because you're a woman (or vice versa).

_____10. Meeting with your professor alone during office hours makes you uncomfortable. You sense an unwelcome attention.

Answers: Every one of these incidents is an example of sexual harassment or discrimination.

As this quiz shows, sexual discrimination can be subtle or blatant. I've experienced both extremes. Here are two examples from my own life:

> *Subtle:* A male professor liked to shake my hand just a bit too long and stand just a bit too close. He never said anything even remotely out of bounds, but I got the message alright.

> *Blatant:* While I was completing my Ph.D., one of my professors actually groped my thigh and asked me to spend the weekend with him. He did it in a joking matter, but it was no joke because a month later, he had to sit on my dissertation committee and vote on my degree. Several years later, he made similar advances to my sister.

Just as harassing people for their skin color or religion is unacceptable, so is harassing people because of their gender or sexual identification. Give respect, and demand respect from others.

Over the Line

Even though they know better, college officials and professors may use their power to intimidate you and get what they want. There are measures you can take to reduce the chances of being discriminated against because of your gender. Here they are:

Crib Notes

The lines between professors and students are usually much more fluid in college than they are in high school. Some professors are distant and intimidating, but many (especially TAs) are likely to be close to you in age. And cute.

Crib Notes

It's not uncommon for college professors to marry their students. It *is* rare in high schools, however.

➤ **Dating and sex.** Don't date or dally with any professor you are studying with now or might study with in the future. I'd avoid doing the hokey-pokey with administrators, too. Once you graduate, you can date anyone you want to.

➤ **Stereotyping.** Sexual harassment occurs equally among male and female professors and students. It's not confined to males coming on to females.

➤ **Office hours.** Don't meet with any professor alone in a closed office. Savvy professors always keep their doors open when they meet with students. Savvy students make sure the door stays open.

➤ **Look, don't touch.** Your professor should not be touching you. You should not be touching him or her. Even the most innocent touching can be misinterpreted.

➤ **Listen to your instincts.** If your professor's behavior makes you uncomfortable, protect yourself. Don't meet with the professor alone; keep your distance. Also, watch how he or she treats other students. See if there is a pattern of inappropriate behavior.

➤ **Keep records.** If you experience what you perceive as sexual harassment, carefully note every instance. You will need these records later if you decide to take official action.

➤ **People in glass houses shouldn't throw stones.** Make sure you're not guilty of the very behavior patterns that you abhor. Don't judge people on the basis of their gender or sexual orientation (nor on their race, religion, or cultural beliefs).

Below "C" Level

Before you get your nose out of joint over potential harassment, be sure your claim has substance. Was there genuine misuse of power, or are you annoyed because the professor gave you a C and you feel you deserved an A? Before you say, "He gave me a C because I wouldn't play footsie with him," be sure that's really what happened. Ruining a person's reputation without cause *is* unforgivable.

The Many Faces of Hate

So far, this chapter has focused on gender and sexual discrimination, but it's a sad fact of life that religious and racial discrimination still exist, even on college campuses. We like to think that institutions of higher education would be on the forefront of equality, but that doesn't always appear to be the case throughout the country.

One student who wishes to remain anonymous told me:

> "People think prejudice is only problems with blacks and whites or gays and straights, but that's just not true. When I got to college, I was shocked to encounter anti-Semitism. I thought that went out in the 1950s, but it was alive and well at my school. The Jewish minority was definitely shunned by the non-Jewish majority."

Another student told me that at her college, black students and white students rarely sit together in the cafeteria. In another college, students steer clear of certain dorms because they're the "black" dorms or the "white" dorms.

You might be racist or religiously bigoted without even realizing it because it was part of the environment you were raised in. Think carefully about your attitude toward people of other races and religions as well as people of different gender or sexual orientation.

Going to the Mat

If you experience any form of discrimination or harassment, you may feel victimized and isolated. Since the law is on your side, there are specific actions you can take. I suggest the following process:

1. **Give the speaker the benefit of the doubt.** Perhaps you misinterpreted the action or comment. Meet with the professor or fellow student and explain why you consider a specific action or comment sexist. Give the person a chance to explain the comment.

2. **Work up the food chain.** If the offensive behavior continues, see the campus affirmative action officer. All campuses are mandated by law to have offices that take care of such issues.

3. **Put it in writing.** Document your complaint, backing up your concerns with specific examples. Send copies to the professor, the department chairperson, and the appropriate dean.

4. **File a formal grievance.** As a last resort, take legal action. This is a serious step and should be undertaken only if you've spoken to your parents at length and retained a lawyer.

5. **Be classy.** If you've been hurt, it's tempting to send an article to the school newspaper, give an interview on the campus radio station, and generally run a media circus. Stand tough and shut up. If you damage a person's reputation unfairly, you can be held liable for slander and libel.

Crib Notes

Familiarize yourself with the hierarchy at your college. In most instances, the chain of command follows this pattern:

professor → department chairperson → dean → provost → vice-president → college president

"Express yourself, don't repress yourself." —Madonna

As Cyndi Lauper wrote in her famous song "True Colors":

> But I see your true colors
> Shining through
> I see your true colors
> And that's why I love you
> So don't be afraid to let them show
> Your true colors
> True colors are beautiful,
> Like a rainbow.

You may have heard you're in college to learn a lot so you can get a good job and earn a pot of money. It's true that all able-bodied adults should be able to support themselves. However, most of all, you're in college to learn about yourself. Develop your talents, abilities, and interests. Don't let anyone destroy your differences; they are what make you unique. And be especially sure you show the tolerance and acceptance that is everyone's right.

The Least You Need to Know

➤ America is becoming increasingly more diverse, making the need for tolerance and understanding more pressing.

➤ Many gays experience misunderstanding and prejudice.

➤ Sexual harassment and discrimination can be present in even the most accepting colleges.

➤ Be sure you have cause before you charge sexual harassment; false charges wreck careers.

➤ Express yourself freely and show tolerance and acceptance to all.

This Dorm Isn't Big Enough for Both of Us

In the best of all possible worlds, your experience with your college roommate(s) will match Kristel Kubart's experience this year at Holy Cross College (Worcester, Massachusetts):

> "Living in the same room with a complete stranger can be a little intimidating. In high school I was not into sports at all, so when I found out that my roommate was going to be on the Holy Cross basketball team I started to panic. She's 6 foot 2 and a complete jock. We have completely different personalities, but in a funny way it works because we learn and grow from each other's different experiences."

Unfortunately, we don't live in the best of all possible worlds, so you're more likely to be in Michael Thomas's shoes (Eastern Kentucky University, University of Iowa):

> "Everybody has a bad roommate at some point. Look at it for what it is, a learning experience, and know that, at the very least, you will have some good stories to tell down the road because of it."

Here, we'll discuss some of the problems you can experience with roommates. To help you understand what issues you might face, I'll share stories I've received from college students around the country. Then I'll teach you effective ways to resolve differences with your roommate(s) so you can concentrate on enjoying college rather than battling with your roommate.

Luck of the Draw

Several members of my panel of experts have given me the same document: "245 Ways to Annoy Your College Roommate." Apparently, it's been making the rounds via the Internet.

Some of the suggestions are silly, such as these:

➤ Burn all your wastepaper while eyeing your roommate suspiciously.

➤ Leave a declaration of war on your roommate's desk. Include a list of grievances.

➤ While your roommate is out, glue your shoes to the ceiling. When your roommate walks in, sit on the floor, hold your head, and moan.

Other suggestions, however, are sadistic:

➤ If your roommate goes away for the weekend, change the locks.

➤ Hit your roommate on the head with a brick. Claim that you were trying to kill a mosquito.

➤ Turn out all the lights and wait for your roommate to come home. Then whack 'em on the head with a golf club.

Below "C" Level

NEVER go after your roommate's sweetheart. This is a sure recipe for disaster.

The sheer number of annoying things on this list—245!—and their combination of silliness and savagery suggests that problems with roommates are widespread and serious.

It only stands to reason: After all, total strangers are thrown into a cage together and told to make the best of it for a year. Add the pressures of being away from home, academic demands, and social issues, and you're sitting on a powder keg.

Often, problems arise with roommates because of cultural differences, honest misunderstandings, outright rudeness, or regrettable stupidity. The following two stories describe typical roommate situations. See how they compare to your own experiences thus far.

Telling Tales Out of School

Both Alison Dorosz of Washington College and Val Delaportas of SUNY—New Paltz (New York) experienced roommate problems because of cultural differences, but their stories turned out differently. Here's Alison's story:

> "When I checked into my residence hall, my roommate greeted me in French. Although I was a freshman, I had been placed in a room with an older exchange student who didn't comprehend American habits or slang. I was jealous of class-mates who were rooming with friends.

> "But by the end of the semester, I realized that I was the lucky one. The friends-as-roommates were squabbling over borrowed clothes, misplaced CDs, and is-sues of personal space.

> "Because we were strangers, we established our own personal space from the very begin-ning. We divided the room equally and agreed to respect each other's clothing and personal items.

> "The language and cultural barriers came down and we became friends who enjoyed sharing our cultures. We certainly had more to talk about than the roommates from the same hometown!"

Crib Notes

Men, a necktie on the doorknob is a traditional signal for "Go away. My sweetie and I are doing the wild thing now."

Val's experience started out almost the same as Alison's, but ended very differently. Here's what Val told me:

> "My school was supposed to send us information on our roommates so we could call and find out who we'd be with. For some reason, I didn't get the in-formation so I couldn't contact my roommates ahead of time.

> "When I arrived on campus, I met our first roommate. She seemed nice and ex-cited about our third roommate, who was her best friend. This scared me be-cause I knew I'd feel left out and strange living in a room with two girls who had known each other from birth. The third roommate moved in. She also seemed nice, so I thought the situation may not be bad.

> "Our parents left. My new roommates decided that we should make a few rules. The first rule they made was, 'Don't curse.' I don't usually curse, but I found it odd that cursing was their biggest concern. They also said they would go to church three times a week, they enjoy gospel music, I might be asked to leave the room when they pray, and that any music I wanted to listen to was fine, un-less it was profane or indecent.

"I thought okay, I can deal with this. After a while, though, I realized this was too much for me to handle. Their gospel music was on all the time and I was kicked out of my own room more than I thought I'd be. I'm not religious, and I couldn't take it anymore.

"Everything they did made me angry. They slept with the light on every night. I was able to deal with it the first few weeks, but one night, it made me crazy. I think it was a combination of the light and the song that was playing while they were falling asleep. My friends have stories about messy or drunken roommates. I would have settled for one of those as opposed to what I had to deal with.

Below "C" Level

Never just assume you can change roommates at will. Check with the college housing office *before* you have problems so you know the policy and procedure.

Crib Notes

Different colleges assign rooms and roommates in different ways. Be sure you understand how this process works at your college. Remember that many colleges give preferential room assignments to students who are substance-free.

"I talked to the resident director about changing rooms. I had given them a month, and I figured that was long enough. The resident director gave me the room number of a girl whose roommate had never showed up. I talked to her, and she encouraged me to move in.

"I really like my new roommate. We get along really well. We have a lot of the same friends so we hang out together, we're in some of the same classes, and we have the same views, taste in music, and even the same sleeping patterns. The past few months have been so much better."

Both Alison and Val were able to solve the problems they had with their roommates. Alison was fortunate that time melted away cultural barriers, but Val was forced to change roommates. It would be nice if all problems resolved themselves in time, but that's not always the case. It's reassuring to know that if the problems you're experiencing with your roommate are severe and ongoing, you almost always have the option of changing roommates. After all, the college authorities want you to succeed—but you can't do your best if you're battling in the dorm. Use the following ideas to help you get along with your roommates.

Bridge over Troubled Waters

If you're having problems getting along with your roommate, try to improve the situation by starting with yourself. The problem might not be with your particular roommate. Rather, you might not want any roommate at all. Here's what Stephanie Muntone of Oberlin College advises:

> "I always lived in dorms because I liked having company readily available in the common rooms or down the hall. However, solitary types preferred to live on their own, preferably off campus."

If you suspect that you're a Lone Ranger, see if you can arrange for a single for the rest of the year. At the next room draw, you can put in for a single.

People in glass houses shouldn't throw stones. Before you're so quick to go on the offensive with your roommate, make sure you're not part of the problem. The following suggestions can help you and you roommate get along more smoothly.

Learn the Lingo

Substance-free housing refers to dorm rooms in which students promise not to drink alcohol, smoke tobacco, or use any illegal drugs.

Be Considerate

A little consideration goes a long way to getting any new roommate relationship off on the right foot. Here are the basics:

➤ NEVER claim a bed, bedroom, or any part of a room before all the other roommates have arrived. Wait until everyone has assembled to decide who gets the bottom bunk (clearly the more desirable berth) and the desk that doesn't wobble.

➤ Turn off the light at a reasonable time.

➤ Get earplugs for your stereo so your roommate isn't assaulted by your music.

➤ Move the party/floating poker game/etc. to someone else's room or the common room.

➤ Pick up your stuff. Put it in drawers, the closet, or wherever it belongs.

➤ Keep the sex stuff private. No one wants to watch you and your honey tickling each other's tonsils ... night after night after night.

Don't Prejudge

Some roommate problems are caused by perceived rather than real differences. You might be worried about rooming with someone who is gay, or someone of a different race, nationality, socioeconomic background, or religion. Suspend your judgments and get to know the person as a *person*.

199

Be Respectful

No matter how closely college officials try to match roommates, it would be a major miracle if the two of you (or four of you) shared the same background, heritage, and beliefs. As a result, you must recognize these differences and respect them if you're going to coexist in the same space.

As Michelle Stern of Mt. Holyoke College suggests, "Be respectful to your roommate. Do not 'sexile' them or be unaccommodating to their customs and culture. They may be coming from a totally different background than you."

Extra Credit

"Cultivate the fine art of listening. I count among my friends from college people I would never have sought out were it not for the close confines of the dorms and campus dining halls. I had discussions with people I never imagined would have opinions as they did. I had arguments that you just do not have time for in 'the real world' with people a lot smarter than me, be they peers, graduate students, or professors."

—Paul Lee, Princeton University

Be Responsible

We all have our hot buttons, things other people do that set us off on a tirade. In nearly all cases, they're caused by a lack of personal responsibility. Start being responsible and you and your roommate are bound to get along more smoothly. Try these suggestions:

➤ Don't borrow things without asking.

➤ Don't keep, lose, or destroy things you borrow.

➤ If you do destroy things you borrow, replace them with things of equal or greater value.

➤ Don't eat food that your roommate has set aside for him- or herself.

➤ Don't expect your roommate to wake you up in the morning. That's your responsibility.

Be Honest

The following hint comes from Lynn Ekstrand of Quinnipiac University in Connecticut: "When you first meet your roommates, be yourself. Don't be fake." If you present a false face from the beginning, you and your roommate won't stand a chance of getting to know each other.

Communicate

Talking about problems from the start is essential. Lynn Ekstrand (Quinnipiac University) realized this. She told me: "I have four roommates. We're in one big room so we have NO privacy; we all listen into each other's conversations. When we had a problem, we all got together in the room and talked it out. It was better to talk it all out before we started having problems. We thought of solutions and worked it all out."

Crib Notes

As Kelly Betts of C.W. Post College on Long Island, New York, advises, "Anything your mom always told you to do—like clean your room—you still have to do. Now it's more important than ever, because your roommate doesn't have to put up with your mess, as your mother did."

Give It Enough Time

It takes a while to get to know anyone. Unless the situation is dangerous, give your roommate several weeks before you throw in the towel and request a transfer. The first few weeks can be rocky, but then you and your roommate might find yourself getting along much better. You might even become friends.

Carol Lash (State University of New York at Albany) has some wise advice, based on her own experience: "I did not do well with my first roommate. We just gave each other as much space as possible and tried to wait it out. I eventually moved to another room for the second term. Not everyone you meet is going to be a friend. All you can do is give the situation as much of a chance as possible."

Below "C" Level

Get a room transfer IMMEDIATELY if your roommate is engaging in dangerous or illegal behavior. Even if you're not the one smoking dope or smuggling in strangers off the street, you can be the one arrested or attacked.

Be Sympathetic

So you're a National Merit Scholarship winner and you never have to study to get straight A's. This does not give you the right to snicker when your roommate flunks her first math test. So your roommate's sweetie cheated on him with his archenemy from high school. This is not the time to announce that your sweetie has knitted you a sweater with "Hunka Hunka Burning Love" spelled out across it.

Give Your Roommate Some Space

The two of you are trapped in a space smaller than the average jail cell and just about as homey. Try to arrange your schedules so you each get a little bit of "down" time alone in your homey little cell.

Take It for What It Is

You don't have to be best buddies to get along with your roommate. Treat each other with respect, consideration, and kindness, and you can often do just fine.

Breaking Up Is Hard to Do

So what can you do if you and your roommate are coming to blows and you haven't been able to resolve the situation? Stephanie Muntone of Oberlin College says, "Don't hesitate to split up if you don't get along with your roommate. I changed rooms and roommates several times and was always better off for the change."

Follow these steps if you've decided the situation is past repair and you and your roommate can't live together any longer:

Crib Notes

"If you break up with someone who lives in your dorm, one of you should consider moving to another dorm. Less stress for one and all. (In my case, I moved out and he stayed!)"

—Stephanie Muntone, Oberlin College

1. **Appeal to a higher authority.** If you and your roommate(s) still aren't getting along, talk to your resident advisor (RA). RAs can provide advice and counseling and can help ensure that residence hall and university regulations are enforced.

2. **Don't give up.** If problems go beyond what an RA can deal with, see the residence hall director or assistant hall director.

3. **Consider informal changes.** Some students take matters into their own hands and make informal room changes. I'd advise you to run all changes through your RA, but if you can rework the arrangements to everyone's satisfaction yourself, you've created a win-win situation for everyone.

As Jonathan Kadishson of Lehigh University suggests:

> "I hope you get lucky. I did. If your roommate is a problem and you are sure after a couple of weeks that you can't get along, consider switching with people from another room. This happened in my hall, and everybody is happier now."

The Least You Need to Know

➤ Virtually all college students have problems with roommates. Fortunately, most problems are resolved fairly easily.

➤ If you're having problems getting along with your roommate, try to improve the situation by starting with yourself. Be considerate, respectful, responsible, and honest.

➤ Share your concerns with your roommate and give the problem at least a few weeks to resolve.

➤ If you can't resolve the problem on your own, talk to your resident advisor (RA). If that doesn't work, see the residence hall director or assistant hall director. You might also want to work out an informal room switch.

Chapter 20

Return of the Party Animal

In This Chapter

➤ Facts about drinking on college campuses

➤ Health risks of excessive drinking

➤ Myths about drinking

➤ Are you drinking too much?

➤ How to curb excessive drinking

On November 10, 1999, University of Michigan sophomore Byung Soo Kim celebrated his twenty-first birthday by trying to drink 21 shots of whiskey. He gulped down 20 shots, passed out, turned blue, and stopped breathing.

As he lay dying in a Michigan hospital later that night, seven college students hopped into a Jeep 500 miles away on the campus of Colgate University. The driver, whom police say was intoxicated, veered off the road and struck a tree, killing four of his passengers.

By the time classes began on Monday, five families who had proudly sent their children off to college were planning their funerals. Even more tragic, these five alcohol-related deaths were just the tip of the iceberg that weekend, that month, and that year.

In this chapter, we'll explore how you can deal with the problem of excessive alcohol consumption at college to make sure you don't become one of these terrible statistics.

The Battle of the Binge

Did you know ...

➤ *Binge drinking* is defined as the consumption of five or more drinks in one sitting by a male, or four or more drinks by a female.

➤ More than half of the students who use alcohol say they drink to get drunk.

➤ Almost one third of college students admit to having missed at least one class because of alcohol or drug use.

➤ Nearly one quarter of students report failing a test or project due to the after-effects of drinking or doing drugs.

➤ Alcohol is a factor in 40 percent of all academic problems and 28 percent of all dropouts.

➤ The average student spends about $900 on alcohol each year. The average student spends $450 a year on books.

(The New York Times, *October 24, 1999*)

Learn the Lingo

Binge drinking is the consumption of five or more drinks in one sitting by a male, or four or more drinks by a female.

According to a survey conducted by the Harvard School of Public Health, more than 50 percent of today's college students binge drink—20 percent of them three or more times in a two-week period. However, only 34 percent of their noncollege counterparts binge drink. We can conclude from these statistics that the college culture encourages binge drinking.

While surveys have documented a significant decline in the use of other drugs by college students, there have been only small declines in binge drinking. College teens drink alcohol at about the same rate they did five years ago.

Crib Notes

"Get used to it: There will be lots of alcohol in college. You should go to college knowing whether you're comfortable with alcohol, how much you can handle, if you want to stay away from it completely, etc. You'll be going to parties, and you alone, not your parents, are responsible for being in control of yourself."

—Jonathan Kadishson, Lehigh University

Drinking and a Parent's Worst Nightmare

"I got into partying too hard first semester freshman year. I didn't get enough sleep, I didn't eat right, and I came down with mono.

I immediately toned it down, and the next semester, I only partied one night of the weekend, and most of the time, it didn't involve alcohol. This year, my friends and I do a lot of nonalcoholic activities, like movies, Nintendo, bowling, the local pool hall, etc. There are always alcohol- and drug-free things to do on and off campus. The party scene got old fast."

—Robyn Smith, Syracuse University

Binge drinking increases the risk for alcohol-related injury, especially for college kids, who often combine alcohol with other high-risk activities, such as impaired driving. According to the Centers for Disease Control and Prevention, the four leading injury-related causes of death among youths under the age of 20 are motor vehicle crashes, homicides, suicides, and drowning. Alcohol is involved in many of these deaths.

Further, according to The Core Institute, 300,000 of today's college students will eventually die of alcohol-related causes, such as cirrhosis of the liver, various cancers, and heart disease.

Drinking and Sexual Violence

"Girls: Avoid drunk boys at parties or you may find yourself having to charge them with date rape. Remember that you are responsible for your own behavior; he is responsible for his."

—Stephanie Muntone, Oberlin College

Sexual encounters—with their inherent risks of pregnancy and sexually transmitted diseases—as well as date rape and other violence occur more often when students are binge drinking. Even sober students who abstain from alcohol can still suffer from the assaults, sex crimes, and poor academic environments that go with heavy drinking.

> **Extra Credit**
>
> College students report that alcohol is more easily available to them today than it was five years ago, and there is a high correlation between availability and use. In addition, alcohol remains inexpensive compared to other beverages. This is especially true of keg beer, often the center of a party.

Out of the Frying Pan into the Fire

As you enter the culture of the college campus, you're confronted with many challenges and opportunities, including:

➤ The opportunity to be independent from your parents

➤ The need to conform

➤ The insecurity of a new social setting

Each of these new challenges can lead to excessive drinking. When combined, they spell disaster for far too many college students.

Perhaps you've fallen for these old myths about drinking. Which ones apply to you?

Myth: "I'm more fun when I drink."

Reality: You're not fun when you're slurring, stumbling all over the place, puking in your pillow, or keeping your roommate up all night. There's a big difference between laughing *with* someone and laughing *at* someone. No one wants to be the dorm's bad joke.

Below "C" Level

Just one night of heavy drinking can impair your ability to think abstractly for up to 30 days, limiting your ability to link reading to class lectures.

Extra Credit

The college binge-drinking pandemic is so severe that 113 college presidents united in 2000 to publicly admit that a generation is in peril. They have authorized a public-service anti-alcohol campaign and a whole slew of educational tactics, including dry rock concerts, dry fraternities, and a series of mock "tail" parties.

Myth: "Everyone drinks a lot at parties so they can chill and hang out."

Reality: Although many people use alcohol to help loosen up in social situations, there are only a few people who get trashed at parties, lose control, embarrass themselves, and endanger their lives—or lose them.

Myth: "After a hard week hitting the books, I need to smoke a little weed while I toss down a six-pack."

Reality: Mixing drugs—including drugs like alcohol and marijuana—has what scientists call an "additive effect." This means you'll feel the intoxication from both. So don't fool yourself into thinking you'll have a few drinks and then "mellow out" by smoking pot. Sure, you may feel mellow, but you're really just plain wasted.

Myth: "It's no one else's business how much I drink. I can handle it."

Reality: Studies show that one person's drinking habits can affect an average of five people other than the drinker. Still think it's nobody else's business?

Myth: "If I didn't drink, there would be nothing to do at my school."

Reality: Learn about the clubs, sports, and service groups your school offers. And if you can't find the club you want, start it.

Myth: "I'm having as much fun as I can while I'm in college. As soon as I graduate, I'll get my act together and stop drinking."

Reality: Excessive drinking habits can keep you from attending class, studying regularly, or getting involved in a career-oriented club or internship. Plus, if you're thinking of going to grad school, you need a good transcript. Even though no one goes to college intending to become an alcoholic, heavy drinking behavior in college can ultimately lead some people to alcoholism for life.

Myth: "Even though my mom or dad is an alcoholic, I know how to drink without letting it get out of hand."

Reality: Maybe, maybe not. Children of alcoholics are three to four times more likely to become alcoholics themselves. Although this doesn't mean you'll definitely have an alcohol problem if one of your parents does, it *does* mean you should pay special attention to your behavior. You are not like people whose parents aren't alcoholics.

Myth: "I'm just a social drinker."

Reality: Drinking with others doesn't make you a social drinker. Social drinkers might drink regularly, but they don't get drunk. Nor does a social drinker exhibit any of the clinical signs of alcohol addiction, like out-of-control behavior while under the influence, inability to control alcohol cravings, severe memory loss, and blackouts.

Below "C" Level

If you have attention-deficit disorder, you are at greater risk for alcohol and drug problems. Drugs and the "party lifestyle" often appeal to impulsive individuals.

Truth or Consequences

Take the following quiz to find out if you drink too much. Circle Yes or No for each question. Be honest, now!

Alcohol Truth or Consequences

1. My personality changes when I drink alcohol.	Yes	No
2. When I'm in a social situation and alcohol isn't provided, I feel uncomfortable.	Yes	No
3. Drinking has caused me to be late for class or work.	Yes	No
4. I sometimes have a drink to fall asleep.	Yes	No
5. I crave a drink at a specific time every day, like after class or after work.	Yes	No
6. My family or friends have expressed concern about my drinking.	Yes	No

continues

continued

7. It is difficult for me to stop drinking after I've had one or two drinks.   Yes   No

8. I use alcohol as an escape when I'm angry, disappointed, or otherwise upset.   Yes   No

9. I've promised myself to slow down or stop drinking, but I can only keep the promise for a few days or weeks.   Yes   No

10. I like certain "drinking buddies" or a specific environment when I drink.   Yes   No

11. I eat very little or irregularly when I'm drinking.   Yes   No

12. My school work has suffered because of my drinking.   Yes   No

13. I've done something sexual that I later regretted while I was under the influence of alcohol.   Yes   No

14. The day after drinking, I have trouble remembering what I did while I was under the influence.   Yes   No

15. I sometimes feel guilty about my drinking.   Yes   No

16. Even after my friends say I've had enough alcohol, I want to continue drinking.   Yes   No

17. I get angry when my family or friends want to discuss my drinking.   Yes   No

18. A large part of my day is spent obtaining, consuming, or recovering from the effects of alcohol.   Yes   No

19. I have been arrested for driving under the influence of alcohol.   Yes   No

20. When I drink, I almost always wind up drunk.   Yes   No

21. I have lost a friend or created a rift with a family member based on their feelings about my drinking.   Yes   No

22. When I'm sober, I regret things I said or did while I was drinking.   Yes   No

23. I have gotten into an argument or a fight while I was drinking.   Yes   No

24. I have a hangover or headache after I've been drinking.   Yes   No

25. When I'm out with friends, I sometimes sneak a few drinks without their knowledge.   Yes   No

Answers: You're in college, so I know you're not stupid. You don't need me to tell you that if you answered "Yes" to even a handful of these questions, you have a problem with alcohol abuse. Read on to find out how you can control your drinking before it totally controls you.

Crib Notes

"Know your alcohol limits and facts about drugs and sex before you get fed misinformation by classmates. I work for the center for alcohol and drug education at my grad school—and it's scary how much trouble kids get into because they just don't know stuff."

—Kathryn Werntz, Alfred University (Alfred, New York)

Alcohol 101

"When I was young and listening to my brothers and sisters talking about their wild parties and getting so drunk in college, I thought it was the coolest thing to do. Now that I'm old enough to drink, I realize that it's not as much fun as I thought it would be. Waking up with a hangover isn't my idea of a great time. When I was binge drinking, I got so sick that I couldn't even remember that I threw up on strangers in the bar. I got kicked out. When I woke up the next morning, I had to go to class. I forgot that I had a test. I struggled to remember the lectures from the week before. It wasn't fun at all."

—Jillian Palmieri, the State University of New York College of Technology at Farmingdale

Contrary to what you've probably heard about college, you don't have to get drunk every night to have fun. In fact, one in five college students doesn't drink at all.

Extra Credit

Which campuses have the heaviest rate of drinking? *The Princeton Review* does the best-known ranking of "party schools." Traditionally, schools with large fraternity systems have more excessive drinking. Some studies also reveal heavier drinking at rural colleges, which have fewer off-campus entertainment options.

Below "C" Level

NEVER drive when you've had a drink—even one—and never get into a car with someone who has been drinking. Take a cab, walk, or sleep it off where you are.

Crib Notes

For additional assistance, check out DRUGHELP (www.drughelp. org), The National Council on Alcoholism and Drug Dependence (www.ncadd.org), and Alcoholics Anonymous (www.aa.org). You can also look in the Yellow Pages under "Mental Health," "Community Services," "Social and Human Services," "Alcoholism," or "Drug Abuse."

Whether you feel you might have a problem with alcohol and want to cut back, or you want to know how to keep your drinking under control, use these guidelines:

Top Ten Ways to Control Alcohol Abuse

1. Write down how many drinks you consume over a month, how you felt when you were drunk, and how being drunk affected your schoolwork.

2. Avoid people who make you feel uncomfortable if you're not drinking. Hang out with friends who are less inclined to include alcohol in their fun.

3. Avoid places where you'll be bored if you're not drinking.

4. Set a liquor limit. For example, don't drink during the week or don't drink more than three drinks on a party night.

5. Eat before you start drinking, and eat while you drink.

6. Drink slowly, spacing alcohol with soda, water, juice, or coffee.

7. Don't play drinking games.

8. Don't keep alcohol in your dorm room. It'll be easier to resist if it isn't there.

9. Go cold turkey for a while. Notice how good you feel while you abstain.

10. Save the cash you don't spend on booze. Treat yourself to something special with the money you've saved by being sober. Go on vacation, buy a great outfit, get some furniture for your room.

Student Kelly Madden (the State University of New York at Farmingdale) sums up the issue of excessive drinking well:

> "Drinking and drugs is a very good way to throw away everything you've worked so hard to accomplish. You'll hear about the boy or girl who died in the college dorm room after overdosing on alcohol. Do you want to become that statistic?

> "College life can be very confusing at first. You might have a hard time managing your time and getting your work done, but as long as you do your best and don't let drugs and alcohol interfere, you will be fine. You just have to focus and resist peer pressure, no matter how hard it may seem at times."

Crib Notes

Many colleges have excellent information on alcohol and drug abuse. I am much indebted to the University of Indiana's superb Web site for much of the information in this chapter.

The Least You Need to Know

➤ More than half of all college students are binge drinkers, males consuming five or more drinks in a sitting and females consuming four or more.

➤ Alcohol is a factor in 40 percent of all academic problems and 28 percent of all dropouts.

➤ If you have a problem with binge drinking, get help. Now.

➤ To keep your drinking under control, track the amount you drink, avoid people who binge drink, and set a liquor limit. Avoid drinking games, don't keep alcohol in your dorm room, and save the money you would otherwise waste on booze.

Part 5

Moving Up, Moving On

"College success is about following your dream, finding your own path, and not those that parents, peers, or society want you to follow. Don't short-circuit this opportunity for self-discovery by doing what's expected. Do what you love and respect yourself at the same time."

—Ally Burleson, Washington College

This guide to college survival concludes with chapters on off-campus housing, semesters abroad, internships, and transferring. I'll also show you how to make the most of your college years as you move toward graduation. Finally, we'll explore the emotional, exhilarating transition from college to the real world.

Chapter 21

A Little Place of My Own

> **In This Chapter**
>
> ➤ Pros and cons of off-campus life
>
> ➤ Types of housing
>
> ➤ How to find an apartment
>
> ➤ Knowing your rights
>
> ➤ Leases and rental agreements

"I'll be a senior next year and I want an apartment because I'll be student teaching and I need my rest. It's too noisy in the dorm, but I'm really going to miss all the social activity there."

—Jessica Swantek, The College of William and Mary

Most freshmen are required to live in official on-campus housing, but upper-class students usually have their choice of remaining in the dorms or moving off campus. Many move off campus for a variety of reasons, which we'll explore in this chapter.

Movin' On

"Particularly unpleasant was my first-year roommate, who filled out her roommate placement form as a nonsmoker—then took up smoking within a week of starting school. I was not amused."

—Shanti

As Shanti points out, dorm living has its downsides—and pesky roommates are the least of it. However, living in the dorms has a lot of advantages: It's fun, convenient, and relatively inexpensive. After all, dorms were designed to make it easy for college students to live so they can concentrate on their education.

Crib Notes

I strongly suggest that you live in the dorm for at least a year. Most of the commuters I've interviewed believe that they've missed a vital part of the college experience by living at home.

Living in an apartment off campus, however, has an undeniable allure. You're free, away from the turmoil of dorm life: marathon music sessions, continual interruptions, and piggy roommates. It's also a great way to take a giant step toward independence. You might decide to live off campus with a roommate or go solo. In either case, the apartment will certainly be quieter than the dorm.

Is it time for you to move off campus? Ultimately, only you can make that decision, but I can lay out the advantages and disadvantages of off-campus housing so you'll have a more complete picture. Study the following chart as you mull over the decision to get a place of your own.

Off-Campus Housing

Advantages	Disadvantages
Private	May be lonely
Quiet	More difficult to meet people
Calm	Chance of reduced social life
Clean and neat	*You* have to keep it clean!
More time	Less time: farther to get to class
May be less expensive	May be more expensive
Freedom, independence	Independence is easily abused
A chance to grow up	Who wants to grow up yet?

Look Before You Leap

So you've decided to get an off-campus apartment: Congratulations! Before you start apartment shopping, here are some factors to consider.

Motive

Why do you want a place of your own? Before you go any further with your plans, make sure your motives are sensible and good for you in the long run. For example:

➤ **Smart reason:** You find the dorm intolerable and you need some peace and quiet.

➤ **Stupid reason:** You want to move in with your honey against the wishes of your family and friends.

Cost

The cost of living in the dorms doesn't vary: Room and board (meals) are fixed. Apartment expenses are variable, however. In the winter, your heating bill can be high enough to induce nose bleeds; in the spring and summer, your electrical bill for air-conditioning can remind you why your parents favored opening the windows.

Here are some costs to consider:

➤ **Monthly rent.** While this expense remains fixed, you might have to sign for a full year (12 months) rather than the academic year (8 to 9 months). That's a lot of extra moolah you have to pony up.

➤ **Security deposit.** The security deposit is usually equal to one month's rent. The landlord holds the security until you move out. If the apartment isn't damaged when you leave, you get all your security back. If there is damage, the landlord deducts the amount of repairs. Therefore, if you don't keep the place up nicely, you can lose a month's rent—or more.

➤ **Utilities.** Whether you're paying the bills directly or have the fee tacked on to your rent, you're still going to have to pay for gas, electricity, and sometimes water. You often have to provide a security deposit for the telephone, too.

➤ **Furnishings.** If the apartment comes furnished, you'll need only what you already have from your life in the dorm: sheets, pillowcases, blankets, towels, and so on. If the apartment is unfurnished, however, you're going to need a bed, chairs, table, drapes or shades, kitchen supplies (cutlery, plates, glasses, pots and pans), etc., etc., etc.

➤ **Food.** Food for one person can be pricey, since you'll have a lot of waste unless you buy carefully.

Learn the Lingo

A **security deposit** is the money you give to the landlord to keep in escrow while you're living in the apartment.

Crib Notes

Want to make sure you get all your security deposit back? Walk through the apartment with the landlord before you move in. Together, compile a list of all the damage you see (such as worn carpet, scratched appliances, and so on). Sign it and have the landlord sign it. If he or she refuses, don't take the place.

219

Roommates

Do you want to live alone off campus or with friends? Many college students live with their buddies to defray the costs. You may want to consider this option.

Below "C" Level

It's not the budgeted costs that sink you; it's the costs you never anticipated. They include the emergency car repair (who knew the brakes were bad?), the outrageous heating bill (such a cold winter), or the huge food bill (but it was a great party).

Crib Notes

If you're the super-responsible type, consider house-sitting rather than renting. When professors take sabbaticals and travel around the globe, they often hire upper-class students or graduate students to stay in their homes rent-free in exchange for chores such as watering the plants, taking care of Fido, and keeping burglars away.

Transportation

How will you get to campus, the food store, and work? If you decide to use a car, make sure you can afford it as well as the apartment. If you're going to use public transportation, check that it's close to the apartment, in a safe area, and easy to get to. You don't want to be tramping two miles in a blizzard through a deserted cornfield to get to the bus. Also, remember that, unlike the shuttle buses on campus, public transportation isn't free.

Personal Style

Finally, are you Little Suzy or Sam Homemaker? Will you like keeping up your apartment lifestyle or find it an insufferable nuisance? Unless you intend to live entirely on take-out, be prepared to do some home cooking. And unless you like living in a pigsty, be ready to spend time scrubbing the bathroom, vacuuming the floors, and dusting away your initials on the end table.

Types of Housing

You're ready to move out of the dorms into the real world, so let's do some apartment shopping. What kind of place best suits your needs? Following are the most common types of housing for college students.

A Room with a View

The least expensive option is renting a single room in a house. You often have to share a bathroom with other people who live in the house. You may be allowed to share the kitchen. Check this option carefully if you intend to cook anything more complex than toaster pastries.

You may have to provide *references*, letters from people who vouch for your ability to pay your rent fully and on time. If you do have to provide references, ask people whom your landlord will respect, such as professors and employers.

Apartments

Most apartments have one, two, or three bedrooms and one or more bathrooms. The apartments may be part of a large house or part of an apartment building. Here are the most common types of apartments:

➤ **Studio apartments.** One room and bathroom. A furnished studio is also called an *efficiency apartment.*

➤ **Duplex apartments.** Rooms on two floors.

➤ **Lofts.** Usually one very large room, often an unfinished space.

➤ **Condominiums or co-ops.** Both types of apartments are usually purchased rather than rented, but sometimes you can sublet (take over the lease from an existing owner or renter). The apartments can be big or small.

Learn the Lingo

References are letters from employers, professors, or friends attesting to your good character, abilities, or accomplishments.

Below "C" Level

If you can't afford an apartment in a safe neighborhood, don't move out of the dorms. Your safety comes before anything else.

Location, Location, Location

According to the old joke, there are three rules of real estate: location, location, location. Yes and no. Location is certainly important because it relates to many other crucial factors. However, there are other important issues to consider when you're looking for an off-campus home. You want your apartment to be:

➤ **Safe.** Number one and most important: Select a location that's safe. Look only in neighborhoods that are well-maintained, well-lighted, and secure.

➤ **Close to campus.** The most desirable apartments (or rooms) are closest to campus, which saves time and transportation money. It also makes it easier for you to remain part of campus life because you can come and go without a long commute.

➤ **Quiet.** My sister, a music major, rented an apartment in a quiet neighborhood and played her trumpet on the balcony every night. Needless to say, she was not one of the nominees for the "Good Neighbor" award. Does anyone want to live next door to a student learning to play the trumpet? Neither do you want to live next door to a construction site, a factory, or an all-night diner.

➤ **Clean.** The apartment should be spic-and-span when you look at it. Look especially for signs of insects: Roaches like to nest under sinks and in dark food cabinets. If you see roaches, get it in writing that the landlord will hire a professional exterminator to take care of the problem *before* you move in (and continue treatments while you're in residence).

The building should also be clean, especially the stairwells, grounds, and sidewalks. In addition to the aesthetic appeal of a clean place, cleanliness is a safety factor: snowy sidewalks, trash-strewn hallways, and overgrown yards are invitations for disaster.

➤ **In good repair.** You can wipe away mold in the bathroom or spiderwebs in the corner. You can't replaster crumbling ceilings or replace an ancient boiler.

Finders Keepers

So how do you find an off-campus place to live? Here are the three most common ways:

➤ Word-of-mouth

➤ Ads

➤ Real estate brokers

Let's look at each method in detail.

I Heard It Through the Grapevine: Word-of-Mouth

You can often find an apartment through a friend who is graduating and moving out. Seniors and graduate students are especially useful. Professors, TAs, RAs, and the on-campus housing office are also great sources for apartments.

Word-of-mouth is a great method because you can find out what's wrong with the apartment—and what's right about it. You can often find out exactly how much rent the former tenant was paying so you know if you're getting gouged. In addition, you can find out how the landlord treats his or her renters.

Let Your Fingers Do the Walking: Ads

Mary Ellen Snodgrass from the University of North Carolina at Greensboro offers this advice:

> "Get off campus and commune with the real world occasionally. Go to a public library to study, buy lunch at the mall, shop at a greenhouse, ride the city bus. Don't let the world boil down to a huge population of people your own age and interests."

In addition to being great advice for keeping yourself centered while you study, Mary Ellen's advice is a great way to find an off-campus apartment. While you're out in the community, look at room and apartment ads on bulletin boards in the Laundromat, church, library, food store, and community center.

Here are some suggestions for using ads to find the best off-campus housing:

➤ Sunday newspapers usually have the most complete housing ads. Pennysavers and other local publications are also good sources.

➤ You snooze, you lose. Get the paper as soon as possible on Sunday morning and start making calls immediately.

➤ If you see a place you like, put down a small deposit to hold it. Make sure the deposit is refundable! I suggest you use a check for this purpose because you can stop payment if there's a problem down the road.

Crib Notes

In most cases, you'll have to sign an agreement with the broker. Be sure to read it carefully.

Get a Pro: Using Real Estate Brokers

Real estate brokers bring buyers and seller together. Brokers do all the legwork, finding the apartments and even driving you to see them. However, brokers charge fees for their services. Sometimes the apartment owner pays the fee; other times, the renter pays. If you decide to use a real estate broker to help you find off-campus housing, always ask about the fee immediately. How much is it? Who pays it?

Know Your Rights!

It's a dog-eat-dog world out there, so you'd better know your legal rights before you start shopping for an apartment.

When people rent or sell a place to live, the law says they cannot discriminate because of a person's race, color, age, religion, or gender. They can't refuse to rent or sell to people because they're handicapped or come from other countries, either.

Unfortunately, some renters and sellers choose to ignore the housing laws. As a result, people are still discriminated against when they try to rent or buy housing. If you find yourself at the receiving end of bigotry, you can take these measures:

➤ Notify the city department of housing.

➤ Notify the state department of human rights.

➤ Notify the U.S. Department of Housing and Urban Development (HUD) at 1-800-669-9777.

Crib Notes

You can find the telephone numbers and addresses for your city's department of housing and your state's department of human rights in the blue pages of the telephone book.

Sign on the Dotted Line: Leases and Rental Agreements

A *lease* (or *rental agreement*) is a legal contract that states the responsibilities of the renter (*tenant*) and the landlord. According to the lease, *you* must pay a set amount of rent at a specific time (often the first of every month). The *landlord* must keep the apartment in good repair.

Most leases include other rules as well. For example, you might not be able to keep pets, make any changes to the apartment, or take in boarders.

Learn the Lingo

A **lease** is a written contract for an apartment or home rental.

Lease Language

While all leases differ in their specifics, they all contain the same general language. Here are some questions to ask yourself as you read the lease:

➤ For how long must I rent the apartment?

➤ What happens if I move out before the lease is over? Will I be liable for the rest of the rent?

➤ How much notice must I give before I move out? Usually, you have to give between 30 and 60 days' notice before you move or you'll be held responsible for the rest of the lease.

➤ Does the rent include utilities?

➤ What restrictions (if any) has the landlord placed on me? These restrictions might include no pets, no sublets, and so on.

Give and Take

NEVER sign a lease (or any legal document, for that matter) that contains language you don't understand or terms you don't agree to. If your signature is on the bottom line, your landlord won't be the one holding the bag—you will.

So what can you do if you don't agree with what's written on the lease? You have the right to talk to the landlord before you sign the lease and work out compromises. Parts of the lease can be crossed out and new parts written in.

Here's the "lease" you need to know:

➤ *Always* **get a lease.** A lease affords you legal protection. NEVER take the landlord's word that "You don't need a lease; we trust each other" or "I'll knock off $50 a month if we don't sign a lease." You must have that legal protection against potential misunderstandings and arguments.

➤ *Always* **read your lease very carefully.** Take the time you need; don't let anyone pressure you to sign quickly.

➤ **Ask for help.** If you're signing a lease for the first time, don't be shy about asking your parents, former RA, or more experienced friends to help you interpret it. Another pair of eyes never hurts, especially when it comes to legal documents.

➤ **Be sure the lease is legal.** If something seems fishy, it probably is. If you think that you're being asked to agree to something illegal, get some help. Your college can help you get free or low-cost legal help.

➤ **Make sure you get a copy of the lease.** Keep the copy in a safe place. You'll need it if problems arise.

Below "C" Level

Warning: To many adults, college students have invisible "Take advantage of me" signs on their backsides. Don't be too cocky, too shy, or too foolish to get help with legal documents such as leases.

Below "C" Level

If you don't honor the lease, the landlord can use legal means to enforce it. You can be hauled into court. Fortunately, you have the same right to seek legal relief if the landlord doesn't hold up his end of the agreement.

College is the ideal opportunity to expand your horizons. Moving off campus can help you assert your independence and learn to deal with the problems of everyday life. If you're ready to take this step, approach it with confidence and enthusiasm.

The Least You Need to Know

➤ Consider your reasons, expenses, roommates, and transportation before you decide to move off campus.

➤ Housing options include single rooms and apartments.

➤ Be sure the neighborhood is safe, close to campus, clean, and quiet.

➤ You can find a place to live through real estate ads, word-of-mouth, and real estate brokers.

➤ Housing discrimination is illegal. If you're a victim of this bigotry, take legal action.

➤ Always get a lease, read it carefully, get help if you need it, and don't be intimidated into signing something you don't understand or cannot honor.

Chapter 22

I Get Around

In This Chapter

➤ Studying abroad

➤ Taking time off

➤ Internships

➤ Transferring to another college

At some point, you'll probably consider spending a semester or a year abroad to immerse yourself in another culture and polish your language skills. Or you might want to take some time off to clear your head and earn some money. Perhaps you want to take an internship to acquire business skills and make valuable industry contacts. Maybe you want to transfer to another college, perhaps to get a wider variety of experiences or to move up a step in the world. In this chapter, we'll discuss all these choices.

A Semester in Spain, a Year in Yugoslavia

You've decided it's time to see the world. Good for you! Here's what Terrence McGlynn of the University of San Diego says about undergraduate study abroad:

> "If you talk to any student who has gone abroad, they really, really, really liked it. Think about where you want to go, and plan your class schedule so that you can do it in your junior year. A year abroad is way better than a semester. Yeah, you'll miss your friends and family and all that, but how often do you get to join another culture?"

Terrence is right on target: While you have the time, energy, and freedom, immerse yourself in another culture. Most colleges sponsor their own overseas programs, and some even have extension campuses in other countries. That way, all your credits are accepted without question.

Washington College in Maryland, for example, sponsors more than 40 study-abroad programs. Alison Dorosz, an environmental studies major at Washington College, took advantage of this bounty and spent the spring semester of her junior year in Siena, Italy. She loved it so much she stayed through the summer. Here's what Alison had to say:

> "I would recommend that every college student study abroad. It is such an amazing experience. You learn so much and you gain a sense of independence and self-reliance because you can't go home to mom and dad to solve every little problem. In learning to make new friends in a foreign country, I grew up so much."

Pack Your Bags

Why study abroad for a semester or a year? Below are my top six reasons why you should be applying for a passport and buying guidebooks:

1. **You save money.** Here's one of the best-kept secrets in higher education: You can usually save a bundle by studying in a foreign college because the tuition and living costs are often far lower abroad.

Crib Notes

A federal government pamphlet, "Study and Teaching Opportunities Abroad," offers useful travel tips, funding ideas, and work opportunities. It's available from the Government Printing Office, Washington, DC 20402.

2. **You broaden your horizons.** You'll get a much broader education by taking classes not available in your home college, studying with a different set of professors, and traveling in a foreign country.

3. **You meet new people.** If you're lucky, your college has students from around the world. In most cases, however, people tend to stick close to home. As a result, your college classmates are just like your high school classmates. It's time to meet people from different cultures!

4. **You get the inside edge.** "As the world changes, it becomes mandatory for more and more majors to spend time abroad, learning how to haggle in the markets or jump on a bus that never stops. These are just some of the skills all students may have to develop," says John Buettner, Washington University.

5. **You improve your language skills.** By studying abroad, you can more easily learn a foreign language or polish the one you mangled in high school.

6. **You have fun.** Savor a freshly baked French baguette by the Seine as the sun dapples the sidewalk. Or listen to Big Ben toll the hour as you sketch the Thames. I've had these experiences, and I'd go back in a flash!

Around the World in Eighty Days

"You can do anything you want in college, and it's a horrible shame not to do everything you want. Unless you need to spend your summers earning money, travel to a place where they don't speak English and you can pay your rent and feed yourself for a few bucks a day. Since most of the world is like this, finding such a place shouldn't be hard."

—Terrence McGlynn, the University of San Diego

The following guidelines can help you find reputable overseas study programs and decide which destination best suits your interests and personality.

1. **Do your homework.** As we've already discussed, you'll have your pick of countries and programs. When you narrow down the list, check with students who have already been on the programs that interest you. Be sure the program is reputable and meets your expectations. Will you be studying with full-time professors or part-time moonlighters? Will your home college accept the credits you earn abroad?

2. **Watch your wallet.** Be sure you understand exactly what you're paying and what you're getting for your money. Check especially for "hidden fees" that aren't stated outright in the contract. Possibilities include necessities such as accident insurance, medical insurance, and cancellation fees.

3. **Look for problems in paradise.** What happens if you get sick while you're abroad? Or if you hate the country? How will the sponsor deal with a family emergency that requires you to return home early? See what arrangements the sponsor has made for students in trouble.

4. **Consider special needs.** If you have special needs, such as dietary or physical restrictions,

Below "C" Level

If you can't get the answers you need from the program sponsors or are treated rudely, drop the program from your list. If the sponsors are distant or obnoxious now, it will only get worse when you're on their home turf.

be sure they can be met. I've been truly fortunate to have traversed huge swathes of the world. As a result, I can state from firsthand experience that Greece, Turkey, England, Ireland, France, Egypt, and Mexico ignore the phrase "handicapped accessible." There are virtually NO special provisions made in these countries for the physically disabled.

Extra Credit

"For travel abroad, get one of those books that claim you can see Europe on $30 a day, or whatever it is now. I spent two months knocking around Europe with that book. It has numbers for hostels and cheap hotels, and vital info for each country. Also I got an unlimited Eurail pass, which helped tremendously."

—Susan Wright, New York University

Crib Notes

ALWAYS carry your current, valid student ID when you study or travel abroad. In many countries, students get in free or at greatly reduced fees to museums, art galleries, and tourist attractions.

5. **Check living arrangements.** American students in general are used to what people in other countries consider luxurious living arrangements. When you evaluate study-abroad programs, check that the housing is in a safe part of town. Be sure it's clean, too. You don't want to find that your promised five-star hotel is really a roach motel.

6. **Don't ignore weather conditions.** If you don't do well in the heat, Egypt or Israel in the summer is likely to send you over the edge. If rain depresses you, cross off much of Europe in the winter. For some people, weather doesn't matter, but others are miserable in certain climes. Know yourself.

7. **Bring a buddy.** Yes, I know you're supposed to be breaking off on your own, but having a buddy along makes foreign travel much easier. You will still meet many new people, but you'll have a backup if there's a problem.

8. **Stick with it.** There's a lot of legwork involved in evaluating an overseas program of study, but it's worth the time and trouble if you're interested in it. Figure on spending at least a full semester finding the program that's right for you.

Stop the World, I Want to Get Off!

Solving complex math equations. Writing mile-long term papers. Studying for brutal tests. Taking brutal tests. Choosing classes. Getting closed out of classes and having to choose again. Dealing with rejection from fraternities, sororities, and other groups. No one said that college was going to be easy.

Perhaps you've decided you need a break from college. Maybe you've just graduated from high school and you don't want to start college right away. In either case, you need time off to catch your breath and decide what shape you want your life to take.

Recognizing that students who are ready for college do far better than those who aren't, many colleges (especially elite ones) recommend that students take a year off between high school and college. If you suspect that college isn't right for you now (and maybe not ever), I advise you to postpone college and get a job. I've had far too many students sitting in my classes just keeping their seat warm. They don't want to be there but they're expected to be. So they sit, breathe, and zone out. No one benefits.

If you're already in college and you're miserable, decide what the problem is—whether it's you, the college, or family factors. Is the college too urban? Too suburban? Are you too far away from home? Too close? Have you given yourself enough time to sort out your feelings about a two- or four-year educational commitment?

Before you make any decisions you might regret, carefully consider the advantages and disadvantages of delaying college enrollment for a year or taking some time off from college once you're already there. Here are the advantages of an education time-out:

Below "C" Level

Be careful here: If you drop out of college, you may have to start repaying your college loans. Before you decide to leave, check the fine print on any college loan agreements you have.

➤ You can earn money to apply to your education.

➤ You won't waste money for credits you're not ready to complete.

➤ You can become more self-confident.

➤ You can become more mature.

And the disadvantages of an education time-out:

➤ Earning your own money can make it difficult to return to school. You'll get used to having the cash and freedom.

➤ It's hard to get a high-paying job without a college degree.

➤ You might waste your time drifting rather than using it constructively.

➤ Time flies and it's much harder to earn a college degree when you're older. You feel out of step and often have greater responsibilities than the other students.

If you do decide to postpone college or leave before getting your degree, think about these suggestions:

➤ Don't burn your bridges. Be sure to leave on good terms with everyone.

➤ Save your money to use on tuition. Your parents may not be willing to foot the bill again.

➤ Use your time well. Don't waste your life daydreaming, playing video games, or hanging out.

Crib Notes

Some schools give credit for "life experience." You're most likely to get this type of credit if you're studying for a degree in business. Check with schools that interest you.

Crib Notes

"If you are short of cash, this is a good tip. If you are at the University of Pennsylvania, New York University, or another big-city school, many places in the city will have student discounts. You can probably get into movies, plays, concerts, and such stuff for a discount. Always have your ID on you."

—Stephanie Muntone, Oberlin College

Hands-On Training: Internships

Jobs are work you do in exchange for money. *Internships* are work you do in exchange for experience in your field of study. If you get lucky, you may find a paid internship, but even the "hot" internships may be freebies.

Internships have several advantages over regular jobs:

➤ Working in your field of study helps you see if you really like that field of study. If not, you can tweak or change your major before you've taken too many classes.

➤ Learning important career skills that you often can't learn in the classroom.

➤ Making valuable contacts. In some cases, summer interns are hired for permanent jobs after they graduate from college.

You can find internships through your college career office and through professors. Many companies post internships on the Internet. Also check campus bulletin boards; companies may post notices for summer and vacation interns there. Finally, companies often send representatives to colleges to recruit interns directly.

We Gotta Get Out of This Place: Transferring

"Give it a full semester before you decide this is the wrong school for you. Give yourself time to fit in and find your feet. You'll be able to transfer your credits, so you won't have wasted your time. However, take into account that if you change schools, you will be the new kid among a bunch of people who have already had time to get to know each other."

—Stephanie Muntone, Oberlin College

Stephanie makes some excellent points. It's rare that you immediately know you're in the wrong place. It takes time to settle in, at least a semester. How can you tell if you should transfer to another school?

Consider transferring when …

➤ Your college doesn't have your major.

➤ Another college decides to offer you a full ride and you need the cash.

➤ You've raised your grades and your first-choice school now accepts you.

➤ There's a family problem and you must be closer to home.

Don't consider transferring when …

➤ You want to be closer to your sweetheart. Beth Bolger, currently a student at Queens College, has transferred twice. She advises: "If you decide to transfer, make sure it's for the right reasons. Transferring to be near your boyfriend/girlfriend will most likely end up in a negative GPA!"

➤ You're vaguely dissatisfied and can't put your finger on the reasons why.

➤ You're searching for a place where you fit in.

Nearly all transfer students lose credits, because not all classes are automatically accepted by every college. As Scott Palma, a transfer student to Hofstra University, says from firsthand experience, "See which school is going to take more of your credits before you transfer. If you can stay at your present college a bit longer and get a degree before you transfer, by all means do it. It is easier to transfer your credits if you have a two-year degree. The degree may make the difference between getting a scholarship from your new school."

In addition, many colleges require you to have at least a C to transfer a grade—and sometimes even a B. Your current school might give you credit for a D, whereas you might not get credit if you transfer. In general, basic classes such as Freshman Composition and Intro to Psychology are more readily accepted for transfer than electives such as The Golem or Underwater Fire Prevention.

Before you decide to transfer, consult with your advisor and your parents. Tour the new college, too, to see if it meets your expectations. If possible, try to spend at least a weekend staying there. Attend classes and meet students.

The Least You Need to Know

➤ Spending a semester or year studying abroad can save you money and broaden your horizons. You'll also become more competitive in the marketplace, learn a foreign language, and have fun.

➤ If you decide to study abroad, do your prep work carefully to make sure you deal with a reputable program and get what you're promised.

➤ Taking a break from college has pros and cons. Think the decision through carefully.

➤ Internships are a great way to decide on a major, acquire important career skills, and make valuable business connections.

➤ Transferring to another college is a serious decision. Speak with your advisor and your parents before you make the break.

Chapter 23

So, What Do You Want to Be When You Grow Up?

In This Chapter

➤ Planning your future

➤ Taking charge of your life

➤ Finding your hidden skills

➤ Participating in extracurricular activities

➤ Understanding the hot skills employers want

Time flies when you're having fun. Nowhere is this reality more true than in college. Blink and suddenly you're a junior. Blink again, and you're a senior. This is scary but not bad, because it means you're getting ready to begin the next part of your life: Grown-Up Adult Person.

To be a Grown-Up Adult Person and deal with the challenges of the wonderful world of work, you've got to start making plans while you're still an undergraduate. This chapter will help you formulate the next part of your life. You'll be better equipped to get the classes and preparation you need before you find yourself out the door.

Sitting in the Hot Seat

➤ "So, what are your plans now that high school is over?"

➤ "Going to enter the family business, eh?"

➤ "We know you're right on track, as always."

➤ "We've always expected you to be a doctor (lawyer, Indian chief, etc.)."

➤ "Got your future all mapped out, right?"

It's a time-honored tradition that at the ripe old age of 18, teenagers are expected to know exactly what they want to do with the rest of their lives. Whether it's entering the work force directly after high school, enrolling in a technical school, earning a two-year associate's degree, or going for a four-year B.A., you're supposed to have your future carved in granite. After all, isn't that all you've been hearing since high school graduation?

Maybe you *do* have a clear idea of your future. If so, congratulations—you're in the minority. A few students have a general idea of their future plans, but most students don't have the slightest idea. As a result, many take general degrees in liberal arts, psychology, English, or business.

Or they let themselves be pushed into careers that seem right or are expected of them. Are you good in math? Then you're clearly destined to be an accountant or engineer. Are you good in biology? No doubt about it: It's medicine for you. Do you have a talent for working with people? Then better high-tail it over to the business department. What if you're really not good at anything much? In that case, you'd better major in computer science because there's a lot of jobs there. You might hate it, but you'll make money and finally get off the family dole.

Below "C" Level

Never assume that you'll be a hot job prospect just because you have a degree—even a degree from an elite school. It takes a lot more than a piece of paper to make a person hirable.

Pretty grim, eh? No wonder 75 percent of all college students change their major at least once!

The stress of the situation is enough to drive anyone crazy. Perhaps so many adults are unhappy with their jobs 10 years after college because they were forced to decide on a career before they even knew who they really were or what they wanted to be.

To Boldly Go Where No One Has Gone Before

So what can you do if you're in the majority and don't know what you want to do? Try the following suggestions.

Take Risks

College is the time to explore different fields. Even if you're 100 percent certain of your career plans, take electives in areas that interest you. After all, this might be the last chance you have to stretch your horizons. And if you don't have any idea what you want to do after college, how better to find out than by taking classes in different areas of study?

Stephanie Muntone from Oberlin College advises:

"Try everything you are interested in as far as classes are concerned. Most people don't know what they want to do with the rest of their lives when they get to college. This is the time to find out. Take classes in all the different subjects you think would be neat. I didn't decide on a major until I was in my final semester. I don't necessarily recommend that, but no need to decide this before you are ready."

Get Your Priorities in Order

Figure out what you want not just in a career but also in life. You'll be much happier if you tailor your career to your personal goals rather than drift into something because it seems easy, convenient, or popular. As you ponder your future, ask yourself these questions:

➤ What is more important to me: challenging work or an easy ride?

➤ How important is earning a lot of money?

➤ How do I feel about the rewards of public service, such as theology, social work, or teaching?

➤ Is fame my goal?

➤ How important is job security? Do I welcome career change or fear it?

➤ Am I more comfortable working with people or ideas?

➤ Do I want to center my life around my job, my family, my community, my faith, or something else?

➤ Do I want a job that carries a great deal of status?

➤ Do I consider myself ambitious or laid-back?

➤ Where do I want to live? In a city or the country? In America or abroad? Someplace warm or cold?

Crib Notes

Second-language proficiency makes you much more appealing on the job market. Now is a good time to polish your language skills by taking extra foreign-language classes.

Learn the Lingo

Freelancers are independent contractors in any field, not just writing. The term "freelance" comes from the Middle Ages, when knights not affiliated with monarchs offered their "lance" for hire.

If you ask yourself nothing else, ask yourself the humdinger: *What's really important to me?* For example, if money is your main priority, make sure you prepare for a career that pays big bucks. Or, if you prefer working on your own, study for a career that rewards lone eagles, such as freelance writing.

Follow Your Heart

Mark Wong, from the Academy of Art College in San Francisco, shared this advice:

> "Do what YOU want to do. Art is my passion and my parents were supportive, so I was lucky. You need to understand that you're going to do this for the rest of your life. Make the choice now and enjoy your craft. That passion has kept me going from the beginning. Now I'm an art director at a marketing agency in Silicon Valley."

But Be Real

It IS important to do what you want with the rest of your life, but that might not always be possible. Few people have the luxury of succeeding as actors or musicians, for example. Follow your heart, but have a backup plan. For every Billy Crystal and Rosie O'Donnell, we have lots and lots of theater majors asking, "Want fries with that?" To make sure you're not one of these McWorkers, explore alternative careers *now* that suit your interests and abilities.

Consider the Marketplace

Your college no doubt offers some fascinating majors—philosophy, psychology, women's studies, ethnic literature, and so on. While these are great subjects to study, what can you do with them? In some cases, you must have a graduate degree in order to use your skills. That's fine if you want a graduate degree—but not so fine if you've already got hefty loans and you're itching to get into the job market.

If you really want to study something unusual such as modern dance but don't see any practical applicability to it, why not make it a minor? Find a major that complements your minor and can lead to a career you enjoy. Modern dance would go well with physical therapy, exercise physiology, or physical education, for example.

Think Outside the Box

Recognize that many jobs you might like don't even exist today. As you rank your priorities and explore different fields, keep yourself open to new possibilities. Perhaps you'll find just the right job—or perhaps you'll create it yourself!

Get Good Skills

To make sure you can leap on opportunities as they arise, arm yourself with the skills you need to succeed. Now is the time to take the more challenging class rather than the easier one. Take a few classes in up-and-coming fields. If you're paying with a flat fee rather than by the credit, why not take a few extra classes in promising areas, such as computer science and finance? Take extra classes in important areas such as English and writing. Make sure you have a solid, well-rounded education.

Don't Be Fooled by Hype

Some careers read better than they play. For example, lawyers make heaps of money—or do they? The market for lawyers is so overcrowded in some areas that many newly minted lawyers are having a tough time paying their rent. Check into a field to make sure it's really what you think it is.

Network

Use the resources available to you on campus to find out about careers. Check out the career counseling office for leads to careers that suit your interests.

All colleges have professors who are leaders in their fields. Find the ones in areas that interest you and spend time learning about the career as well as the skills it requires. Mark Wong (Academy of Art College, San Francisco) was lucky enough to realize this early: "My instructors were actual working professionals. I was able to pick their brains and learn a lot about the art field."

Here are some other ways to get information about careers:

➤ Read, read, read. Check trade journals in your field, the occupational guides available in the library, yearly stock reports, and the daily newspapers.

➤ Speak to alumni when they visit campus. Ask them what their jobs are really like. How do they see the prospects in the field for new graduates?

➤ Discuss careers with parents, relatives, and neighbors. Do they like their jobs? Why or why not?

➤ Talk with former bosses, especially people with whom you interned. Do they think you'd like their specific jobs? Why or why not?

➤ Talk to people through informational interviews.

➤ Try out careers by shadowing professionals. To do so, follow them around as they carry out their daily tasks.

The help is out there, but it's not going to come to you. You have to seek it out.

Go for It!

Whatever you decide to do, do it with passion and gusto. You stand a far better chance of succeeding if you're enthusiastic about your career plans. Care about what you're doing, or change your major.

It's terrifying to think about your future, but you can't be a student forever. Too many people enter graduate school not to pursue further education, but to avoid having to make a decision about a career.

You're not a failure if you don't have the rest of your life mapped out—but don't let the days slip by in a pleasant haze, either. Today is the first day of the rest of your life. It's a cliché, but today *is* a fresh start. Resolve to plan your career *now*.

Hidden in Plain Sight

Of course, none of my advice will hold water unless you recognize your skills and abilities, your strengths and weaknesses. So before we go any further, it's time to zero in on what makes you special and what makes you happy.

Don't panic if you've never given this any thought before; after all, in high school you most likely signed up for the regular complement of classes—English, history, science, math, and so on—without giving it much thought. Even if you hated some of these classes, you didn't have a choice: They were required for graduation. And even if you loved art, music, gym, psychology, and other "enrichment" classes, there probably wasn't much room in your schedule for more than a handful.

Below "C" Level

Weigh all the information you get carefully. Some relatives, for example, are quick to offer warnings about certain career fields—although they have little knowledge of those fields. Friends, roommates, classmates, and significant others often offer similar warnings, frequently based on what they've heard from someone else.

Now you *do* have a choice. You might not be able to match all your interests with your college classes, but you *can* tailor your education to suit your unique personality. This is especially true when you reach your junior and senior years. Start by figuring out what you're good at.

Talent Scouts

➤ A professional wrestler runs for governor of Minnesota and wins.

➤ My favorite neighborhood chef is a former cleaning-supply salesman.

➤ An opera singer becomes a computer hotshot for Oracle computers.

How did these people get where they are today? Through a combination of luck, confidence, and lots of self-awareness. As you contemplate where your own career might take you after college, it's impossible to know what opportunities fate may throw your way. What you can do, however, is identify your interests, talents, and values, then explore occupations that might make good use of them. If you follow the three-step process in the next section, "What Are Friends For?" you won't just be sitting back waiting for jobs to land in your lap. You'll be working toward discovering what makes you happy.

What Are Friends For?

Ironically, other people can often spot skills in you that you never realized you had. That's because many of us are simply too close to ourselves to recognize our own abilities. Sometimes it's difficult to see what's right in front of you.

Try the following easy three-step process to see what I mean:

1. Ask two or three friends to jot down all the skills and abilities they think you have. Here are some possibilities:

   ➤ Knowing how to develop a Web site

   ➤ Dealing well with people

   ➤ Writing well and quickly

2. Write down what skills *you* think you have.

3. Compare lists. You'll find that you've listed some skills your friends don't know about. You'll also discover that some of your friends listed skills you didn't include.

Your favorites among these skills will likely point you in an appealing career direction to explore—one you may not have considered.

Crib Notes

Most employers like to hire grads who can show that they've worked with a wide range of people in a variety of settings. Being involved in extracurricular activities can give you that crucial edge when the job comes down to you and one other candidate.

Kid 'n' Play

Participating in extracurricular activities can help you find and develop hidden talents. If you are not yet involved in any on-campus activities, there's still time to join.

Try to hold an office within an organization, since this can help you decide whether you prefer to lead or follow. If you don't have time to hold an office in an organization (or if you don't get elected), look for other leadership opportunities, such as heading up committees.

As a bonus, on-campus involvement can strengthen a resumé as well as any off-campus experience can. It can also introduce you to people whom you might not otherwise have met.

Hot Skills Employers Want

Experts who study trends in hiring find that most employers, regardless of the industry, look for the same basic skills when hiring. Fortunately for you, you're most likely to develop these skills during college. Here are the skills and abilities you need to be a hot prospect on the job market:

➤ Being proficient in writing and speech

➤ Synthesizing information and understanding what you read

➤ Understanding and showing an interest in other cultures

➤ Getting along with diverse groups of people

➤ Knowing how to conduct research

➤ Taking the initiative while knowing your place in the corporate structure

➤ Having a strong work ethic

➤ Working well in teams as well as on your own

➤ Setting goals and working to fulfill them

➤ Being willing to learn new skills

➤ Being well-groomed, well-mannered, and pleasant

As a college student, you already possess a number of these hot skills. Now that you know what you need, you can fill in any gaps. Right now, you can choose electives with an eye to building some of these necessary skills. For example, why not take some classes in small-group communication, research techniques, and public speaking? Position yourself for success in life—just as you've positioned yourself for success in college.

The Least You Need to Know

➤ Take risks, get your priorities in order, and follow your heart, but consider the marketplace.

➤ Think outside the box, acquire key skills, and don't be fooled by hype. Network to shape your future.

➤ Recognize your skills and abilities so you can build on your strengths and minimize your weaknesses.

➤ Participate in extracurricular activities to find and develop hidden talents.

➤ Take classes now to build the skills you'll need in the marketplace.

Chapter 24

Moving Toward Graduation

In This Chapter

➤ Verifying degree requirements

➤ Planning for graduation

➤ Enjoying the Big Day: Commencement

➤ Considering graduate school

➤ Getting your first job

One door closes and another one opens, the pundits say. They're right. As your college career winds down, it's time to look ahead.

Oh, Was This a Four-Year Program?

Yes, it was. Assuming that you attend college full-time, a two-year degree is meant to be completed in two years; a four-year degree, in four years. This isn't to say you can't take longer to complete your degree if you need to, but eventually you should finish your degree and graduate. "Eventually" should be sooner rather than later.

As you move into the fast lane for graduation, check to make sure you have all your requirements and enough credits to graduate. At least once a year, verify that …

➤ All your grades have been recorded in the registrar's office. Glitches in the system and instructor errors are not uncommon.

➤ All your credits have been correctly totaled. Yes, errors in addition do occur, even with computers.

➤ Any transfer credits or study-abroad credits have been included.

➤ You have satisfied degree requirements completely.

Below "C" Level

Students who don't turn in proof of inoculations can have their grades purged. Make sure you're up to date on all your required inoculations and that you've filed the proof with the health office.

All of this is your responsibility, not your advisor's, the registrar's, or your parents'. If there is a problem with your record, the sooner you discover it, the easier it will be to resolve.

Erika Timar of the University of California at Davis found out the importance of keeping her records timely the hard way. Here's what Erika told me:

"I miscalculated the number of units I needed for a minor, and my advisor didn't catch it. She was a semi-famous artist who didn't really want to be working as an advisor. I wish I had asked someone else to double-check my course list before graduation, because I would have taken another art class, and I could now be teaching it."

Getting Your Ducks in a Row

By senior year, you should get everything set up for graduation. Since this is such an important day for you and your family, you want everything to go smoothly. Follow these steps to ensure a wonderful graduation experience:

1. **Meet with your advisor.** You've already checked your transcript. Now schedule a meeting with your advisor to go over your papers once again. Thank your advisor for his or her help over the years. If your advisor has been especially helpful, write a formal thank-you note.

2. **File all graduation forms.** In most cases, you must file an "Intent to Graduate" form. You might also have to pay a fee. Keep copies of all the forms you file and a copy of your canceled check.

3. **Order your cap and gown.** Usually, this is done through the bookstore. Get it done, because you won't be allowed to march in the procession without the proper academic garb.

4. **Pay all fees (library, traffic, etc.).** You won't be allowed to graduate if you owe the university money. Make sure that your account is fully paid. If there's a problem, work out a payment schedule.

5. **Get graduation tickets.** You may or may not need tickets for family members and friends. Find out well ahead of time so you can get your tickets before they're all given out.

6. **Make hotel reservations.** Over 33,000 students flock to Boston every year to attend college. Imagine what the town looks like when all those colleges are holding graduation ceremonies! Smaller towns may have even more trouble accommodating visitors. If you expect people from home to share your moment of triumph, make sure you've made hotel reservations well in advance. Rooms get booked fast, so figure at least six months lead time on this.

A Milestone to Celebrate

Commencement—graduation—is a tradition that reaches back nearly 1,000 years. It symbolizes not so much the culmination of years of effort on the part of both students and teachers but rather the beginning (the commencement) of a productive social and professional life, a life of continued learning.

> **Learn the Lingo**
>
> Graduation ceremonies are called **commencement** exercises because they are the beginning of your professional life.

Cap and Gown

There are three basic parts of the academic outfit: the *cap,* the *gown,* and the *hood.* Three factors determine each aspect of the uniform: the degree (B.A., M.A., Ph.D.), the branch of knowledge (art, science, engineering, business administration, etc.), and the university granting the degree. Let's look at each part of the commencement outfit so you can appreciate its significance:

➤ **The cap.** The cap is black with a tassel fastened at midpoint. The tassel is worn to the left side until a B.A. has been conferred; it is then worn on the right.

➤ **The gown.** The gown is black for Bachelor's degrees, worn closed. Many American universities now have gowns of characteristic color for doctoral graduates. For instance, the graduates of Harvard may wear crimson gowns.

➤ **The hood.** The hood's shape and size represent the degree of the wearer. The hood's lining indicates the university granting the degree. The velvet trim on the hood indicates the major field of knowledge.

Everyone Loves a Parade

Commencement begins and ends with the academic procession, led by the chief marshal carrying the mace (a wooden, torch-like club). The ceremony officially begins when the mace is placed before the graduates and ends when the chief marshal retrieves it and leads the recession. The color guard follows the marshal, with the candidates for degrees marching behind in reverse order of seniority (Bachelor's first,

Master's next, and Doctoral third). The faculty follows, also proceeding in reverse order from assistant professor to full professor. The final group to enter is the platform party, composed of academic deans, administrative officers, trustees, honorary degree recipients, and the university president.

It's a glorious day, and you should not miss it!

Extra Credit

The University of Bologna, the first university, was founded in Italy in 1162 and offered specialized education in the major professional fields of the medieval world: law, medicine, government, and theology. From Bologna, the concept of a university education spread throughout Europe and later to America. The pageantry and symbolism of commencement are represented by the cap and gown, the everyday dress of medieval scholars.

Here are some hints to get the most enjoyment from your moment of well-earned glory:

➤ Don't skip the rehearsals. You want to know what you're doing when you march down the aisle.

➤ The university issues commemorate booklets. They are handed out at the door or placed on seats. Be sure to get one because they make lovely keepsakes.

➤ There is almost always a reception after commencement. This is one of the traditional photo ops, as your classmates, professors, deans, and university officials will be there to pose for pictures with you.

➤ Academic robes are heavy and graduation days are usually warm, so wear something cool, comfortable, and appropriate under your robe.

➤ If you rent your robe, don't forget to return it. Otherwise, you'll forfeit your security deposit.

Below "C" Level

Some dopes invariably disrupt this solemn, special day by throwing things and talking during the speeches. Act with decorum to help maintain the dignity of the occasion.

Let the Good Times Roll

Home Sweet College. It's so tempting to stay for a few more years, especially when the outside world seems so cold and harsh. After all, the real world has all those 6:30 A.M. commuter trains and buses, and you managed to avoid 8:00 classes for four years.

How do you decide whether to go to graduate school, and if so, when? In some cases, you don't have a choice. You can't be a lawyer without graduating from law school; ditto for doctors and medical school. You *must* have graduate credentials to get the job.

> **Crib Notes**
>
> If you finish all your course work and graduate in the winter or summer, come back and participate in the big spring commencement. It's worth the trip.

You Snooze, You Lose

If your career goal demands a graduate degree, you're best off soldiering straight through without a break. Here are some important reasons:

➤ The sooner you start, the sooner you finish.

➤ You're likely to have fewer personal commitments now than you'll have later.

➤ The cost of the degree will only go up, so the sooner you study, the less you'll pay.

➤ If you pause in your education, you might lose momentum and end up doing something you really don't want to do.

The Pause That Refreshes

If you *do* have the choice of whether or not to continue straight on to graduate school, I strongly advise you to work for several years before you return to school. Entering the work force gives you valuable hands-on experience that can help you decide if you really do need a graduate degree. Some graduate programs (especially those in business) believe so strongly in work experience that they won't even accept you until you've been working for several years. Furthermore, a surprisingly large number of employers will pay for your education if they decide it's in their best interests to have you acquire further training.

Ask yourself these questions as you ponder the decision to stay in the academy a few more years:

1. What will this degree get me that I don't already have?

2. Do I *need* this degree or do I *want* it?

3. Am I sure this is a field I want to pursue or am I floundering?

4. Can I afford to incur more debt?

5. Will there be a job for me when I complete this degree?

November of your senior year is the latest date to think realistically about applying to grad school for next year. If you do decide to attend graduate school, check into programs carefully. In some careers (such as corporate law, business, and academic medicine) the best jobs go to graduates of the most prestigious schools. In other fields, such as education and engineering, the choice of schools is not as crucial.

Playing with the Big Kids

"Get serious about graduating. I didn't understand the corporate interview concept and had very few in my senior year because of it."

—Mike Flynn, Georgetown University

Crib Notes

Graduate schools are highly political places with professors and students jockeying for power. The prizes—jobs, fellowship, publication opportunities—go to the sharks. Be sure you can swim in these waters before you dive in.

Here's the first cold, brutal truth about getting a job: If you place all your trust in any person, system, piece of paper, or electronic mechanism to help you find your first job out of school, you might as well go bury yourself in graduate school while you wait for the world to change.

But the world won't change. American business isn't in business to hire people. The sooner you learn that, the quicker you'll be on your way to becoming a profitable employee for a great company.

Extra Credit

"You won't find your dream job right out of school, and many people are working in jobs that have no relevance to what they majored in. So I think it's best to actually go through college learning about a subject area you are interested in. Liberal arts majors are more well-rounded anyway because of it."

—Jill Semko, Indiana University

No matter what you've heard about the booming economy, it's all meaningless if you don't take career matters into your own hands. No matter how high your GPA, how many campus recruiters you've met, or how many hours you've spent in the career center, the job market can crush you under a mountain of no's.

The task of choosing a career field and breaking into it can seem overwhelming, so here are a few concrete actions you can take to get the process rolling. (I've placed the job search information after the graduation material in this chapter, but I know that you've been searching for a job since the second half of your senior year. And maybe even earlier.)

Crib Notes

For help with resumé writing, check out monster.com's content.monster.com/resume/. Also visit your campus career center for assistance.

1. **Start your career research.** Choose companies or organizations that you think you might like to work for and learn something about them. Look up their Web sites and call companies' public relations or human resources offices to request some literature on them.

2. **Write a resumé or revise an old one.** You need to have an up-to-date resumé on hand.

3. **Start or expand a portfolio.** Gather material that reflects your accomplishments and skills, such as writing samples, letters of recommendation, certificates or honors, and work samples from internships or class projects.

Learn the Lingo

A **portfolio** is any formal collection of your best work, such as art, musical compositions, writing, or computer programs, for example.

4. **Get the clothes.** You've got to dress the part to get the part. Buy yourself clothing appropriate to the career you wish to pursue: a banker's good navy blue suit, briefcase, and business shoes, for example. Then you're all set when you're called for interviews.

   And while we're here: Unless you're an artist, you should probably ditch the piercings, cover the tattoos, and let the mohawk grow out and return to its original color.

5. **Learn the manners.** If you're rusty on table manners, it's time to brush up. Ditto on phone etiquette, spelling, and all the conventions of civilized adults.

6. **Go on informational interviews.** Do lots of networking and go on as many informational interviews as possible, preferably *before* you graduate. You'll get valuable advice about your career options and your job search strategy. You'll also make contacts that could be helpful in the future.

7. **Join a networking organization.** If you haven't already done so, find out about student memberships in professional associations in fields that interest you.

8. **Attend a career-related event.** Such events include job fairs or career panels in which alumni come back to campus to talk about their jobs.

9. **Identify skills to develop.** Would you like to try your hand at managing people or do you need to improve your written communication skills? Now is the time to work on self-improvement.

10. **Stick with it.** Searching for a job isn't easy, and it can be discouraging when prospective employers don't come banging down your doors. If things go badly at first, take a deep breath and keep going.

One of the great adventures of your life has drawn to a close, and a whole new life is beginning. You've learned many valuable skills, made a slew of friends, and had some serious fun. But now it's time to move on to your next great adventure.

The Least You Need to Know

➤ Well before graduation, check that you have all your requirements and enough credits to graduate.

➤ Meet with your advisor, file all necessary forms, order your cap and gown, pay all fees, get graduation tickets, and make hotel reservations for the folks.

➤ Commencement is wonderful: Don't miss it.

➤ Unless graduate school is mandated for your career, you're usually better off working for several years before you earn a graduate degree.

➤ Pursue jobs intelligently and diligently.

Chapter 25

Your Brave New World

In This Chapter

➤ Being true to your school

➤ Relating to family on a new level

➤ Obtaining health and car insurance

➤ Paying college loans

➤ Dealing with legal issues

➤ Planning for your financial future

Commencement is over. Your parents have gone home; your friends have scattered around the globe. You're ready to begin an exciting new phase of your life. Congratulations! Now, take a deep breath and consider your next step.

Don't Be a Stranger

You've graduated from college, but that doesn't mean you sever all ties with your *alma mater*. There are many important reasons to keep in touch with the university as well as with your college friends:

➤ **Networking.** College professors and friends can help you make valuable business connections as you begin your career.

➤ **Career counseling.** College career officials can provide useful career assistance as you get those first jobs.

➤ **Continuing education.** Technology is changing so quickly that it's almost certain you'll have to brush up your skills—or develop new ones. You might take classes at your alma mater in the future or return for a graduate degree.

➤ **University resources.** College libraries are often far more complete than community libraries, which make them helpful for in-depth research. In addition, many large universities have museums, art galleries, health clubs, and other resources you can use for free or a nominal fee.

➤ **Social events.** It's fun to return to college for reunions, homecoming, and cultural events. (It's even more fun if you've aged better than your classmates.)

To make it easier for the alumni association to keep in touch with you, consider these suggestions:

Learn the Lingo

An **alma mater** is the school, college, or university from which a person has graduated. The term is Latin for "dear mother."

Crib Notes

Have your professors place copies of their recommendations with the career office. You can then request that your materials be sent to prospective employers.

1. **Keep your address current.** Send change-of-address cards to your college alumni association when you move.

2. **Maintain your e-mail account.** Increasingly, colleges are allowing students to keep their e-mail accounts for life, for free. Upon graduation, your student account automatically becomes your alumni account. Right now, Macalester College in St. Paul and Emory University in Atlanta offer free lifetime e-mail forwarding. Think of it as a virtual class ring.

3. **Join the alumni association.** In most cases, you're automatically enrolled in the alumni association when you graduate. If you have to fill out a form to join, do it. Even if you don't think you want to keep in touch, your feelings might change down the road.

4. **Give back.** Your college was good to you, so be good to it. Contribute a few dollars when you can afford it. If you want, earmark the funds for a cause close to your heart: a scholarship fund in the name of a departed friend, refurbishment of the soccer field, books for the library, and so on. Also contribute your time. Make calls for fund-raising campaigns; help muster support for building programs.

5. **Go back for visits.** Visit the campus now and again. You don't want to become one of those ridiculous grads who hangs around campus and gets all misty-eyed at football games, but neither do you want to forget where you spent some of the most important years of your life.

6. **Be true to your school.** Every school has its strengths and weaknesses. Even if your experience in college was less than positive, don't trash your school to others. If you can't say anything nice, don't say anything at all.

Crib Notes

Alumni often interview prospective candidates for admission. Consider becoming part of this worthwhile program.

You Can't Go Home Again—Even If You Do

"Start to develop a friendship with your parents."

—Terrence McGlynn, the University of San Diego

When you graduate from college, you might get a plum job immediately and move into an apartment on your own or with some friends. Or you may get a good job, marry your college honey, and start a sweet little love nest. Perhaps you begin graduate school on a full fellowship. Your parents smile, send e-mail once a month, and move on with their lives.

In many cases, however, recent college graduates move back in with their parents. They might be saving up for a place of their own or decide to attend graduate school close to home. Sometimes, events don't shake down the way the graduates thought and they're forced to return to their parents.

Don't assume that parents are automatically thrilled to have you back. They love you, but they also love their newfound closet space and all the quiet. They've no doubt turned your bedroom into a study, exercise center, or bedroom for your little sister, and they don't want to turn it back into your room. Much as they adore, worship, and venerate you, the sands of their life have shifted to fill your space.

It can be difficult for college graduates to accept that life has changed back home. If you *do* move back in with mom and dad after graduation, try these suggestions for avoiding nuclear explosions:

1. Understand that you can go home again, but it will never be the same as it was before you went to college four years ago.

2. Accept that you are no longer the center of the universe. That space may have been taken by a younger sibling, a pet, or an elderly parent, or may not yet be filled.

3. Recognize that your parents have lives of their own. They do not exist to serve you, pay for you, or do your laundry. Neither is it their job to cook for you, buy your clothes, or service your car. You're old enough to take care of yourself.

4. Pay rent. Even if it's a token amount, show that you're an adult by shouldering some of the economic responsibilities of running the household.

Below "C" Level

Be on your guard: The death of a pet can be extraordinarily difficult for newly returning graduates because the death comes to symbolize all the upsetting changes in their life.

5. Get off your keister. If you're not working, look for a job very actively. You're not on an extended vacation during which you play video games, experiment with new hairstyles, and sleep until 2:00 every afternoon.

6. Acknowledge that the family pet may not respond to you in the same outgoing friendly way. The pet might even have decamped to the Daisy Hill Puppy Farm.

7. You neighbors may look at you strangely and wonder who you are. Smile and nod.

8. Most important, realize that home will never be quite the same. It is that place you will probably always call home. However, it is the place you never plan to return to on a permanent basis. (Thanks to Ellen Nelson.)

College over, Financial Education Begins

Now that you've graduated, it's time to start your financial education in earnest. The typical college student graduates with a brain crammed with knowledge, some serious debts, and no health insurance.

Some of the most pressing financial issues new graduates like yourself face include health insurance, car insurance, college loans, legal issues, and planning for their financial future. Let's take a look at each issue in detail.

Don't Leave Home Without It: Insurance

Once students receive their diplomas, they are often unceremoniously dropped from their parents' health insurance policies. When this happens, you *must* buy health insurance that will cover you until benefits kick in with your new employer. Health insurance is one of your most important needs. Without it, one serious illness or accident could wipe you out financially—for life.

COBRA

First, check to see if you're eligible to extend the health coverage you had under your parents' plan through *COBRA (Consolidated Omnibus Budget Reconciliation Act)*. COBRA is often an expensive option, but the coverage is continuous.

You may want to use COBRA if you ...

➤ Had comprehensive medical benefits under your parents' policy.

➤ Like your current doctor.

➤ Have health problems or a history of medical problems.

➤ Must take expensive medications.

➤ Have been refused private health insurance.

➤ Had an accident within the 60-day window of enrollment.

➤ Are pregnant or planning to get that way.

Learn the Lingo

COBRA means **Consolidated Omnibus Budget Reconciliation Act,** a federal law that makes it possible for most people to continue to get health coverage for at least 18 months after their insurance is terminated.

In addition to exploring COBRA, ask your college if it offers temporary health benefits for graduates. Many colleges do. This is often a less expensive option than COBRA, although the coverage will likely not be as complete.

If you decide to buy a stop-gap health insurance policy, run a cost comparison with private insurance companies to see which option offers you the most coverage for the least money.

Never Assume ...

Not all employers offer health insurance. You might find this to be the case with your job, especially if you work for a small business or work part-time. If your employer doesn't offer health insurance, you might be able to get group insurance through membership in a labor union, professional association, club, or other organization.

If your employer doesn't offer group insurance or if the insurance offered is very limited, you can buy an individual policy. You can get fee-for-service, HMO (Health Maintenance Organization), or PPO (Preferred Provider Organization) protection.

Compare your options and shop carefully because coverage and costs vary from company to company. Individual plans may not offer benefits as broad as those in group plans.

Below "C" Level

Beware of single-disease insurance policies that offer protection for only one disease, such
as cancer. If you already have
health insurance, your regular
plan probably already provides
all the coverage you need.

Caveat Emptor

Before you buy any health insurance policy, make sure
you know what it will pay for and what it won't. To
find out about individual health insurance plans, you
can call insurance companies, HMOs, and PPOs in
your community, or speak to the agent who handles
your car or house insurance.

Follow these tips when shopping for individual insurance:

➤ Shop carefully. Policies differ widely in coverage
and cost. Contact different insurance companies and compare policies.

➤ Make sure the policy protects you from costly
medical costs.

➤ Read and understand the policy. Make sure it provides the kind of coverage
that's right for you.

Pooling the Risk: Car Insurance

While you were in college, you might not have needed your own car. Perhaps your
parents let you use the family wheels when you were home on vacation and they gra-
ciously picked up the tab for the insurance and gas.

But now you're on your own and you probably want and need a car. Here's the good
news for your parents: According to the Independent Insurance Agents of America,
auto-insurance premiums may drop by two-thirds once a younger, high-risk driver is
off their policy. Here's the bad news for you: You have to get your own policy and
pay for it yourself. Now that you've graduated, you are responsible for your insurance
needs. It's also safer from an insurance standpoint for you to have your own policy,
not to stay on your parents' policy.

Student Loans

About half of all college graduates leave school with debt. Among those, graduates of
public colleges owe an average of $11,950, while their counterparts at private schools
owe $14,290, according to the American Council on Education. Generally, student-
loan payments start six months after a student leaves school.

If you're in debt and have some extra cash—perhaps from graduation gifts—I strongly
suggest that you put it toward paying down loans. Here are your priorities:

➤ Pay the loans with the highest interest rate.

➤ Pay the loans that start accumulating interest the earliest.

If you enter a field where employers are fiercely competitive for workers, wait until you've been made an offer. On that sweet day, ask if the company will help pay your student loans. It's not uncommon to get this perk if you're a hot property in a hot field.

Legal Issues

Remember what you learned in Chapter 21, "A Little Place of My Own," about leases? Nothing has changed: The person whose name is on the lease and utility contracts is liable for the bills. If you want someone to share the responsibility with you, see if the landlord will allow more than one name on the lease.

If you don't have a job or a credit history and have a poor record paying bills, you may need your parents to co-sign a car loan or an apartment lease. Your parents will be on the hook if you renege on payments.

It's impossible to become financially independent if your parents are co-signing your loans. If you can't afford to buy or lease a new car, take public transportation and save your money until you can afford one. If you must have a car, buy an inexpensive used one and drive it until you can afford a better one.

Saving for a Bright Future

"Are you crazy, Rozakis?" you shout. "I don't have money for a bagel and schmeer, much less stock investments." So pack your own lunch and stop moaning. It's never too soon to start saving. Even if you can only sock away $10 a week, do it. Here are some ways to get a leg up on a secure financial future:

Extra Credit

Who gets the tax deduction when college grads are supported by parents for part of the year but self-supporting the rest of the year? Parents covering more than half a child's yearly expenses are entitled to the tax deduction. If a parent makes less than $250,000, it's almost always advantageous for the parent to take the deduction.

Crib Notes

"Working in the 'real' world is much like working on campus. Be punctual, take your work seriously, and be detail-oriented. Don't be afraid to ask questions, don't try to be everyone's friend. Know what your job duties are and don't let people dump their work on you because you're new."

—Sharon Li, University of San Francisco

➤ If it's available to you, participate in your employer's 401(k) retirement plan. Try to put in as much as you can.

➤ Open a Roth IRA (Individual Retirement Account).

➤ Learn as much as you can about financial investments. Read, read, read.

➤ Track your expenses and savings on a spreadsheet. Know where your money is and where it's going.

This year, salaries for new graduates range from the upper $20,000s (education and nonprofit jobs) to the high $40,000s (technical work). This means you should be on your feet shortly, earning good money and building an exciting new life. It's been a pleasure helping you on your way!

The Least You Need to Know

➤ Keep in touch with your alma mater.

➤ Your relationship with your family will change now that you've graduated. Forge adult friendships with your parents.

➤ Be sure you have health and car insurance.

➤ Start paying off college loans.

➤ Establish yourself as financially independent by signing your own apartment and car leases.

➤ Save for the future.

Glossary

alma mater   The school, college, or university from which a person has graduated. The term is Latin for "dear mother."

alumni   Graduates of a specific school or college.

area advisors (AAs)   Upper-class students hired to oversee underclass students. Also called *resident advisors* and *student advisors*.

ATMs   Automated teller machines.

balancing your checkbook   Doing the math to make sure your checkbook balance matches the bank's balance. (See also *reconciling a checkbook*.)

binge drinking   The consumption of five or more drinks in one sitting by a male, or four or more drinks by a female.

blue books   Test booklets, so called because of their blue covers.

bouncing a check   Writing a check for which you have insufficient funds in your checking account.

budget   A record of the way you manage your money.

cashing a check   Exchanging a check at the bank for money.

class   An individual's economic ranking based on wealth and the sources of wealth.

clinical depression (or unipolar depression)   A mood disorder in which the individual may feel sad, helpless, and hopeless, as if life is just too overwhelming. Depressed individuals have a decreased interest in activities and little pleasure in anything, including sex. (Source: American Psychiatric Association)

COBRA   Consolidated Omnibus Budget Reconciliation Act, a federal law that makes it possible for most people to continue to get health coverage for at least 18 months after other coverage is terminated through job loss or other means.

commencement exercises   Graduation ceremonies.

conjunctions   Parts of speech that link words, phrases, and sentences. There are three types of conjunctions: *coordinating* (and, but, so, or, for, yet); *subordinate* (if, when, because, etc.); and *correlative* (not only … but also, etc.)

core requirements   Classes that every student must take to qualify for graduation.

credit   Deferred payment.

culture   The collective behavior patterns, beliefs, and values unique to a community that are socially transmitted to individuals and to which individuals are expected to conform.

debit card   A card used to withdraw money from your account. A debit card is not a credit card.

Dr.   A title used for college professors who have earned a doctorate (Ph.D.).

electives   Classes that do not fulfill a specific core requirement.

expository writing   Writing that explains, shows, or tells.

finance charges   See *interest or finance charges*.

freshman orientation   Organized programs offered before classes start for the purpose of helping freshmen and transfer students make friends and get integrated into the university community.

gender   The psychological makeup of an individual based on cultural perceptions of femaleness and maleness (such as femininity, masculinity, androgyny).

Greek system   Fraternities and sororities.

homophobia   An intense, irrational fear of same-sex relationships.

inference   A conclusion made by "reading between the lines" to find information or an opinion the author does not directly state.

interest or finance charges   The fee you pay for the convenience of using someone else's money.

intramural sports   Sports that are open to all students. To get involved, you just sign up.

Ivy League   The eight most prestigious universities in the United States—Brown, Columbia, Cornell, Dartmouth, Harvard, Princeton, University of Pennsylvania, and Yale.

lease   A written contract for an apartment or home rental.

major   The subject you specialize in at college. A major usually requires a minimum of 36 credit hours of classes in a specific subject.

minor   A subspecialty. A minor usually requires a minimum of 18 credit hours of study in a specific subject.

mnemonics   Memory aids such as rhymes and songs.

objective tests   Tests in which each item has one correct answer. True/false, matching, multiple-choice, identification, and sentence completion are all objective test items.

office hours   Set times during which professors meet with students in their office.

parenthetical documentation, footnotes, endnotes   Ways of giving credit to sources used in a research paper.

periodical literature   Material published on a regular basis, such as newspapers, magazines, and journals.

persuasive writing   Writing that uses reason, ethics, or emotion to sway an audience to action or belief.

plagiarism   Using someone else's words without giving adequate credit.

portfolio   any formal collection of your best work, such as art, musical compositions, writing, or computer programs.

power   The ability to influence and enforce decisions in a community; control of valued resources.

prejudice   An unfavorable preconceived idea, judgment, or belief directed toward a racial, religious, cultural, or ethnic group.

primary sources   Reference materials created by direct observation. Primary sources include autobiographies, diaries, eyewitness accounts, and interviews.

professor   A title of honor used to address college teachers.

"publish or perish"   The common practice of retaining and promoting only those professors who publish copious high-quality scholarship.

race/ethnicity   People grouped according to a common racial, national, tribal, religious, linguistic, or cultural origin.

racism   An assumption that there is inherent purity and superiority of certain races and inferiority of others.

rape   When a woman or man is forced to have non-consensual sex.

reconciling a checkbook   Deducting any checks from your balance, adding any deposits, and making sure the bank has correctly computed your balance. Another term for "balancing your checkbook."

references   Letters from professors, friends, or employers attesting to your good character, abilities, or accomplishments.

research paper   A persuasive paper that presents and argues a thesis. (See also *thesis statement.*)

resident advisors (RAs)   Upper-class students hired to oversee underclass students. Also called *student advisors* and *area advisors.*

sabbatical   A leave with or without pay for the purpose of completing scholarship. Sabbaticals are usually granted to professors for one or two semesters at a time.

secondary sources   Reference materials written by people with indirect knowledge. Secondary sources include biographies, almanacs, encyclopedias, and textbooks.

security deposit   The money you give to the landlord to keep in escrow while you are living in an apartment.

sexism   A belief in the inherent purity or superiority of one gender over the other.

sexual harassment   Discriminating against a person based on his or her gender or sexual orientation.

sexually transmitted diseases (STDs)   Illnesses that are passed through intercourse or other sexual acts. STDs include AIDS, chlamydia, gonorrhea, and herpes.

skimming a text   Scanning the words to get the general idea or find an important fact.

status   The respect that a person commands in a community.

student advisors (SAs)   Upper-class students hired to oversee underclass students. Also called *resident advisors* or *area advisors.*

syllabus   A listing of class activities, requirements, readings, tests, and quizzes.

teaching assistants (TAs)   Graduate students who run small classes and grade papers for large classes in exchange for free tuition.

term paper   An expository essay that provides information about a topic. (See also *expository writing.*)

thesis statement   The central point you're proving in your research paper.

transitions   Words and phrases that signal connections between and among ideas.

work-study programs   On-campus student jobs, often part of the student's financial aid package.

writing process   A series of activities that start when a writer begins thinking about the topic and ends when the writer completes the last draft.

Index

265